P9-DNY-771

Holidays In Cross-Stitch 1987

The Vanessa-Ann Collection

The Vanessa-Ann Collection Staff

Owners:
Jo Packham and
Terrece Beesley Woodruff
Executive Editor:
Margaret Shields Marti
Editor: Monica Smith
Art Director: Trice Boerens
Needlework Director:
Nancy Whitley
Graphic Artist: Julie Truman
Graphing Director:
Susan Jorgensen
Operations Director: Pam Randall
Administrative Assistant:
Barbara Milburn

Designers

Trice Boerens
Lynda Calvert
Linda Durbano
Margaret Marti
Jo Packham
Tina Richards
Julie Truman
Terrece Woodruff

Holidays In Cross-Stitch
1987
The Vanessa-Ann Collection
Oxmoor House®

January 1987

Dear C,

Just a short note to say "thank you" for having had faith in our talents, for offering help where it was needed, and for being our friend.

With affection,
T J M T

Book Division of Southern Progress Corporation
P.O. Box 2463, Birmingham, Alabama 35201

Library of Congress Catalog Number: 86-62285
ISBN: 0-8487-0697-8
ISSN: 0890-8230
Manufactured in the United States of America
First Printing 1987

Executive Editor: Candace N. Conard
Production Manager: Jerry Higdon
Associate Production Manager: Rick Litton
Art Director: Bob Nance

Holidays In Cross-Stitch 1987

Editor: Linda Baltzell Wright
Editorial Assistant: Lenda Wyatt
Copy Chief: Mary Jean Haddin
Designer: Diana Smith Morrison
Artist: Earl Freedle
Photographers: Brent Herridge, Jim Bathie, Courtland W. Richards

1 9 8 7

Contents

Introduction

Our calendars are filled with holidays, and for years cross-stitchers have looked for designs to celebrate these special occasions. But they had to really search, and often in vain, to find appropriate designs. Now every holiday can be a cross-stitch holiday!

Holidays In Cross-Stitch celebrates the traditional, the surprising, and the often whimsical holidays in America and around the world. We have included designs and projects for every stitcher and for every home. Our book honors occasions from New Year's to Christmas, from the patriotic to the personal, with ideas for gifts and good wishes.

We at the Vanessa-Ann Collection welcome you into our homes through our designs and hope our hand-worked treasures will add warmth to your special celebrations. Every page of *Holidays In Cross-Stitch* is like a note from one of us to one of you, wishing you many memorable holidays throughout the year.

1987

JANUARY

S	M	T	W	T	F	S
				1	2	3
4	5	6	7	8	9	10
11	12	13	14	15	16	17
18	19	20	21	22	23	24
25	26	27	28	29	30	31

FEBRUARY

S	M	T	W	T	F	S
1	2	3	4	5	6	7
8	9	10	11	12	13	14
15	16	17	18	19	20	21
22	23	24	25	26	27	28

MARCH

S	M	T	W	T	F	S
1	2	3	4	5	6	7
8	9	10	11	12	13	14
15	16	17	18	19	20	21
22	23	24	25	26	27	28
29	30	31				

APRIL

S	M	T	W	T	F	S
			1	2	3	4
5	6	7	8	9	10	11
12	13	14	15	16	17	18
19	20	21	22	23	24	25
26	27	28	29	30		

MAY

S	M	T	W	T	F	S
					1	2
3	4	5	6	7	8	9
10	11	12	13	14	15	16
17	18	19	20	21	22	23
24	25	26	27	28	29	30
31						

JUNE

S	M	T	W	T	F	S
	1	2	3	4	5	6
7	8	9	10	11	12	13
14	15	16	17	18	19	20
21	22	23	24	25	26	27
28	29	30				

JULY

S	M	T	W	T	F	S
			1	2	3	4
5	6	7	8	9	10	11
12	13	14	15	16	17	18
19	20	21	22	23	24	25
26	27	28	29	30	31	

AUGUST

S	M	T	W	T	F	S
						1
2	3	4	5	6	7	8
9	10	11	12	13	14	15
16	17	18	19	20	21	22
23	24	25	26	27	28	29
30	31					

SEPTEMBER

S	M	T	W	T	F	S
		1	2	3	4	5
6	7	8	9	10	11	12
13	14	15	16	17	18	19
20	21	22	23	24	25	26
27	28	29	30			

OCTOBER

S	M	T	W	T	F	S
				1	2	3
4	5	6	7	8	9	10
11	12	13	14	15	16	17
18	19	20	21	22	23	24
25	26	27	28	29	30	31

NOVEMBER

S	M	T	W	T	F	S
1	2	3	4	5	6	7
8	9	10	11	12	13	14
15	16	17	18	19	20	21
22	23	24	25	26	27	28
29	30					

DECEMBER

S	M	T	W	T	F	S
		1	2	3	4	5
6	7	8	9	10	11	12
13	14	15	16	17	18	19
20	21	22	23	24	25	26
27	28	29	30	31		

JANUARY 1

New Year's Day

Traditionally a time to celebrate the year past and make resolutions for the year to come, New Year's begins our calendar. Preserve the memory of 1987 (or any other important year in your life) in this sampler, A Year To Remember. Refer to General Instructions for the Smyrna Cross and Herringbone stitches.

A Year To Remember

SAMPLE
Stitched on cream Belfast Linen 32 over three threads, the finished design size is 10⅛″ x 11″. The fabric was cut 16″ x 17″. For the best results, stitch this design only on Belfast Linen 32. To stitch a year other than 1987, first graph the appropriate Roman numerals; then center and stitch in place of "MCMLXXXVII."

Conversion Chart

1987 MCMLXXXVII
1988 MCMLXXXVIII
1989 MCMLXXXIX
1990 MCMXC
1991 MCMXCI
1992 MCMXCII
1993 MCMXCIII
1994 MCMXCIV
1995 MCMXCV
1996 MCMXCVI
1997 MCMXCVII

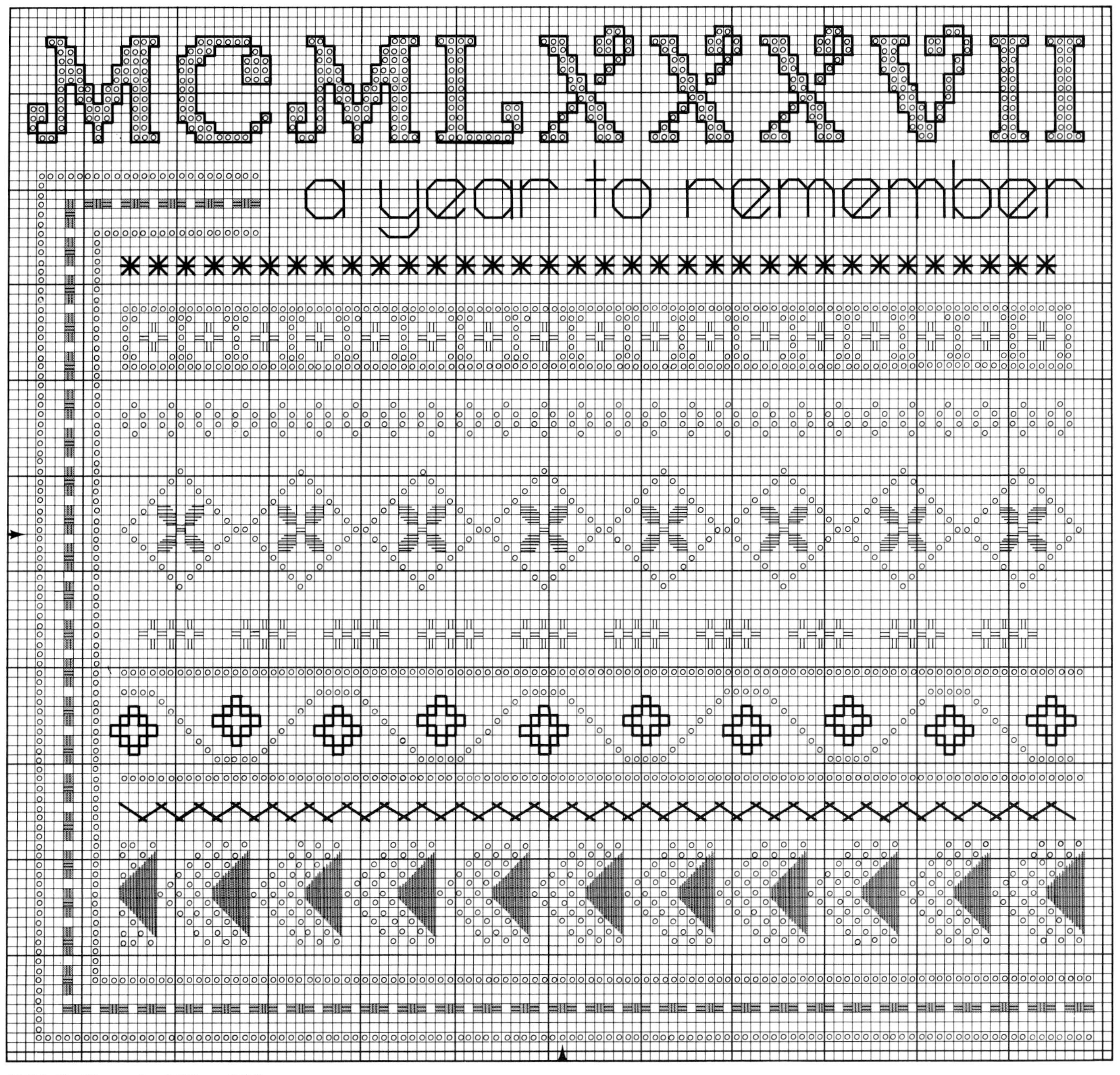

Stitch Count: 115 x 106

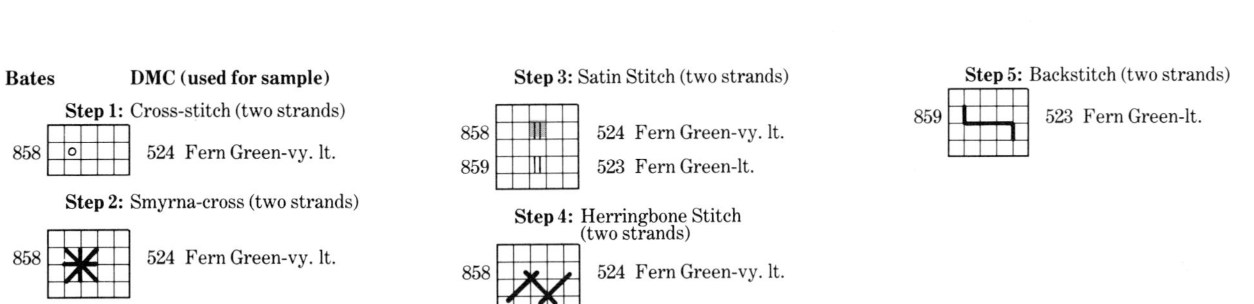

Bates
DMC (used for sample)
Step 1: Cross-stitch (two strands)
858
524 Fern Green-vy. lt.
Step 2: Smyrna-cross (two strands)
858
524 Fern Green-vy. lt.
Step 3: Satin Stitch (two strands)
858
524 Fern Green-vy. lt.
859
523 Fern Green-lt.
Step 4: Herringbone Stitch (two strands)
858
524 Fern Green-vy. lt.
Step 5: Backstitch (two strands)
859
523 Fern Green-lt.

FEBRUARY 14

Valentine's Day

The feast day of St. Valentine, patron saint of engaged couples, has become an occasion for the universal display of love and affection. Sending affectionate and humorous greetings to loved ones has become an indispensable part of our celebration today. Bearing time-tested sentiments, these five designs will inspire you to stitch a message of love for your favorite Valentine.

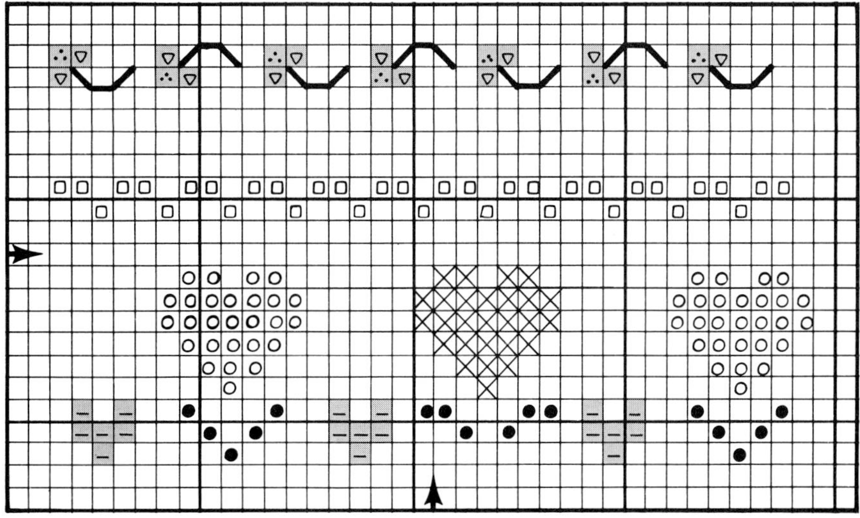

Stitch Count: 36 x 19

Valentine Doll

SAMPLE
Stitched on cream Belfast Linen 32 over two threads, the finished size for the pinafore design is 5″ x 1¼″. (A fabric with this stitch count must be used so that the design will fit the pinafore.) The fabric was cut 9″ x 7″. Trace the pinafore skirt front pattern onto the fabric with a dressmakers' pen (see General Instructions). Position the stitching as desired (see the photo). Repeat the borders, alternating the hearts as indicated on the graph.

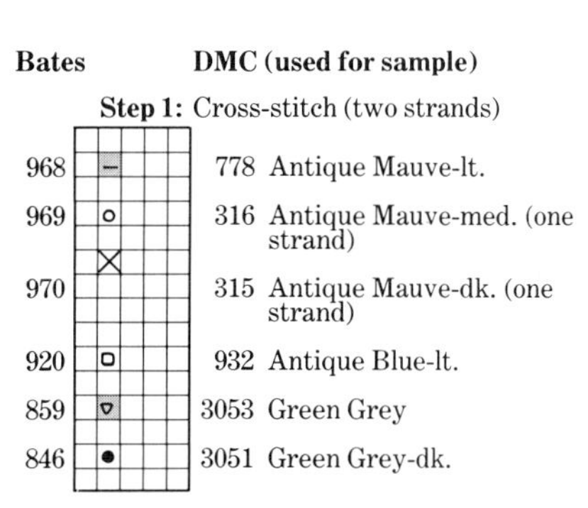

Bates		DMC (used for sample)
	Step 1: Cross-stitch (two strands)	
968	–	778 Antique Mauve-lt.
969	o	316 Antique Mauve-med. (one strand)
970	X	315 Antique Mauve-dk. (one strand)
920	▫	932 Antique Blue-lt.
859	▽	3053 Green Grey
846	•	3051 Green Grey-dk.

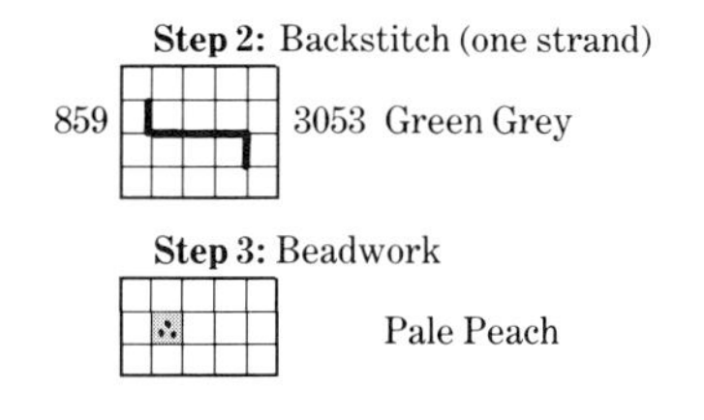

Step 2: Backstitch (one strand)

859	3053 Green Grey

Step 3: Beadwork

∴	Pale Peach

Be Mine

SAMPLE
Stitched on white Belfast Linen 32 over two threads, the finished design size is 6¾″ x 6½″. The fabric was cut 13″ x 13″.

Bates **DMC (used for sample)**

Step 1: Cross-stitch (two strands)

Bates	Symbol	DMC	Color
887	–	3046	Yellow Beige-med. (bead over cross-stitch)
968	▫	778	Antique Mauve-lt.
968	∴	778	Antique Mauve-lt. (bead over cross-stitch)
970	☒	315	Antique Mauve-dk.

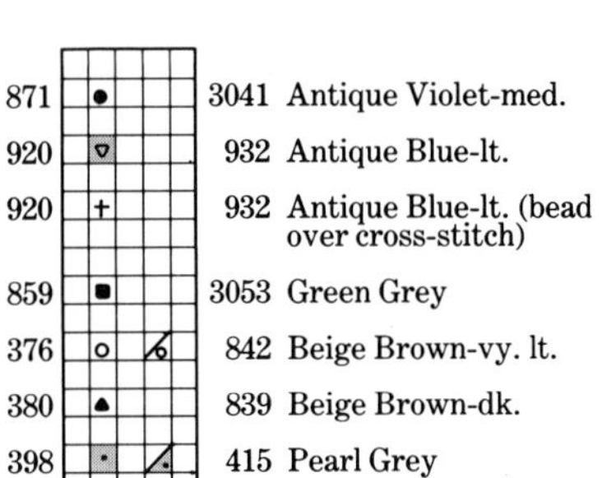

Bates	Symbol	DMC	Color
871	●	3041	Antique Violet-med.
920	▿	932	Antique Blue-lt.
920	+	932	Antique Blue-lt. (bead over cross-stitch)
859	■	3053	Green Grey
376	○	842	Beige Brown-vy. lt.
380	▲	839	Beige Brown-dk.
398	·	415	Pearl Grey

Stitch Count: 109 x 103

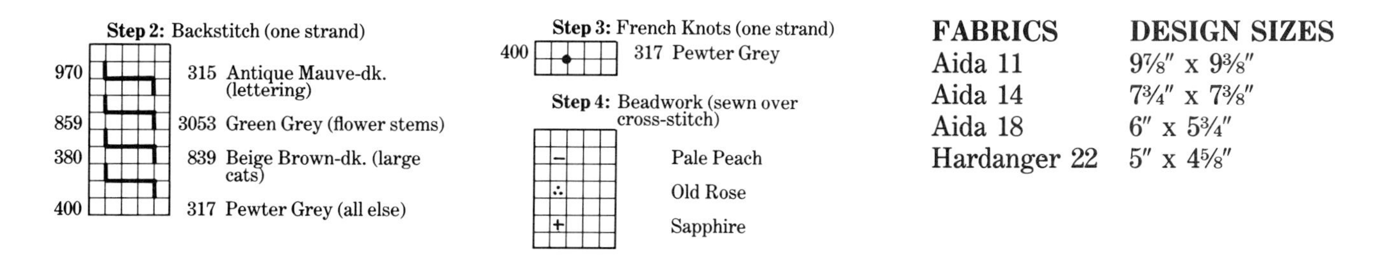

FABRICS	DESIGN SIZES
Aida 11	9⅞″ x 9⅜″
Aida 14	7¾″ x 7⅜″
Aida 18	6″ x 5¾″
Hardanger 22	5″ x 4⅝″

Valentine

SAMPLE
Stitched on white Belfast Linen 32 over two threads, the finished design size is 6¼″ x 9¼″. The fabric was cut 12″ x 15″.

Bates		DMC (used for sample)
	Step 1: Cross-stitch (two strands)	
887	∴	3046 Yellow Beige-med. (bead over cross-stitch)
968	○	778 Antique Mauve-lt.
968	–	778 Antique Mauve-lt. (bead over cross-stitch)
969	·	316 Antique Mauve-med.
970	●	315 Antique Mauve-dk.
72	▲	902 Garnet-vy. dk.
869	○	3042 Antique Violet-lt.
871	X	3041 Antique Violet-med.
920	▽	932 Antique Blue-lt.
859	□	3053 Green Grey
846	■	3051 Green Grey-dk.
398		415 Pearl Grey
400	X	414 Steel Grey-dk.
	Step 2: Backstitch (one strand)	
970		315 Antique Mauve-dk. (lettering)
859		3053 Green Grey (yellow flowers)
846		3051 Green Grey-dk. (pink flowers)
400		414 Steel Grey-dk. (all else)
	Step 3: French Knots (one strand)	
400	●	414 Steel Grey-dk.
	Step 4: Long Stitch (one strand)	
846		3051 Green Grey-dk.
	Step 5: Beadwork	
	∴	Pale Peach (sewn over cross-stitch)
	–	Old Rose

FABRICS	DESIGN SIZES
Aida 11	9⅛″ x 13½″
Aida 14	7⅛″ x 10⅝″
Aida 18	5½″ x 8¼″
Hardanger 22	4½″ x 6¾″

Insert flower motif
from chart
on page 13.
VALENTINE

Stitch Count: 100 x 149

You Will Always Be My Valentine

SAMPLE
Stitched on cream Belfast Linen 32 over two threads, the finished design size is 6⅝" x 5⅝". The fabric was cut 14" x 12".

Step 1: Cross-stitch (two strands)

Bates	Symbol	DMC (used for sample)	
778	•	948	Peach Flesh-vy. lt.
893	∴	224	Shell Pink-lt.
894	▲	223	Shell Pink-med.
108	–	211	Lavender-lt.
104	⊠	210	Lavender-med.
117	■	341	Blue Violet-lt.
158	∵	828	Blue-ultra lt.
159	○	827	Blue-vy. lt.
130	● /	799	Delft-med.
214	I	966	Baby Green-med.
186	o	993	Aquamarine-lt.
875	•	503	Blue Green-med.
878	⊠	501	Blue Green-dk.
942	□	738	Tan-vy. lt.

Step 2: Filet Cross-stitch (one strand)

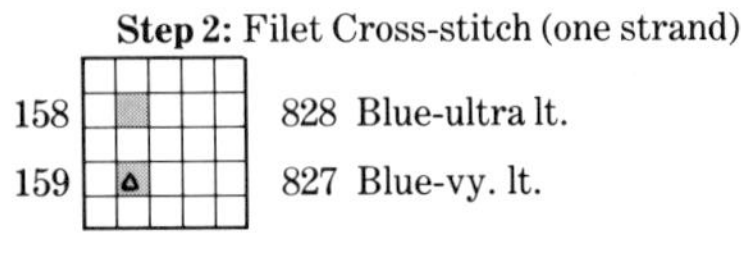

Bates	DMC	
158	828	Blue-ultra lt.
159	827	Blue-vy. lt.

Step 3: Backstitch (one strand)

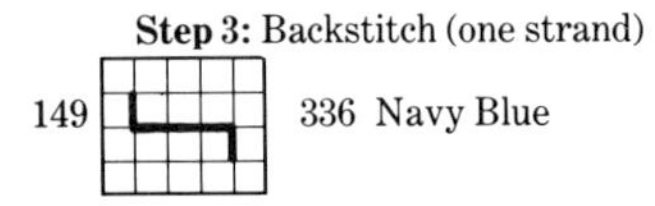

Bates	DMC	
149	336	Navy Blue

FABRICS	DESIGN SIZES
Aida 11	9⅝" x 8⅛"
Aida 14	7⅝" x 6⅜"
Aida 18	5⅞" x 5"
Hardanger 22	4⅞" x 4⅛"

MATERIALS
- Completed cross-stitch on cream Belfast Linen 32 and matching thread; see sample information
- One 9" x 11" piece of cream Belfast Linen or a matching fabric for the back
- One 9" x 11" piece of cream net lace for the back
- 1¾ yards of 3½"-wide cream lace
- 1¾ yards of 5½"-wide cream lace
- 1 yard of ⅛"-wide lavender silk ribbon
- 2 yards of ⅛"-wide green silk ribbon
- 1 yard of ⅛"-wide blue silk ribbon
- 1 yard of ⅛"-wide cream lace
- Stuffing
- ½ cup of potpourri
- Dressmakers' pen

Stitch Count: 106 x 90

DIRECTIONS
All seam allowances are ½″ wide.

1. Cut the linen 9″ x 11″ with the design centered. Mark the center of each edge.

2. Place the 3½″-wide lace over the 5½″-wide lace. Align the unfinished edges and stitch together to form one strip. Divide the lace into quarters and mark.

3. Stitch gathering threads through both layers of the lace. Gather the lace to fit the pillow front, matching the quarter marks on the lace to the center marks on the linen. With right sides together, stitch the lace to the front, allowing extra fullness at the corners and rounding slightly.

4. To construct the pillow back, place the net lace over the right side of the linen. Stitch around edges, leaving a 2″ opening. Insert potpourri and stitch closed.

5. Stitch the right sides of the pillow front and back together, tucking the lace ruffle inside and sewing on the stitching line of the ruffle. Leave a 5″ opening. Turn the pillow right side out and stuff. Slipstitch the opening closed.

6. Cut the green ribbon in half. Handling all the pieces of ribbon and the ⅛″-wide lace as a single unit, tie them into a bow. Tack bow to corner of design and trim ends to desired length.

Ewes Coverlet

SAMPLE
Stitched on green Linen 29 over two threads, the finished design size is 5⅞" x 4¾". The fabric was cut 14" x 14". The yarn used is lightweight mohair. Refer to the General Instructions for the Turkish Tufting Stitch used on the lambs.

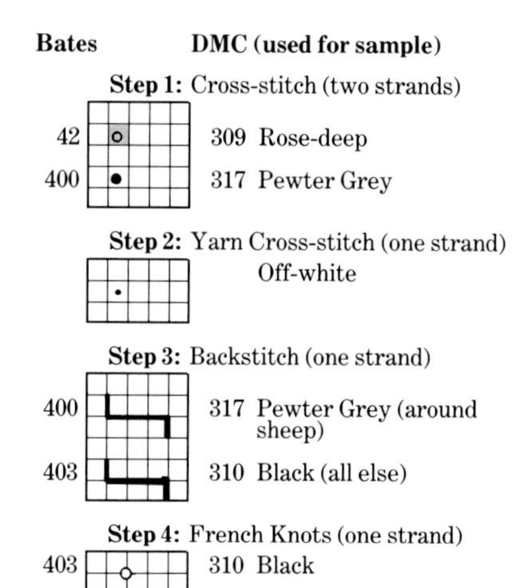

Bates
DMC (used for sample)
Step 1: Cross-stitch (two strands)
42
309 Rose-deep
400
317 Pewter Grey
Step 2: Yarn Cross-stitch (one strand)
Off-white
Step 3: Backstitch (one strand)
400
317 Pewter Grey (around sheep)
403
310 Black (all else)
Step 4: French Knots (one strand)
403
310 Black

Stitch Count: 85 x 69

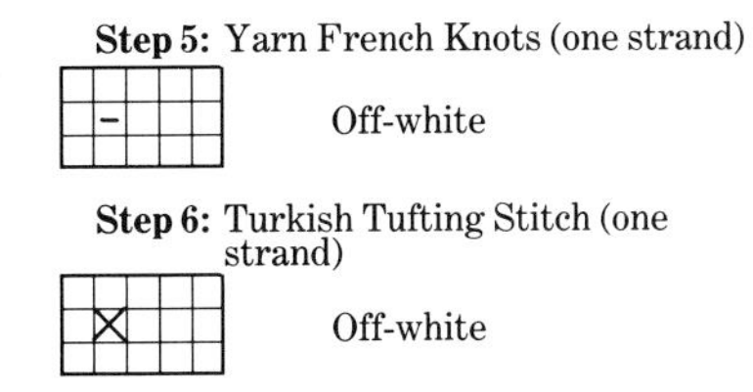

FABRICS	DESIGN SIZES
Aida 11	7¾" x 6¼"
Aida 14	6⅛" x 4⅞"
Aida 18	4¾" x 3⅞"
Hardanger 22	3⅞" x 3⅛"

MATERIALS

Completed cross-stitch on green Linen 29 and matching thread; see sample information
⅞ yard of 45"-wide print fabric for border; matching thread
¼ yard of 45"-wide cream fabric
2¾ yards of ¼"-wide pink double-fold bias tape or ⅜ yard of 45"-wide pink fabric to make binding
⅝ yard of polyester fleece
Dressmakers' pen

continued . . .

. . . Ewes Coverlet continued

DIRECTIONS
All seam allowances are ½″.

1. Cut the linen 11″ x 11″ with the design centered.

2. From the print fabric, cut one 22½″ x 22½″ piece for the back and four 24″ x 5¼″ pieces for the front.

3. From the cream fabric, cut four 3″ x 13″ strips.

4. Sew the cream strips to the linen (Diagram A). Press the seams away from the design.

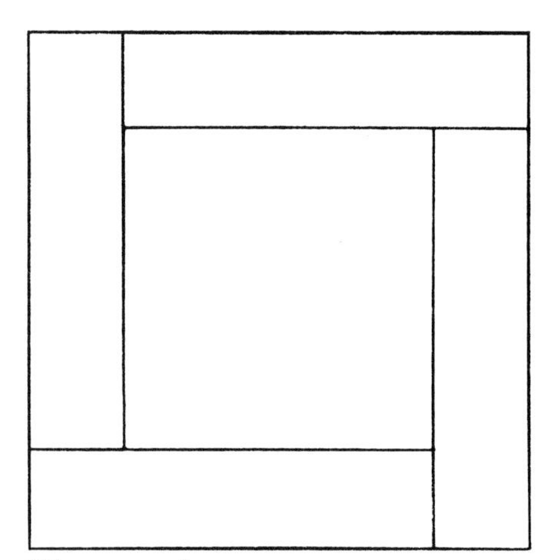

Diagram A

5. Mark the center of the outside edge of each cream strip and the center of one edge of each of the four print pieces. Stitch a cream strip to each print piece, right sides together and centers matching. Sew to within ½″ of each corner of the cream fabric. Press the seams away from the design.

6. To miter the corners, fold the right sides of two adjacent strips together and stitch at a 45-degree angle (Diagram B). Trim the seam to ½″ and press. Repeat for each corner.

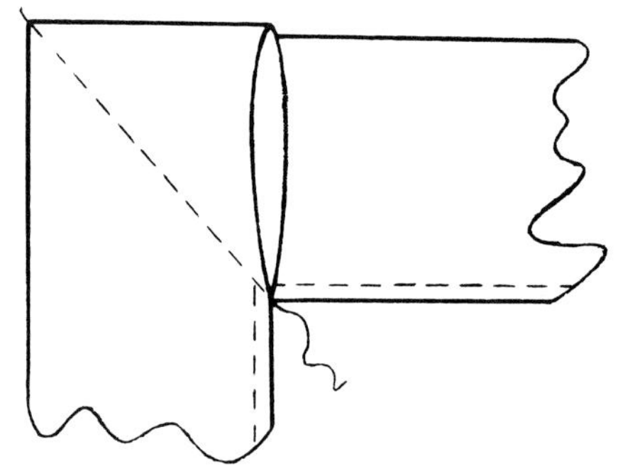

Diagram B

7. Layer the blanket front, right side down; the fleece; and the blanket back, right side up. Baste all three layers together.

8. Using the dressmakers' pen, mark the quilting lines (Diagram C). Use green thread to quilt the cream strips and matching thread to quilt the print strips.

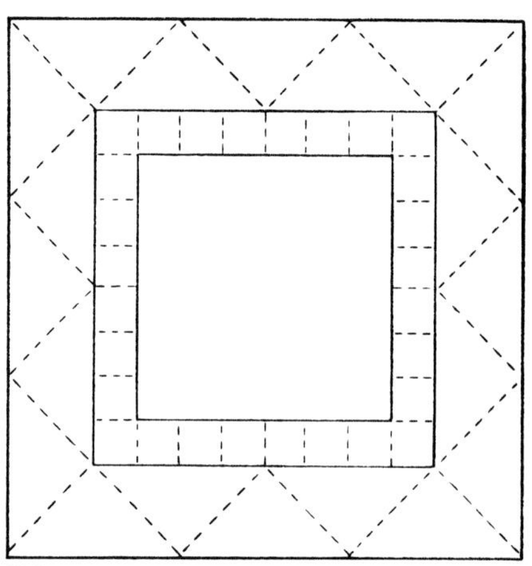

Diagram C

9. Pin the bias tape to the front of the coverlet, right sides together and raw edges aligned. Fold ¼″ of the tape to the back of the coverlet; fold again and slipstitch.

MARCH 1

National Pig Day

A little-known, but nonetheless important, national holiday honors one of man's most intellectual domesticated animals, the pig. This cross-stitched cover, depicting the deserving member of the Suidae family, wraps around a loose-leaf notebook, which is ideal for keeping old family recipes and adding new favorites.

Ham & Eggs

SAMPLE
Stitched on cream Hardanger 22 over two threads, the finished design size is 6⅝″ x 6¾″. The fabric was cut 12″ x 12″. (A fabric with this stitch count must be used so that design will fit notebook.)

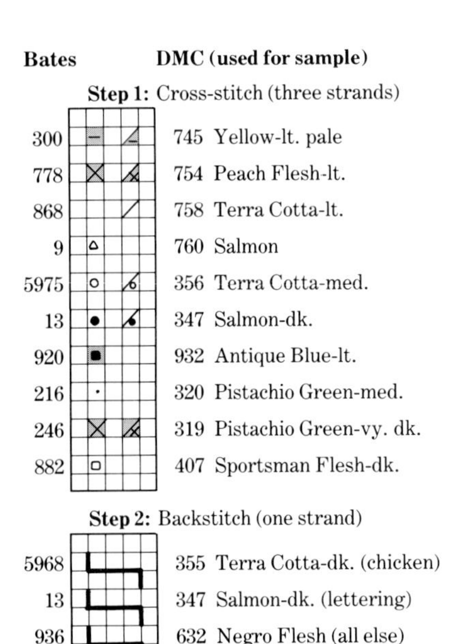

Bates	DMC (used for sample)
Step 1: Cross-stitch (three strands)	
300	745 Yellow-lt. pale
778	754 Peach Flesh-lt.
868	758 Terra Cotta-lt.
9	760 Salmon
5975	356 Terra Cotta-med.
13	347 Salmon-dk.
920	932 Antique Blue-lt.
216	320 Pistachio Green-med.
246	319 Pistachio Green-vy. dk.
882	407 Sportsman Flesh-dk.
Step 2: Backstitch (one strand)	
5968	355 Terra Cotta-dk. (chicken)
13	347 Salmon-dk. (lettering)
936	632 Negro Flesh (all else)
Step 3: French Knots (one strand)	
13	347 Salmon-dk.

Stitch Count: 73 x 74

MATERIALS
- Completed cross-stitch on cream Hardanger 22; see sample information
- ½ yard of 45″-wide tan print fabric; matching thread
- ⅜ yard of 45″-wide green print fabric; matching thread
- ⅜ yard of 45″-wide muslin for lining
- 2 yards of small cording
- 2½ yards of ⅛″-wide pink satin ribbon; matching thread
- ½ yard of ¼″-wide light green satin ribbon; matching thread
- ½ yard of polyester fleece
- Purchased three-ring notebook with 1¼″ rings
- Stuffing
- Dressmakers' pen
- Tracing paper for patterns

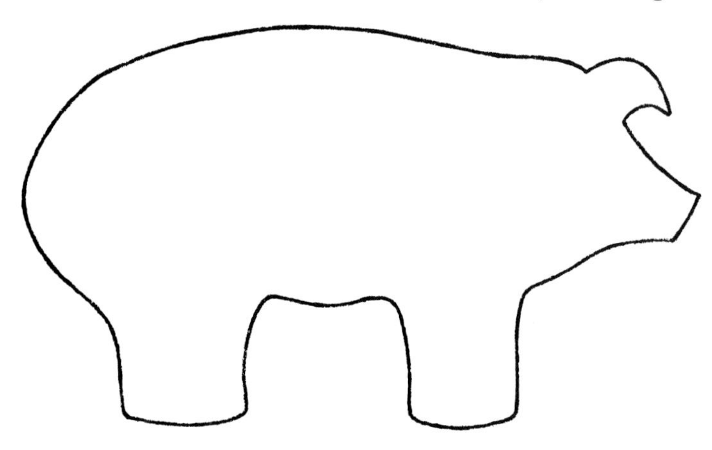

DIRECTIONS
All seam allowances are ½″.

1. Open the notebook on top of the tracing paper so that the spine and back lie flat. Trace the outline of the entire notebook onto the paper, marking the fold line of the spine. Add a ½″ seam allowance to all sides. For the facings, trace the outline of the notebook only to the fold line of the spine. Add a ¼″ seam allowance to all sides.

2. From the tan print fabric, cut four 2½″ x 13″ strips. Also cut one 13″ square for the back and spine of the cover.

3. To construct the front, cut the Hardanger 9″ x 9″ with the design centered.

4. Mark the centers of the fabric strips for the front of the notebook and the centers of all edges of the design piece. With right sides together and center marks matching, sew one 2½″ x 13″ strip to one edge of the design piece, stopping ¼″ from the corner of the design piece. Backstitch. Sew the remaining strips to the remaining edges.

5. To miter the corners, fold the right sides of two adjacent strips together and stitch at a 45-degree angle (Diagram A). Trim the corner to a ½″ seam allowance; press. Repeat for each corner.

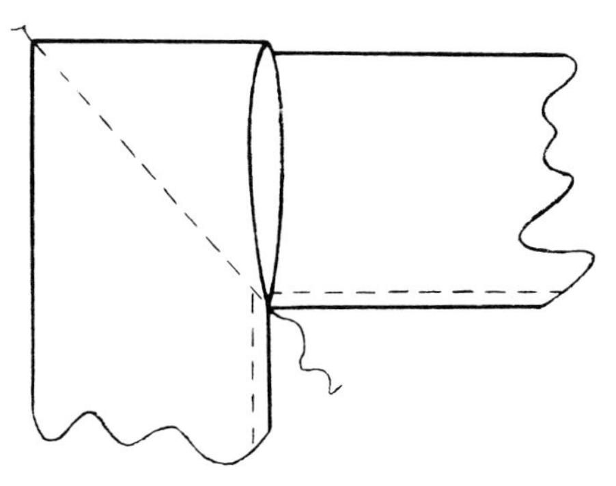

Diagram A

6. Trim 1½″ from the edge of the left border only. With right sides together, stitch the 13″ x 13″ back and spine piece to the trimmed edge. Press.

7. Place the large pattern for the notebook over the fabric. Align the seam with the fold line for the front of the spine. Vertically center the design on the front of the cover and trim the fabric to match the pattern.

8. Again using the large pattern, cut one piece of muslin and one piece of fleece.

9. From the tan print fabric, cut two facing pieces. Also cut two pigs for the bookmark, using the pig pattern.

10. From the green print fabric, cut a 1½″-wide bias strip, piecing as needed to equal 54″. Cover the cording.

11. With a dressmakers' pen, mark the quilting pattern on the cover front (Diagram B). Layer the cover, right side up, over the fleece and muslin and baste all three layers together. Machine-stitch on the quilting lines.

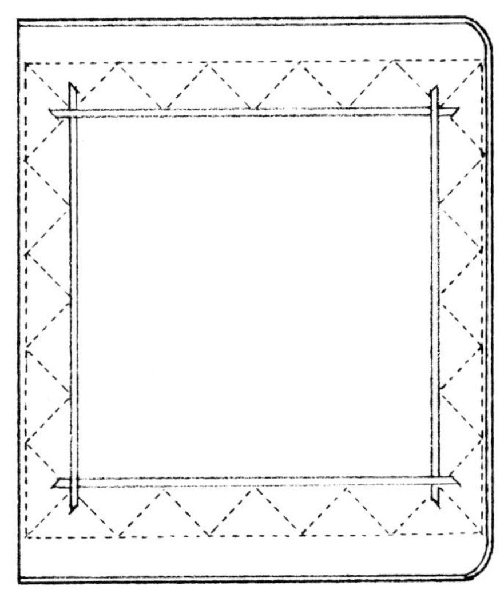

Diagram B

12. Stitch the cording to the right side of the cover, aligning the raw edges and rounding the corners to match the shape of the notebook.

13. To finish the edges of the facings, turn up a ¼″ double hem on the straight edge of each facing and stitch.

14. Place the cover right side up on a flat surface. Place the facings on the cover with right sides together and curved edges aligned. Stitch on the stitching line of the cording.

15. Turn right side out and slip the cover on the notebook. It should fit snugly but not bind, and the seam lines should be on the notebook's edge. Remove the cover and make any necessary adjustments.

16. From the pink ribbon, cut four 9″ lengths. Slipstitch the ribbon to the edges of the cover design, along the seam of the Hardanger and print fabric. Cut two more lengths of ribbon, one 15″ and one 24″. With the 15″ length, form two 3″ loops with 1½″ ends. Wrap the 24″ length around the center of the loops and tie with an additional 3″ bow, leaving 9″ ends. Tack the bow to the corner of the design.

17. Place the pig pieces right sides together. Stitch around the pig, leaving 1″ open at the top. Turn right side out and stuff. Insert one end of the green ribbon and secure it while slipstitching the opening closed. Trim the ribbon to 13½″. Sew the ribbon to the top of the inside back edge of the cover next to the spine. Place the cover on the notebook.

MARCH 17

St. Patrick's Day

In Ireland, this day highlights a full week of festivity in honor of St. Patrick, that country's patron saint. The shamrock greens and floral brights in this cross-stitch piece lend Irish cheer to the romantic sentiment.

An Irish Blessing

SAMPLE

Stitched on white Belfast Linen 32 over two threads, the finished design size is 7¼" x 6¼". The fabric was cut 14" x 13".

Bates	Symbol	DMC (used for sample)
		Step 1: Cross-stitch (two strands)
301	– / ◺	744 Yellow-pale
323	∴	722 Orange Spice-lt.
326	▢	720 Orange Spice-dk.
49	∵	3689 Mauve-lt.
66	o	3688 Mauve-med.
69	◪	3687 Mauve
104	+	210 Lavender-med.
101	●	327 Antique Violet-dk.
167	(shaded)	519 Sky Blue
168	+	518 Wedgewood-lt.
162	△	517 Wedgewood-med.
213	I	369 Pistachio Green-vy. lt.
215	▢	368 Pistachio Green-lt.

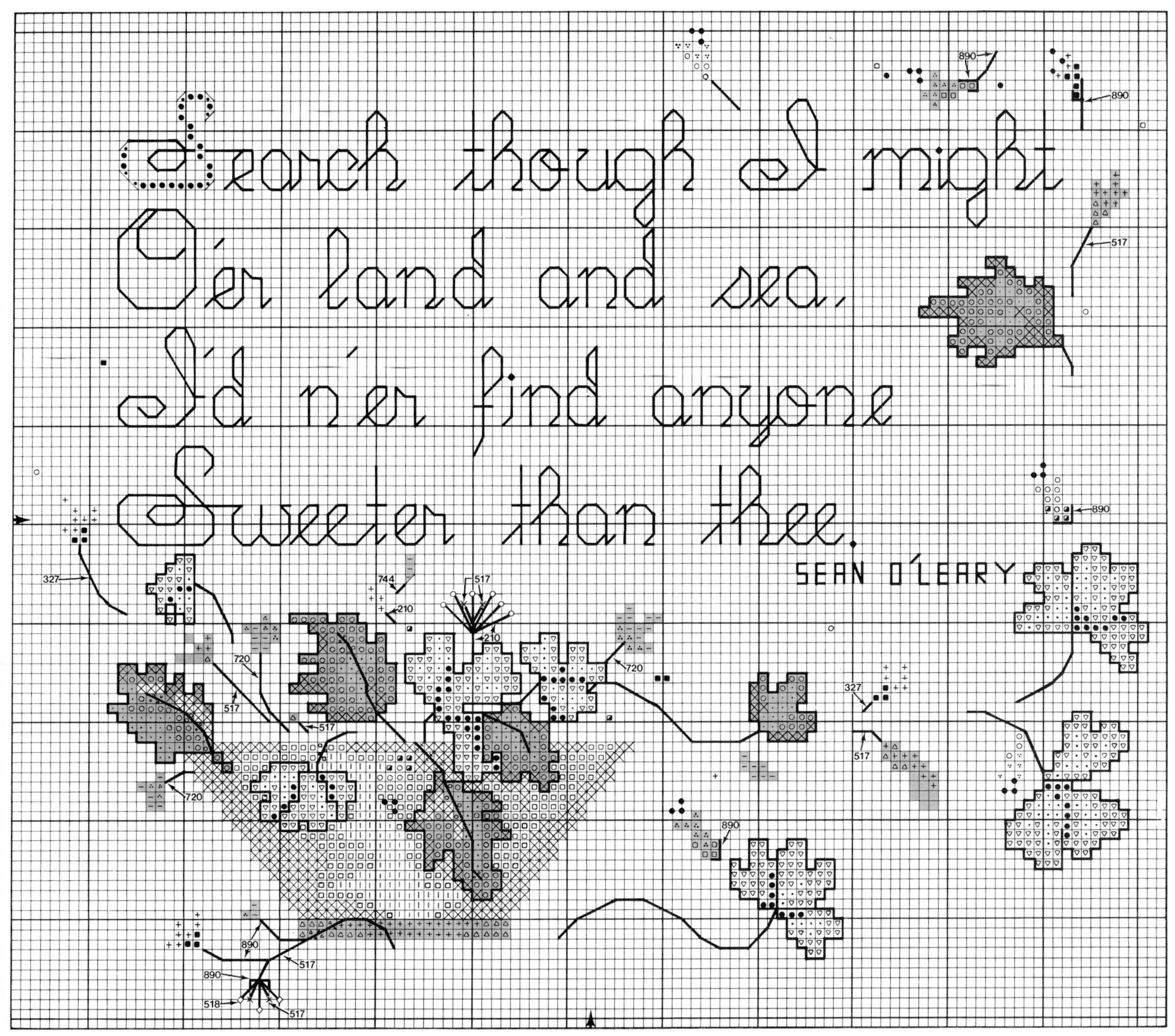

Stitch Count: 117 x 99

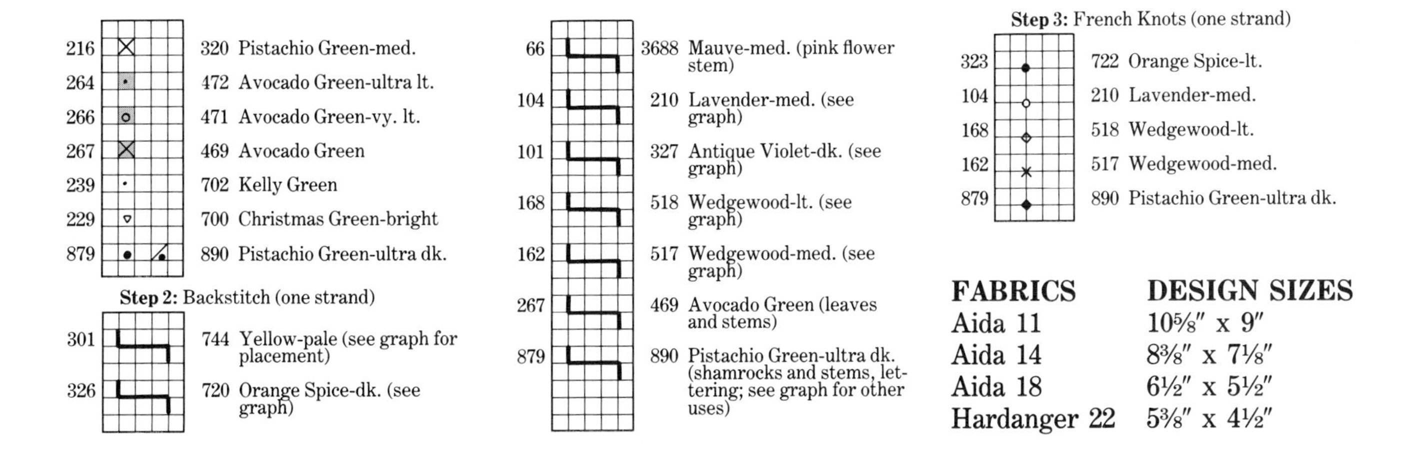

216 320 Pistachio Green-med.
264 472 Avocado Green-ultra lt.
266 471 Avocado Green-vy. lt.
267 469 Avocado Green
239 702 Kelly Green
229 700 Christmas Green-bright
879 890 Pistachio Green-ultra dk.
Step 2: Backstitch (one strand)
301 744 Yellow-pale (see graph for placement)
326 720 Orange Spice-dk. (see graph)
66 3688 Mauve-med. (pink flower stem)
104 210 Lavender-med. (see graph)
101 327 Antique Violet-dk. (see graph)
168 518 Wedgewood-lt. (see graph)
162 517 Wedgewood-med. (see graph)
267 469 Avocado Green (leaves and stems)
879 890 Pistachio Green-ultra dk. (shamrocks and stems, lettering; see graph for other uses)
Step 3: French Knots (one strand)
323 722 Orange Spice-lt.
104 210 Lavender-med.
168 518 Wedgewood-lt.
162 517 Wedgewood-med.
879 890 Pistachio Green-ultra dk.
FABRICS DESIGN SIZES
Aida 11 10⅝" x 9"
Aida 14 8⅜" x 7⅛"
Aida 18 6½" x 5½"
Hardanger 22 5⅜" x 4½"

APRIL 19

Easter

Easter, the most joyous holiday of the Christian year, is a celebration of new life. Some of our holiday traditions, however, began before the Christian feast. In ancient times, the Egyptians and Persians dyed spring eggs for gifts. The custom continued, with early Christians exchanging colored eggs on Easter as a symbol of life returning to the world in spring.

Easter Doll

SAMPLE
Stitched on white Belfast Linen 32 over two threads, the tiny chick design is taken from the Chick Egg. Finished design size for bodice front or back is 3½" x 3/16"; for chick, 1⅛" x 1⅛"; and for three hearts, ¾" x ¼". (A fabric with this stitch count must be used so that the design will fit the pinafore.) The fabric was cut 9" x 7" for skirt and 3¾" x 2½" for bodice. Trace the pinafore bodice front and back and skirt front onto the fabric with a dressmakers' pen (see General Instructions). Position the stitching as desired (see the photo). Stitch count varies.

Bates	Symbol	DMC (used for sample)
		Step 1: Cross-stitch (one strand)
50	o	605 Cranberry-vy. lt.
104	–	210 Lavender-med.
130	X	809 Delft

Step 2: Beadwork

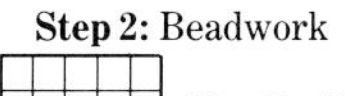

For the bird feed, scatter seven yellow beads as desired (see the photo).

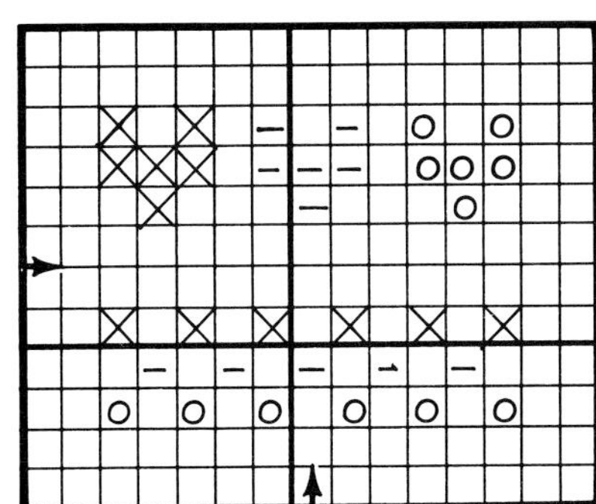

Rabbit Egg

SAMPLE
Stitched on white Linda 28 over two threads, the finished design size is 4½" x 6¼". The fabric was cut 10" x 10". (A fabric with this stitch count must be used so that the design will fit the egg.)

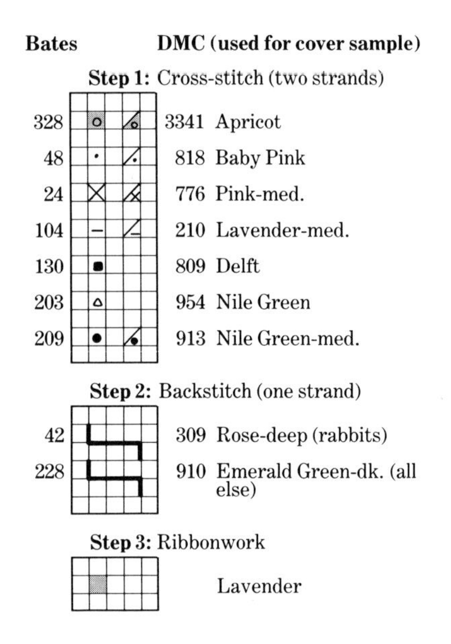

Bates
DMC (used for cover sample)
Step 1: Cross-stitch (two strands)
328
3341 Apricot
48
818 Baby Pink
24
776 Pink-med.
104
210 Lavender-med.
130
809 Delft
203
954 Nile Green
209
913 Nile Green-med.
Step 2: Backstitch (one strand)
42
309 Rose-deep (rabbits)
228
910 Emerald Green-dk. (all else)
Step 3: Ribbonwork
Lavender

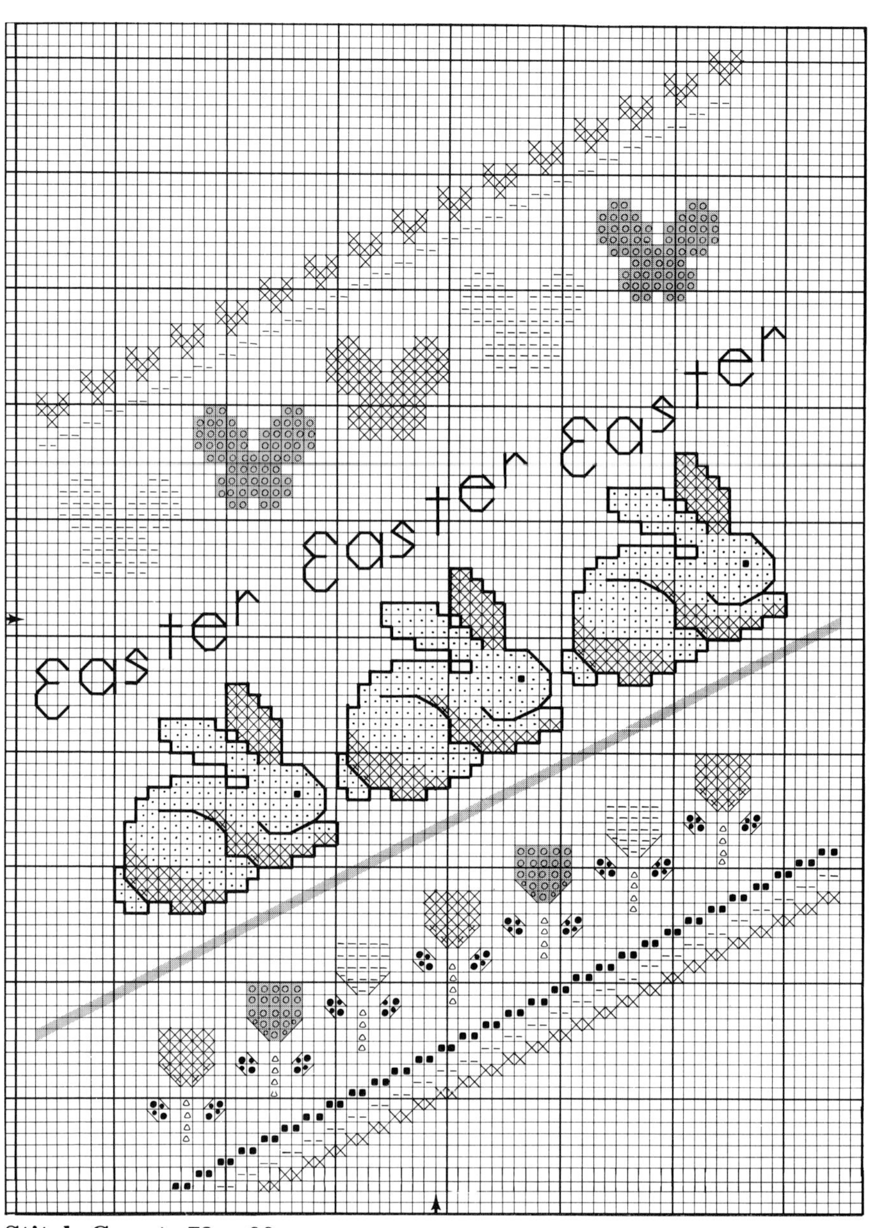

Stitch Count: 72 x 99

MATERIALS
- Completed cross-stitch on white Linda 28; see sample information
- ¼ yard of 45"-wide pink print fabric
- ½ yard of 1"-wide gathered white lace
- ½ yard of ¼"-wide flat white lace
- ¾ yard of lavender tubular satin cording
- 5" of 1/16"-wide lavender satin ribbon
- 7" Styrofoam egg

DIRECTIONS
1. Score the vertical center all the way around the egg to make an indentation for inserting the fabric and lace. Also score 1" in front of and parallel to the vertical center.

2. Cut one 8" x 9" piece of fabric. Also cut one 1" x 20" strip.

3. Center the large fabric piece over the back of the egg and tuck it into the indentation. Trim any fabric extending from the indentation. Starting at bottom of egg, wrap fabric strip around 1"-wide band created by second score. Tuck in fabric and trim. With design centered, place Linda over front of egg. Tuck in edges and trim.

4. Insert the 1"-wide gathered lace into the vertical center indentation. Insert the ¼"-wide lace into the front indentation. Place the satin cording between the ¼"-wide lace and the Linda, tying the bow just to the left of the center top. Trim the ends.

5. Place the lavender satin ribbon diagonally under the rabbits. Glue the ends in the indentation.

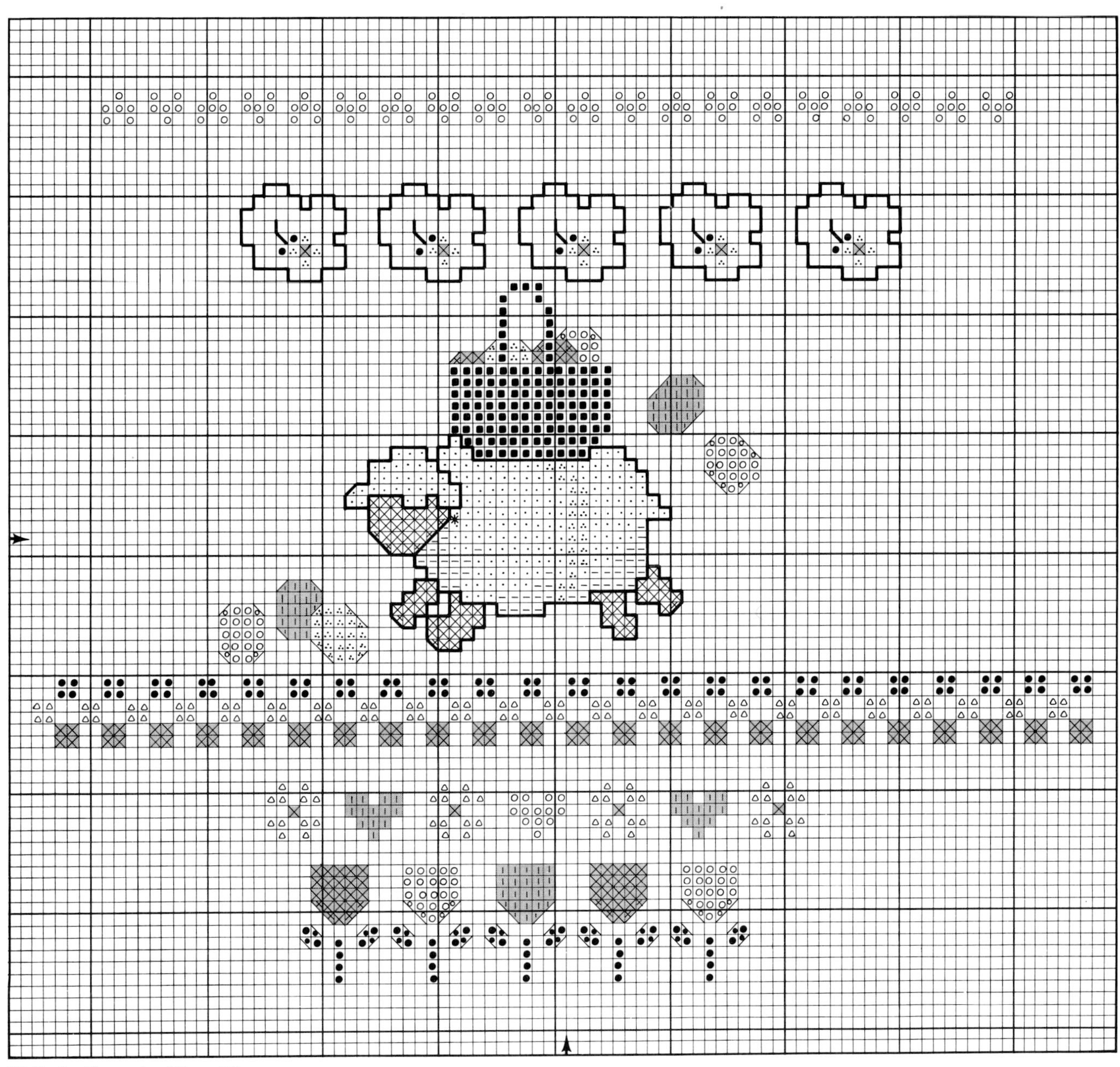

Stitch Count: 92 x 83

Lamb Egg

SAMPLE

Stitched on white Linda 28 over two threads, the finished design size is 5¾" x 5¼". The fabric was cut 10" x 10". (A fabric with this stitch count must be used so that the design will fit the egg.)

Bates DMC (used for sample)

Step 1: Cross-stitch (two strands)

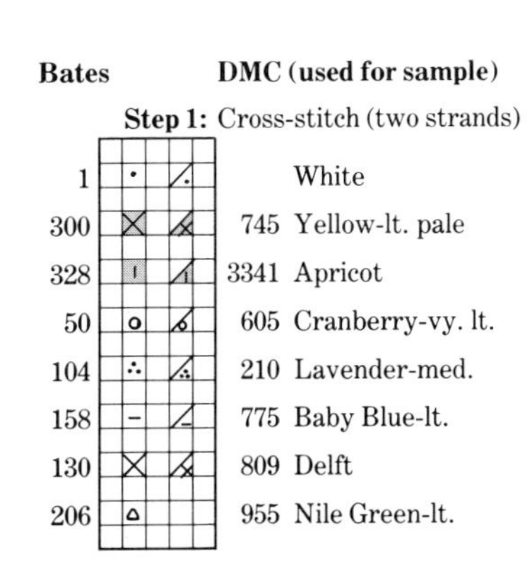

Bates	DMC	
1		White
300	745	Yellow-lt. pale
328	3341	Apricot
50	605	Cranberry-vy. lt.
104	210	Lavender-med.
158	775	Baby Blue-lt.
130	809	Delft
206	955	Nile Green-lt.

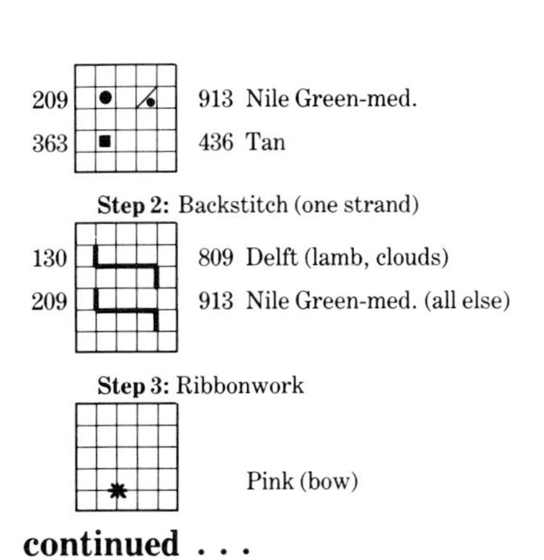

Bates	DMC	
209	913	Nile Green-med.
363	436	Tan

Step 2: Backstitch (one strand)

Bates	DMC	
130	809	Delft (lamb, clouds)
209	913	Nile Green-med. (all else)

Step 3: Ribbonwork

Pink (bow)

continued . . .

. . . **Lamb Egg continued**

MATERIALS

Completed cross-stitch on white Linda 28; see sample information
8″ x 9″ piece of lavender seersucker fabric
½ yard of ¾″-wide gathered white eyelet
1½ yards of ¹⁄₁₆″-wide lavender satin ribbon
⅝ yard of ¹⁄₁₆″-wide purple satin ribbon
¼ yard of ¹⁄₁₆″-wide bright pink satin ribbon
7″ Styrofoam egg
Glue

DIRECTIONS

1. Score the vertical center all the way around the egg to make an indentation for inserting the fabric and the eyelet.

2. Center the fabric piece over the back of the egg and tuck it into the indentation. Trim any fabric extending beyond the indentation. With the design centered, place the Linda over the front of the egg. Tuck in the edges and trim.

3. Insert the eyelet into the indentation around the egg.

4. Cut two 5″ lengths of lavender ribbon. Place one length above the top row of stitching. Glue the ends into the indentation. Place the second length below the bottom row of stitching and glue the ends in place. See photo for pink ribbon.

5. Fold the remaining lavender ribbon into 2½″ loops, leaving 6″ to 8″ ends. Tie the purple ribbon around the center of the loops. Trim the ends. Glue the bow on the egg to the right of the center top.

Chick Egg

SAMPLE

Stitched on white Linda 28 over two threads, the finished design size is 5⅝″ x 5⅞″. The fabric was cut 10″ x 10″. (A fabric with this stitch count must be used so that the design will fit the egg.)

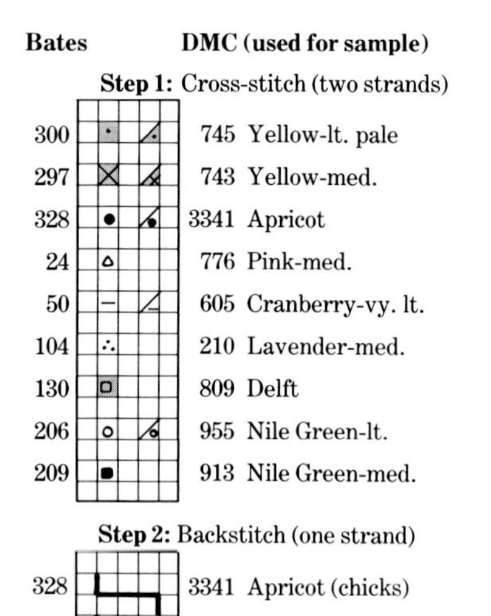

Bates	DMC (used for sample)	
Step 1: Cross-stitch (two strands)		
300	745	Yellow-lt. pale
297	743	Yellow-med.
328	3341	Apricot
24	776	Pink-med.
50	605	Cranberry-vy. lt.
104	210	Lavender-med.
130	809	Delft
206	955	Nile Green-lt.
209	913	Nile Green-med.
Step 2: Backstitch (one strand)		
328	3341	Apricot (chicks)
130	809	Delft (clouds)
209	913	Nile Green-med. (all else)

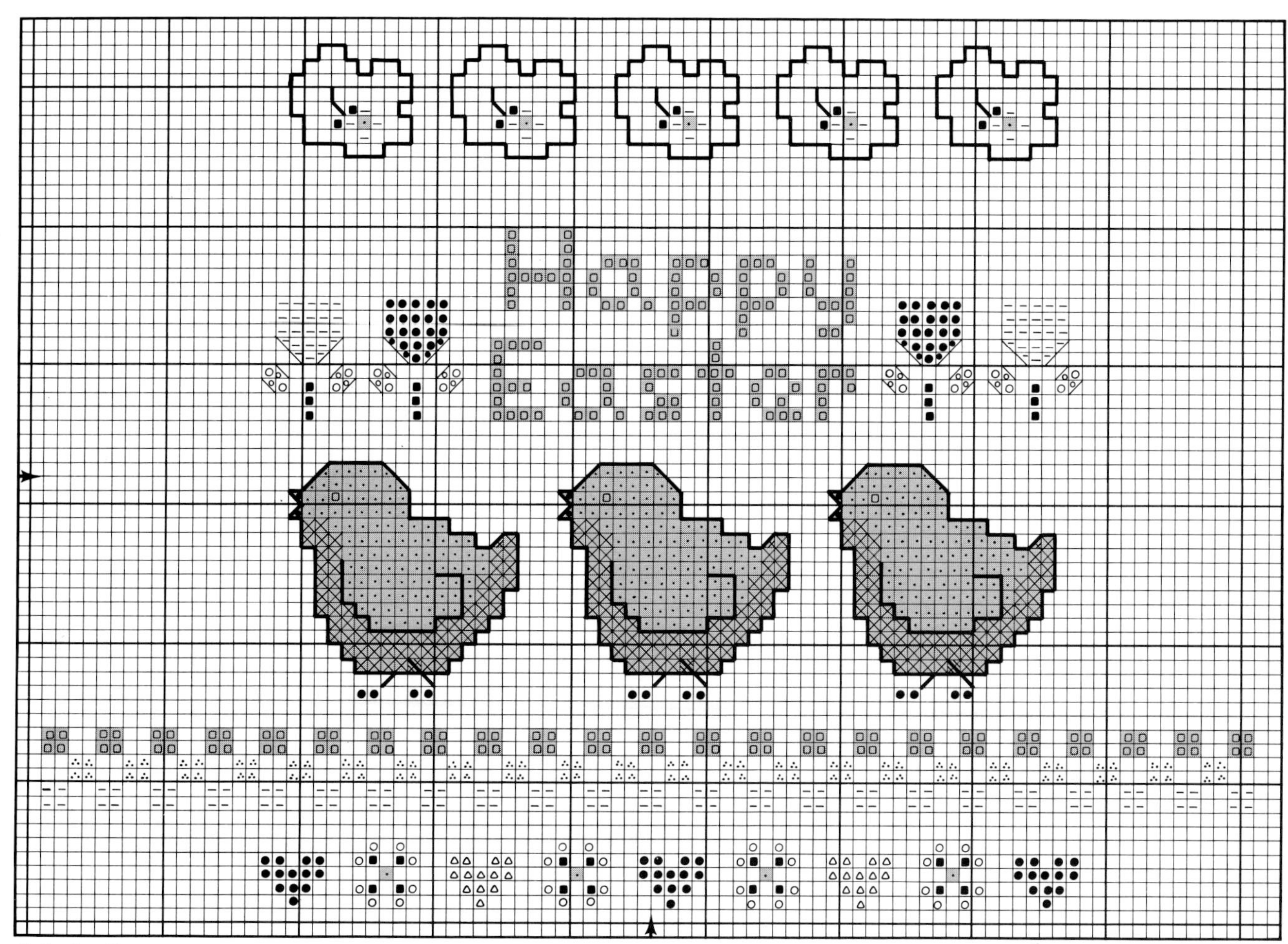

Stitch Count: 90 x 62

MATERIALS

Completed cross-stitch on white Linda 28; see sample information

¼ yard of 45″-wide blue-and-white striped fabric; matching thread

1½ yards of 1/16″-wide pink satin ribbon

¾ yard ⅛″-wide pink satin ribbon

7″ Styrofoam egg

Glue

DIRECTIONS

1. Score the vertical center all the way around egg to make an indentation for inserting fabric.

2. Cut one 8″ x 9″ piece of fabric. Also cut a 1″-wide bias strip, piecing as needed to equal 1½ yards.

3. Center the fabric piece over the back of the egg and tuck it into the indentation. Trim any fabric extending beyond the indentation. With the design centered, place the Linda over the front of the egg. Tuck in the edges and trim.

4. Stitch a gathering thread close to one edge of the bias strip and gather to 18″ (the thread will not be removed). Tuck the gathered edge into the indentation.

5. Cut the 1/16″-wide ribbon into two equal lengths. Handling all the ribbon lengths as one unit, tie them into a 3″-wide bow. Glue the bow to the egg just to the left of the center top.

Stenciled Eggs

SAMPLE
Stitched on white Hardanger 22 over two threads, the finished design sizes vary. The fabric was cut 6" x 6". (A fabric with this stitch count must be used so that the design will fit the egg.) The cross-stitch portions of the eggs are taken from the graphs for the Chick, Rabbit, and Lamb eggs; refer to the individual sample information for the designs listed below. Position the stitching as desired, allowing room for the stenciled designs.

Blue Hearts: The checkerboard pattern and cloud are from the Chick Egg.

Green Tulips: The cross-stitch tulips and checkerboard pattern are from the Rabbit Egg.

Pink Tulips: The hearts are from the border above the tulips on the Lamb Egg. Repeat the pink heart to form a row, allowing two stitches between the hearts. The checkerboard pattern is from the Chick Egg.

Green Heart: The top border is the row of tiny pink hearts on the Lamb Egg. The bottom border is also from the Lamb Egg.

MATERIALS (for one egg)
Completed cross-stitch on white Hardanger 22; see sample information
Pink, blue, and green acrylic-based paint
6¼" x 7½" piece of print fabric
1½ yards of ⅛"-wide contrasting satin ribbon
4" Styrofoam egg
Glue or pins

DIRECTIONS
1. Make stencils for the tulips or heart; see General Instructions for stenciling.

2. Center the stencil design between the cross-stitch rows, and stencil (see photo for colors).

3. Cut the Hardanger 4½" x 5½" with the design centered.

4. Score all around the egg vertically, ½" forward of center, to make an indentation for the fabric.

5. Center the print fabric over the back of the egg, and tuck it into the indentation. Trim any excess fabric. With the design centered, place the Hardanger over the front of the egg. Tuck it into the indentation and trim any excess.

6. Cut two 27" lengths or three 18" lengths of ribbon. Handling equal ribbon lengths as one unit, mark the center. Place the center of the ribbon unit at the top of the indentation and glue or pin it along the line, twisting slightly. Tie a bow near the bottom of the indentation where the ends meet and glue or pin in place. Trim ends.

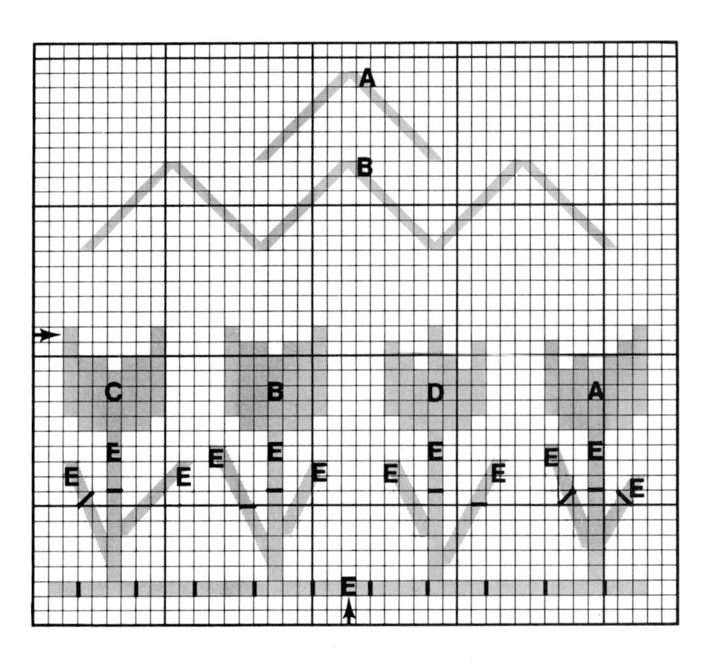

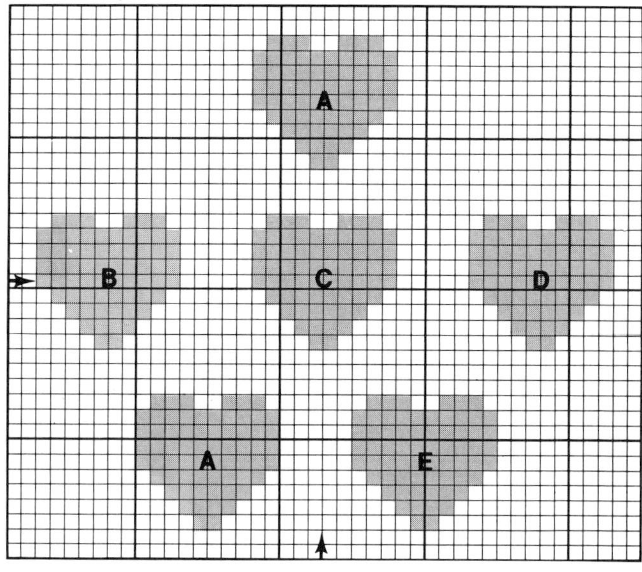

Ribbon Eggs

SAMPLE
Stitched on white Linda 28, the finished design size is 2½" x 2¼". The fabric was cut 5" x 5". (A fabric with this stitch count must be used so that the design will fit the egg.)

Tulips:

Step 1: Ribbonwork

A	Blue
B	Light Pink
C	Lavender
D	Light Yellow
E	Light Green couched with matching thread

Hearts:

Step 1: Ribbonwork

A	Light Pink
B	Lavender
C	Light Yellow
D	Light Green
E	Blue

MATERIALS (for one egg)
Completed ribbon design on white Linda 28; see sample information
One 5" x 6½" piece of unstitched white Linda 28 or contrasting fabric for the back
Heart Egg: ⅞ yard of ⅛"-wide pink satin ribbon and ⅞ yard of ⅛"-wide blue satin ribbon
Flower Egg: 1½ yards of ⅛"-wide pink satin ribbon
4" Styrofoam egg
Glue and pins

DIRECTIONS
1. Score the vertical center all the way around the egg to make an indentation for the fabric and the ribbon.

2. Center the fabric piece over the back of the egg and tuck it into the indentation. Trim any fabric extending beyond the indentation. Attach the stitched piece of linen to the front of the egg in the same manner.

3. Heart design: Fold the blue ribbon in half. Handle both layers as a single unit and pin the ends at the center bottom of the egg inside the indentation. At ¾" intervals, pin 1" loops of ribbon into the indentation. Beginning at the upper right side of the egg, loosely weave pink ribbon through the loops of blue ribbon. Tie the pink ribbon into a bow on the right side of the egg and trim the ends.

4. Flower design: Beginning at the center bottom, tuck 1" loops of ribbon into the indentation as close together as possible. Secure with glue or pins.

Easter Pinafore & Hatband

SAMPLE
Pinafore: Stitched on white Belfast Linen 32 over two threads, the finished design size will vary with the size of the pinafore. Cut the fabric 5½″ wide. To determine the length to cut the fabric, add 3″ to the width of the pinafore front. Begin stitching the rabbits 1½″ from the left end of the fabric and continue stitching until the design is the width of the pinafore front.

Bates	DMC (used for cover sample)
Step 1: Cross-stitch (two strands)	
48	818 Baby Pink
24	776 Pink-med.
130	809 Delft
Step 2: Backstitch (one strand)	
42	335 Rose

SAMPLE
Hatband: Stitched on white Belfast Linen 32 over two threads, the finished design size will vary with the size of the hat. Cut the fabric 3½″ wide. To determine the length to cut the fabric, add 2″ to the circumference of the hat. Use the butterfly graph and colors from the Rabbit Egg, placing the butterflies side by side, two stitches (4 threads) apart. Begin stitching the butterflies 1″ from the left end of the fabric and continue stitching until the design equals the circumference of the hat.

MATERIALS
Completed cross-stitch on white Belfast Linen 32; matching thread; see sample information for pinafore and hatband
¼″-wide lavender satin ribbon to fit around hat and once across front of pinafore skirt; matching thread
¼″-wide yellow satin ribbon to fit twice across front of pinafore skirt; matching thread
1⁄16″-wide lavender satin ribbon to fit once across front of pinafore skirt and 1½ additional yards for a bow; matching thread
Purchased white pinafore or purchased pattern
Purchased white straw hat

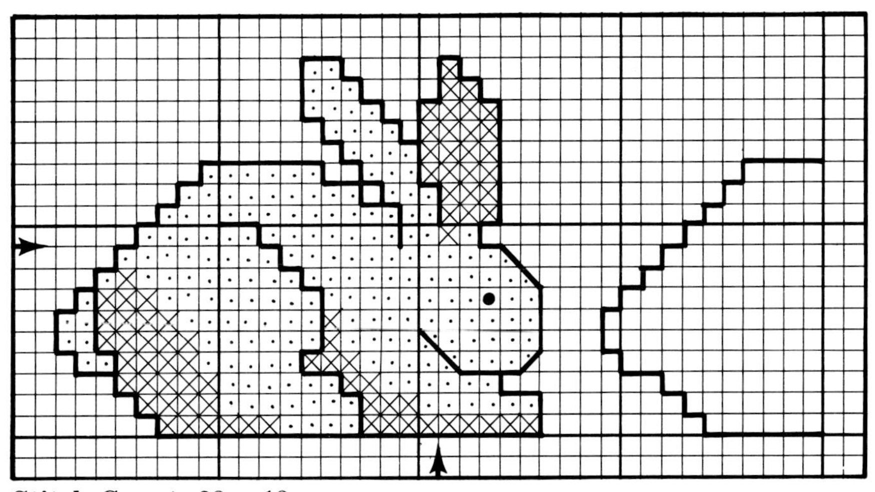
Stitch Count: 38 x 18

DIRECTIONS
Note: If applying the design to a purchased pinafore, turn under the seam allowances at each end and slipstitch. If you are making a pinafore, the seam allowances will be included when you stitch the hem on the sides.

1. With the rabbit design centered, cut the linen in a strip 3″ wide and long enough to extend across the front of the pinafore skirt with a ½″ seam allowance on each end.

2. Pin the linen 2½″ from the bottom of the pinafore. Stitch along both long edges of the stitched linen with a zigzag stitch.

3. From the yellow ribbon, cut two lengths equal to the length of the stitched design. Place one length of ribbon over the bottom edge of the linen and slipstitch both edges of the ribbon to the pinafore. Use the other ribbon to cover the top edge of the linen.

4. From the ¼″-wide lavender ribbon, cut a length long enough to extend across the pinafore skirt with a ¼″ seam at each end. Cut an equal length from the 1⁄16″-wide ribbon. Slipstitch both edges of the ¼″-wide ribbon to the pinafore, ¼″ above the upper length of yellow ribbon. Slipstitch both edges of the 1⁄16″-wide ribbon to the pinafore, ¼″ below the lower length of yellow ribbon.

5. Cut the remaining 1⁄16″-wide ribbon into one 22″ and two 16″ lengths. Fold the 22″ length into three 3″ loops. Tie the 16″ lengths around the center of the loops to form a bow. Tack the bow to the pinafore next to the ¼″-wide lavender ribbon (see the photo). Trim the ends to a desired length.

6. Measure the circumference of the hat. With the design centered, cut the linen 3″ wide by the circumference plus 1″.

7. With right sides together, fold the hatband to measure 1½″ wide. Stitch the long edges with a ¼″ seam. Turn right side out and press with the design centered.

8. Slipstitch both edges of the ¼″-wide lavender ribbon ¼″ below the design.

9. Place the band around the hat. Overlap the ends and slipstitch securely. It may be necessary to slipstitch the band to the hat all along the top edge.

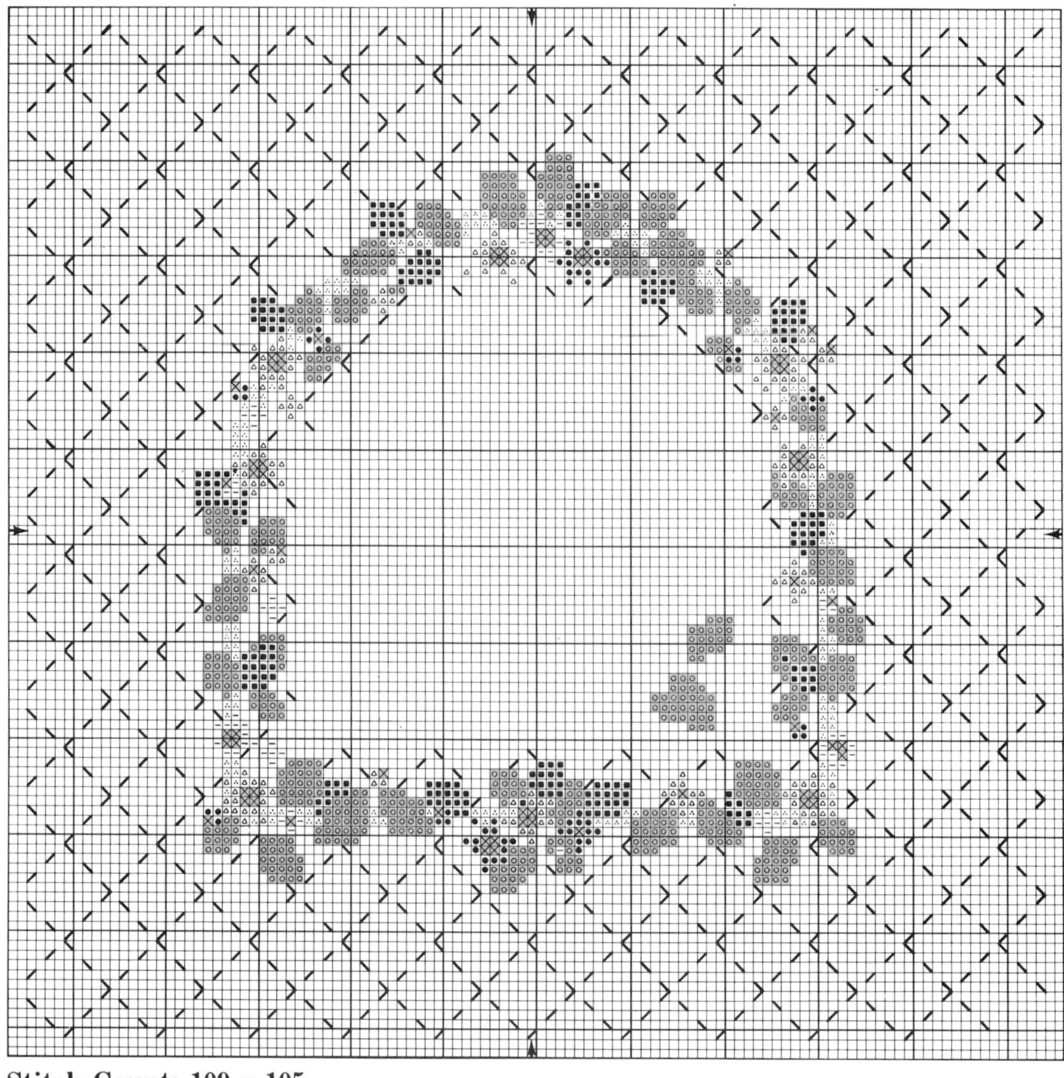

Stitch Count: 109 x 105

MAY 1

May Day

Spring's first blossoms have inspired celebrations since ancient times, and festivals with maypoles and dancing are still common in England and parts of the U.S. Welcome spring to your home with a pretty pillow.

Trellis Pillow

SAMPLE
Stitched on teal Jobelan 28 over two threads, the finished design size is 7¾″ x 7½″. The fabric was cut 15″ x 15″. (A fabric with this stitch count must be used so that the design will fit the pillow.)

Bates		DMC (used for sample)
	Step 1: Cross-stitch (two strands)	
893	–	224 Shell Pink-lt.
894	△	223 Shell Pink-med.
5975	•	356 Terra Cotta-med.
920	∴	932 Antique Blue-lt.
876	■	502 Blue Green
189	○	991 Aquamarine-dk.
397	☒	3072 Beaver Grey-vy. lt.
	Step 2: Backstitch (one strand)	
921	⌐	931 Antique Blue-med.

MATERIALS
Completed cross-stitch on teal Jobelan 28 and matching thread; see sample information
½ yard of 58″-wide additional teal Jobelan for ruffle and back
Small pieces of white chintz for appliqué
11″ x 11″ piece of muslin
13″ x 13″ piece of polyester fleece
3 yards of 2″-wide white flat eyelet lace
3 yards of ⅛″-wide turquoise satin ribbon
Stuffing or 12″ x 12″ pillow form
Dressmakers' pen
Tracing paper for patterns

DIRECTIONS
1. Trace the patterns for the appliqué flower on tracing paper. Then trace the pattern onto the Jobelan with a dressmakers' pen.

2. From the white fabric, cut the flower pieces, adding a ¼″ seam allowance. From the polyester fleece, cut the flower pieces without any seam allowance.

3. Layer the fleece and the fabric in the center of the cross-stitch design and slipstitch in place. Quilt and embroider the flower as indicated on the pattern.

4. Cut the stitched Jobelan 11″ x 11″, with the design centered. Also cut one 11″ x 11″ piece of Jobelan for the back and one 8″-wide bias strip for the ruffle, piecing as needed to equal 100″.

5. Cut one 11″ x 11″ piece from the muslin and another from the fleece. For the pillow front, stack the muslin, the fleece, and stitched Jobelan, right side up. Baste together. Mark a quilting guideline ⅜″ outside the edge of the stitched design with a dressmakers' pen. Quilt by hand with matching thread.

6. Stitch the short ends of the bias strip together, forming one continuous piece. Fold the strip in half lengthwise, wrong sides together, and press. Place the eyelet right side up on the Jobelan bias, aligning the raw edges. Divide the strip into quarters and mark with a dressmakers' pen.

7. Stitch gathering threads through all the layers of the Jobelan and eyelet. Gather to form a ruffle to fit the pillow front. With right sides together, pin the ruffle to the pillow front, matching the quarter marks to the corners and allowing extra fullness at each corner. Stitch with a ½″ seam.

8. With right sides of the pillow front and back together, stitch on the stitching line of the ruffle, leaving a 6″ opening. Turn the pillow right side out and insert the form or stuffing. Slipstitch the opening closed.

9. With a large-eyed needle, thread the ribbon through the eyelet ruffle, securing the ends.

MAY 3-9

Be Kind to Animals Week

This holiday was established to promote humane treatment of animals. And who exemplifies such kindness better than Noah! A sampler with a contemporary design in warm colors reminds us of our animal friends.

Noah's Ark

SAMPLE
Stitched on Glenshee Egyptian Cotton quality D over two threads, the finished design size is 6½" x 10¾". The fabric was cut 13" x 17".

Bates	DMC (used for sample)
	Step 1: Cross-stitch (two strands)
352	300 Mahogany-vy. dk.
903	3032 Mocha Brown-med.
889	610 Drab Brown-vy. dk.
905	645 Beaver Grey-vy. dk.
	Step 2: Backstitch (one strand)
382	3371 Black Brown
	Step 3: Long Stitch (twelve strands) The staff is six strands couched with one strand.
352	300 Mahogany-vy. dk.

FABRICS	DESIGN SIZES
Aida 11	7⅝" x 12⅝"
Aida 14	6" x 9⅞"
Aida 18	4⅝" x 7¾"
Hardanger 22	3⅞" x 6⅜"

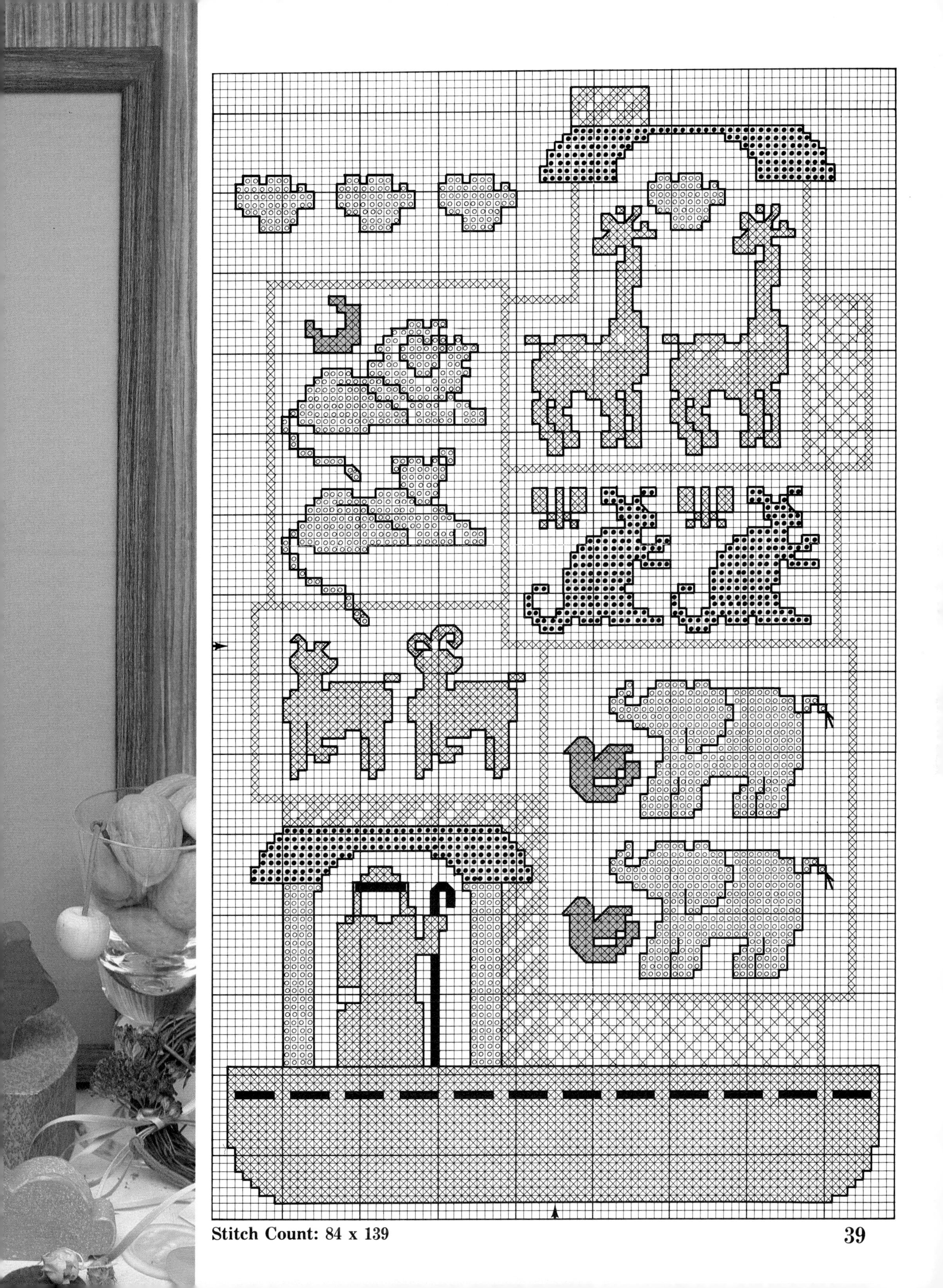

Stitch Count: 84 x 139

MAY 10

Mother's Day

Mothers are the world's most important people! President Woodrow Wilson must have felt this when, in 1915, he proclaimed Mother's Day as a national observance. Mothers will always appreciate a few of the more private expressions of gratitude, too—such as the distinctive card, boxes, and intricate sampler shown here.

ABCDEFGHIJK
LMNOPQRSTU
VWXYZ 1234567890
Once upon a memory
Someone wiped away a tear,
Held me close and loved me,
Thank you, Mother dear.

A Mother's Day Sampler

SAMPLE
Stitched on white Belfast Linen 32 over two threads, the finished design size is 11½" x 7¼". The fabric was cut 18" x 13". Refer to General Instructions for the Herringbone stitch.

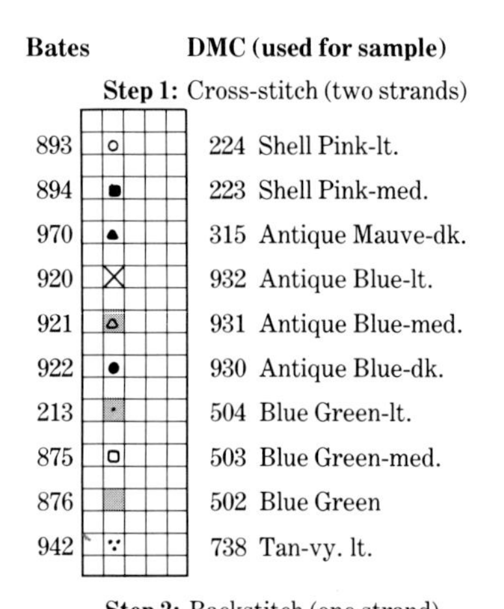

Bates		DMC (used for sample)
		Step 1: Cross-stitch (two strands)
893	○	224 Shell Pink-lt.
894	■	223 Shell Pink-med.
970	▲	315 Antique Mauve-dk.
920	☒	932 Antique Blue-lt.
921	△	931 Antique Blue-med.
922	●	930 Antique Blue-dk.
213	·	504 Blue Green-lt.
875	□	503 Blue Green-med.
876	▒	502 Blue Green
942	∵	738 Tan-vy. lt.

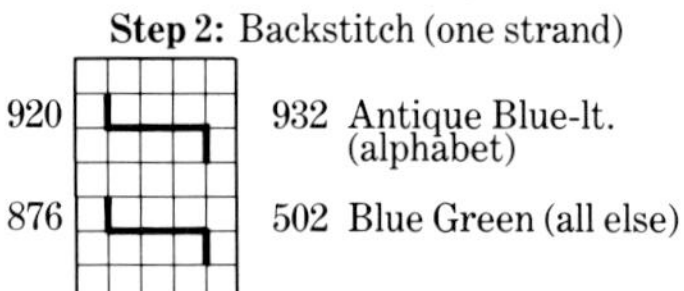

Bates	DMC
	Step 2: Backstitch (one strand)
920	932 Antique Blue-lt. (alphabet)
876	502 Blue Green (all else)

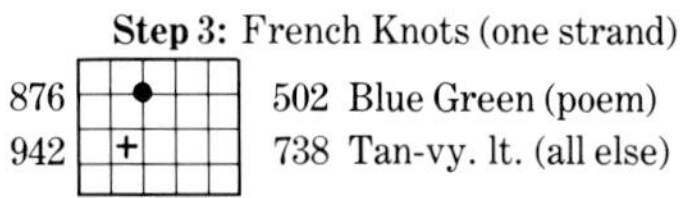

Bates	DMC
	Step 3: French Knots (one strand)
876	502 Blue Green (poem)
942	738 Tan-vy. lt. (all else)

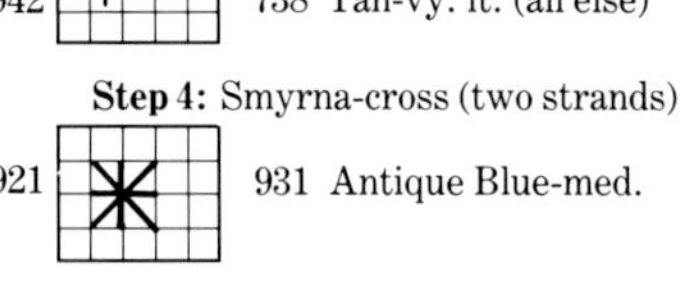

Bates	DMC
	Step 4: Smyrna-cross (two strands)
921	931 Antique Blue-med.

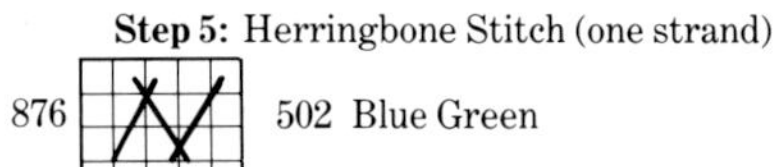

Bates	DMC
	Step 5: Herringbone Stitch (one strand)
876	502 Blue Green

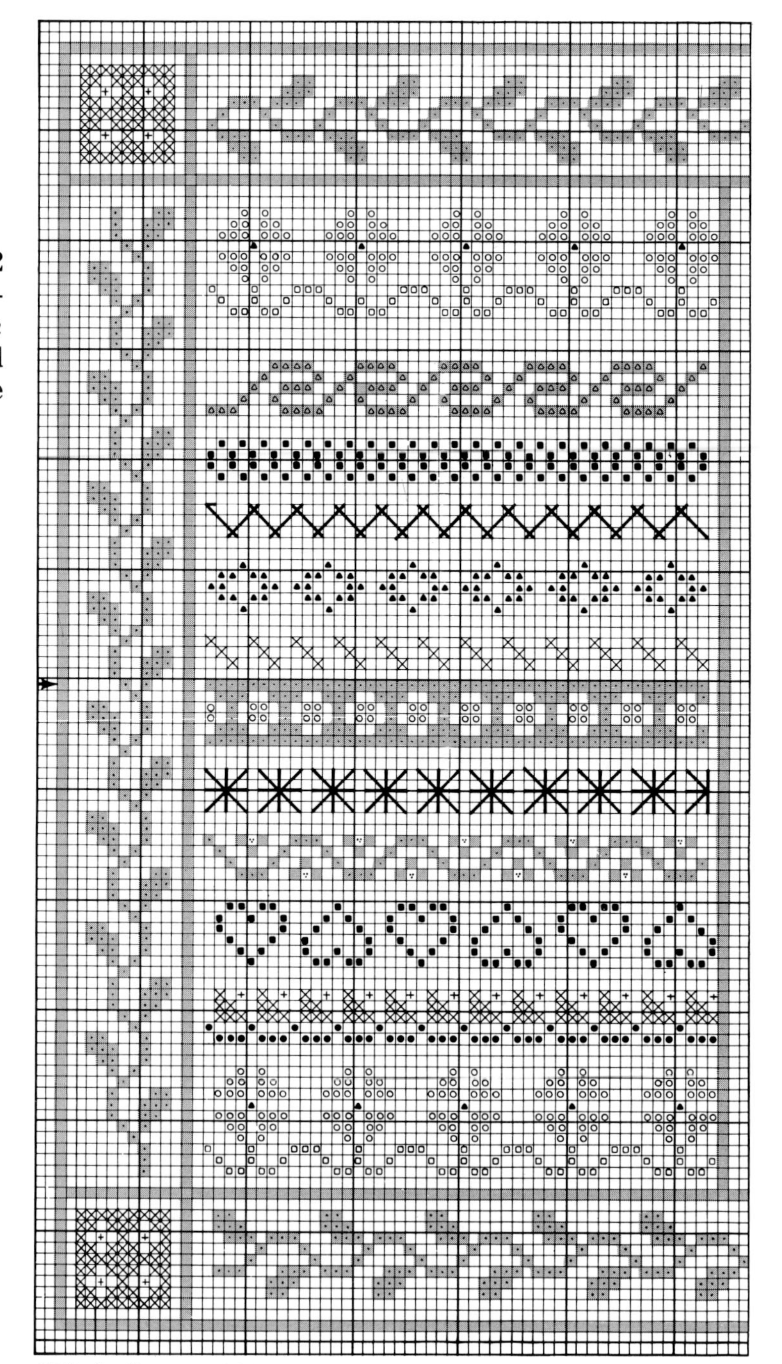

Stitch Count: 185 x 117

FABRICS	DESIGN SIZES
Aida 11	16⅞" x 10⅝"
Aida 14	13¼" x 8⅜"
Aida 18	10¼" x 6½"
Hardanger 22	8⅜" x 5⅜"

ABCDEFGHIJK
LMNOPQRSTU
VWXYZ 1234567890
Once upon a memory
Someone wiped away a tear,
Held me close and loved me,
Thank you, Mother dear.

A Mother's Day Card

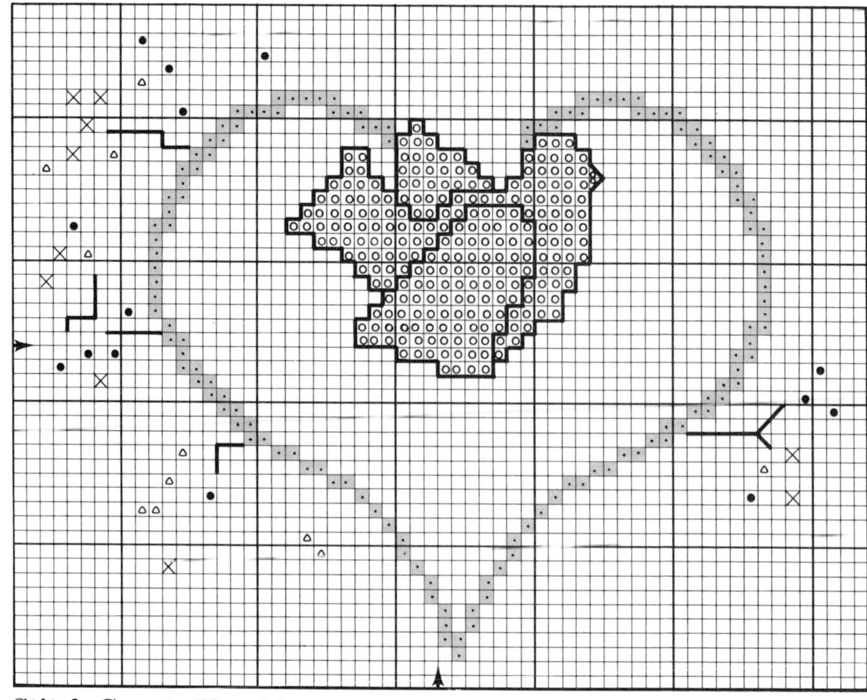

Stitch Count: 58 x 44

SAMPLE
Stitched on white Belfast Linen 32 over two threads, the finished design size is 3⅝" x 2¾". The fabric was cut 6" x 6". (A fabric with this stitch count must be used so that the design will fit the card.)

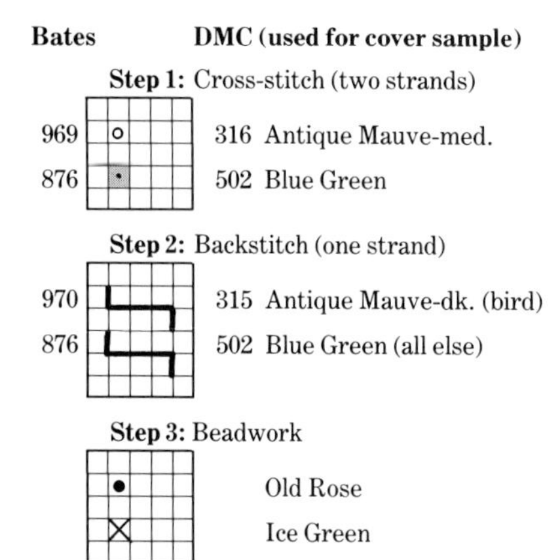

MATERIALS
Completed cross-stitch on white Belfast Linen 32; see sample information
9" x 14" piece of unstitched white Belfast Linen 32
2½ yards of ⅜"-wide white cotton lace; matching thread
5" x 5" piece of polyester fleece
Two mat-board hearts
Two 6" x 8" pieces of white mat board
1½ yards of narrow variegated light green ribbon
¾ yard of narrow light green silk ribbon
½ yard of narrow dark green silk ribbon

Ribbon flowers: three light green, two mauve, two yellow, and one pink or 3″ of ¼″-wide ribbon to construct each flower
Small piece of paper for tag
Crystal heart ⅜″ wide
8″ of white plastic tape
Fusing material
Glue
Dressmakers' pen
Tracing paper for pattern
Optional: 7½″ x 11½″ piece of decorative paper

DIRECTIONS

1. Cut the piece of fleece, using the heart pattern. Glue it to one mat-board heart.

2. Center the heart pattern on the cross-stitch design. Trace around it with a dressmakers' pen; then add a ¾″ seam allowance. Cut out the design piece.

3. Center the fleece side of the heart against the wrong side of the design piece. Clip the seam allowance as needed, wrap the fabric to the back of the padded heart, and glue.

4. Cut a 45″ length of lace and set it aside. Stitch gathering threads close to one edge of the remaining length of lace and gather it to 15″. Slipstitch the lace ruffle to the back of the padded heart with the ruffle extending beyond the heart.

5. Glue the second mat-board heart to the back of the padded heart.

6. Write a message on the paper for the tag. Trim the tag to ⅝″ x ¾″. Trim the corners diagonally. Using one strand of embroidery floss, sew through the corner of the tag and attach it to the bird's beak.

7. Using two light green, one mauve, one pink, and one yellow ribbon flower, stitch an arrangement to the lower left side of the cross-stitch heart. (To make ribbon flowers, see General Instructions.) Attach the crystal heart. From the light green silk ribbon, cut an 8″ length and tie it into a small bow. Attach it to the padded heart.

8. To construct the card, lay the mat-board pieces with the 8″ edges side by side. Run tape down these edges to join them. This becomes the inside of the card.

9. Trace around the opened-out card on fusing material. Fuse the unstitched linen piece to the outside front of the card only. Then wrap the linen to the back, allowing for the spine of the card, and fuse. (Follow the manufacturer's directions for fusing.) Trim fabric to fit card.

10. Glue reserved lace along the outside edges of the linen. Center and glue the padded heart to the card, ½″ from the lower front edge.

11. Cut a 9″ length of light green variegated ribbon. Fold the remaining ribbons into 4″-wide loops. Tie the 9″ length around the center of the loops. Center and glue the bow to the card, ½″ from the top front edge. Glue one light green, one mauve, and one yellow ribbon flower over the knot.

12. Write a message on the inside of the card.

13. Optional: Fold the decorative paper to measure 5¾″ x 7½″. Glue the fold lightly to the spine on the inside of the card. Write a personal message on the paper.

Porcelain Boxes

SAMPLES

Small Round Box: Stitched on white Belfast Linen 32 over two threads, the finished design size is ⅝" x ¾". The fabric was cut 3" x 3". (A fabric with this stitch count must be used so that the design will fit the box.)

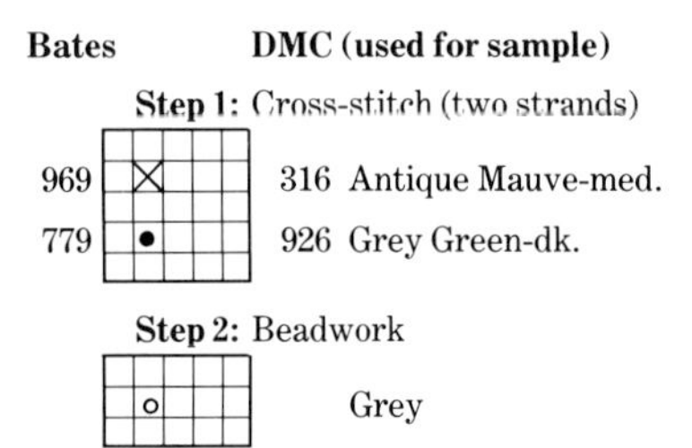

Bates		DMC (used for sample)
	Step 1: Cross-stitch (two strands)	
969	X	316 Antique Mauve-med.
779	•	926 Grey Green-dk.
	Step 2: Beadwork	
	o	Grey

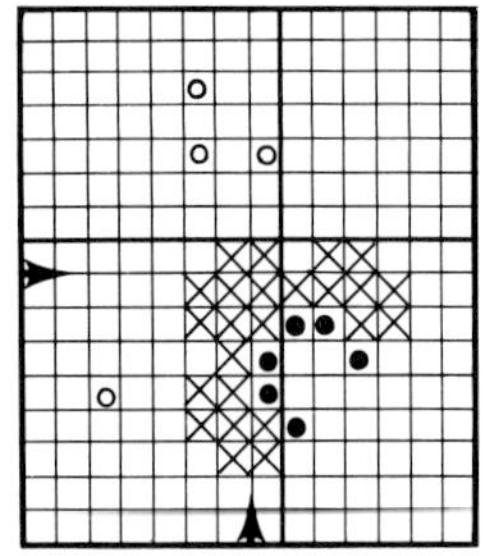

Stitch Count: 10 x 12

Small Oval Box: Stitched on white Belfast Linen 32 over two threads, the finished design size is 1¼" x ½". The fabric was cut 3" x 2". The initial is taken from the Mother's Day Sampler. (A fabric with this stitch count must be used so that the design will fit the box.)

Large Round Box: Stitched on white Belfast Linen 32 over two threads, the finished design size is 2⅝" x 2⅞". The fabric was cut 5" x 5". (A fabric with this stitch count must be used so that the design will fit the box.)

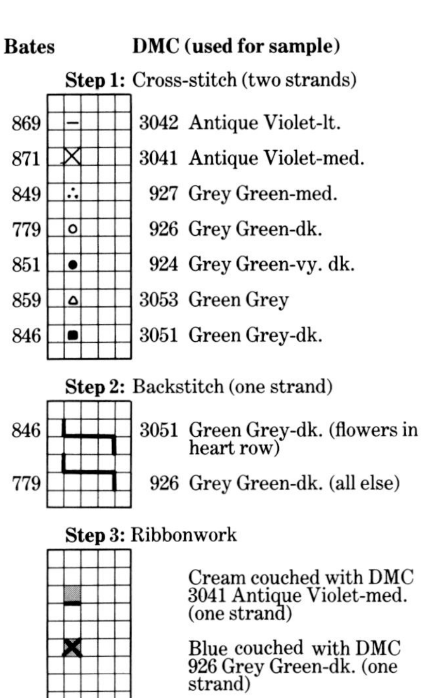

Bates	DMC (used for sample)
Step 1: Cross-stitch (two strands)	
869	3042 Antique Violet-lt.
871	3041 Antique Violet-med.
849	927 Grey Green-med.
779	926 Grey Green-dk.
851	924 Grey Green-vy. dk.
859	3053 Green Grey
846	3051 Green Grey-dk.
Step 2: Backstitch (one strand)	
846	3051 Green Grey-dk. (flowers in heart row)
779	926 Grey Green-dk. (all else)
Step 3: Ribbonwork	
	Cream couched with DMC 3041 Antique Violet-med. (one strand)
	Blue couched with DMC 926 Grey Green-dk. (one strand)
	Green couched with DMC 3053 Green Grey (one strand)

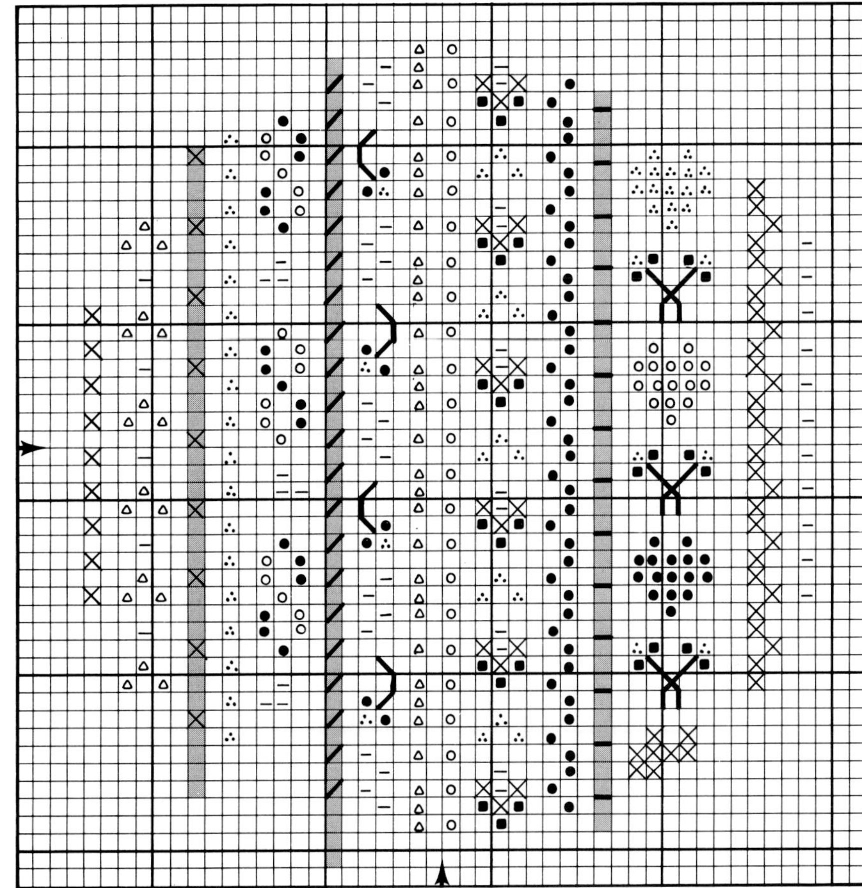

Stitch Count: 43 x 45

Large Oval Box: Stitched on white Belfast Linen 32 over two threads, the finished design size is 3" x 1½". The fabric was cut 5" x 4". (A fabric with this stitch count must be used so that the design will fit the box.)

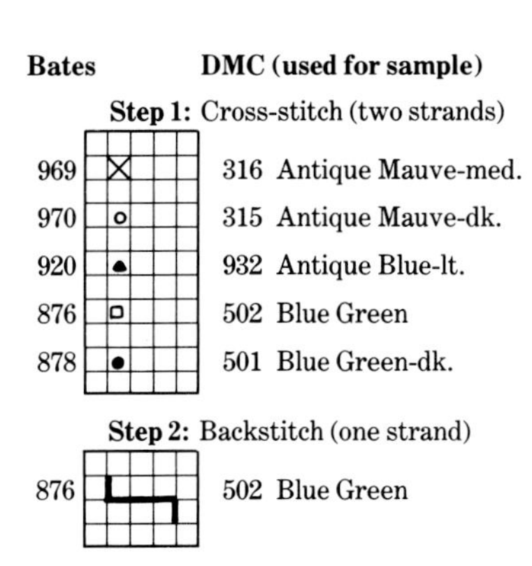

Bates	DMC (used for sample)
Step 1: Cross-stitch (two strands)	
969	316 Antique Mauve-med.
970	315 Antique Mauve-dk.
920	932 Antique Blue-lt.
876	502 Blue Green
878	501 Blue Green-dk.
Step 2: Backstitch (one strand)	
876	502 Blue Green

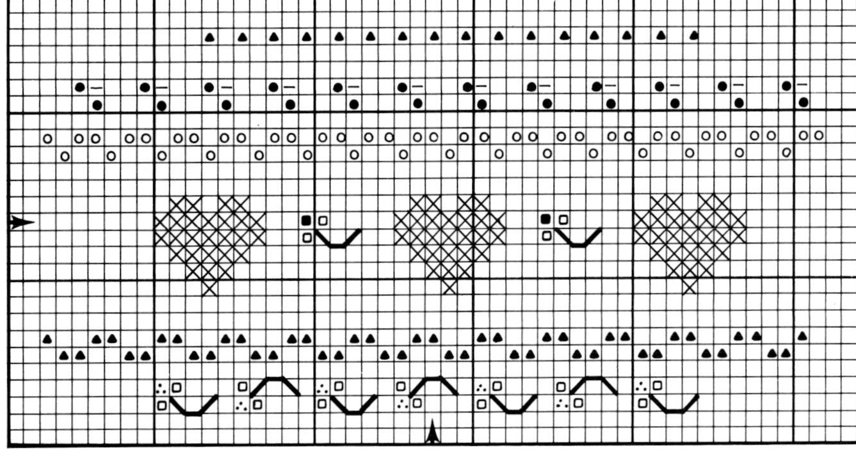

Stitch Count: 49 x 23

Step 3: Beadwork

Pale Peach

Amethyst

Garnet

JUNE 15

Friendship Day

It's a holiday set aside to recognize friends, both old and new! Send these sunny greetings with a personal note inside.

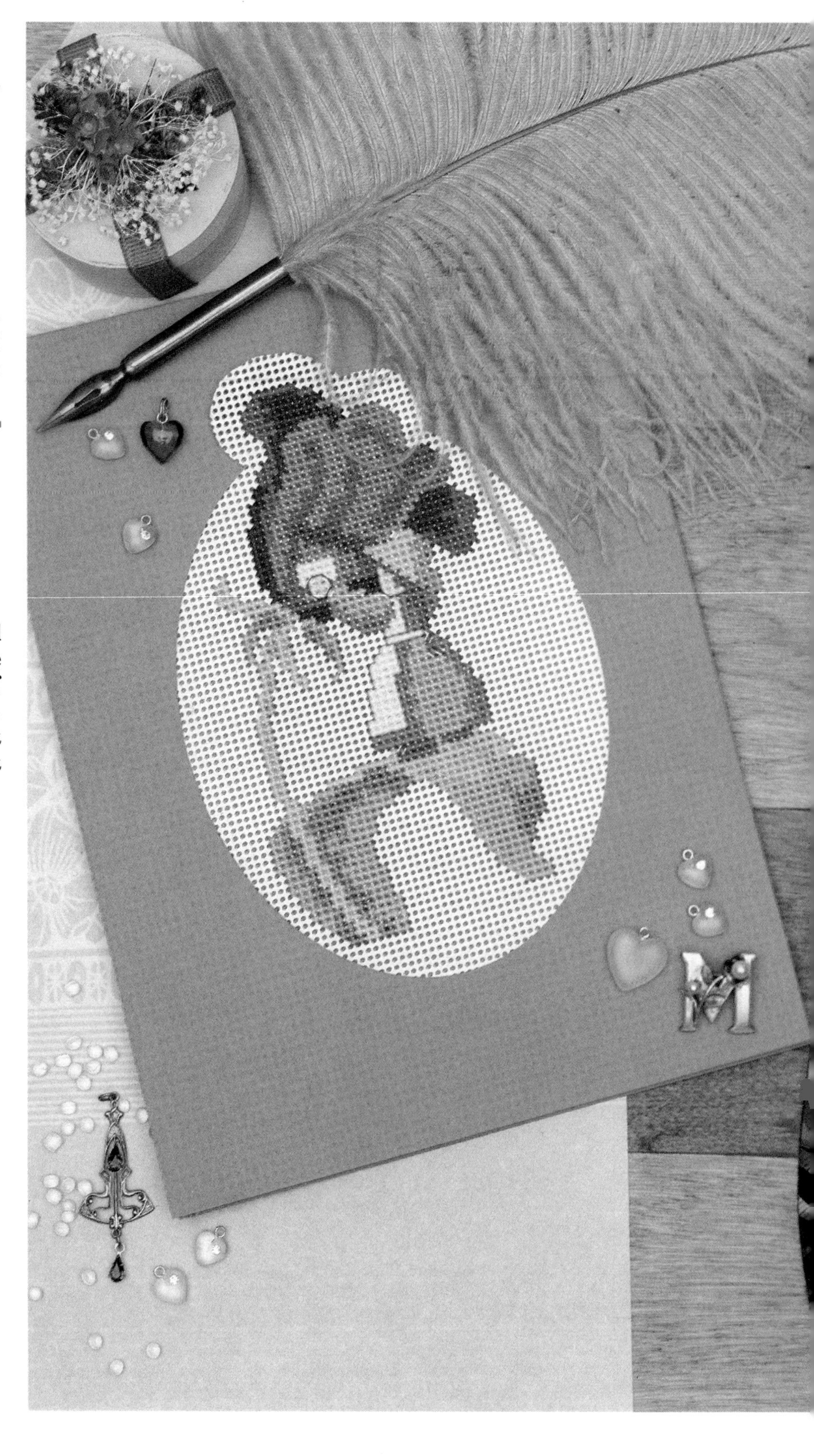

Tulip Card

SAMPLE
Stitched on white Perforated Paper 15, the finished design size is 2½" x 5¼". A 9" x 12" sheet of Perforated Paper was used. (Paper with this stitch count must be used so that the design will fit the card.)

Step 1: Cross-stitch (three strands)

Bates	DMC (used for sample)	
1		White
306	725	Topaz
778	948	Peach Flesh-vy. lt.
8	353	Peach Flesh
10	352	Coral-lt.
66	3688	Mauve-med.
69	3687	Mauve
70	3685	Mauve-dk.
99	552	Violet-dk.
203	954	Nile Green
209	913	Nile Green-med.
205	911	Emerald Green-med.
307	783	Christmas Gold
309	781	Topaz-dk.

Step 2: Backstitch (one strand)

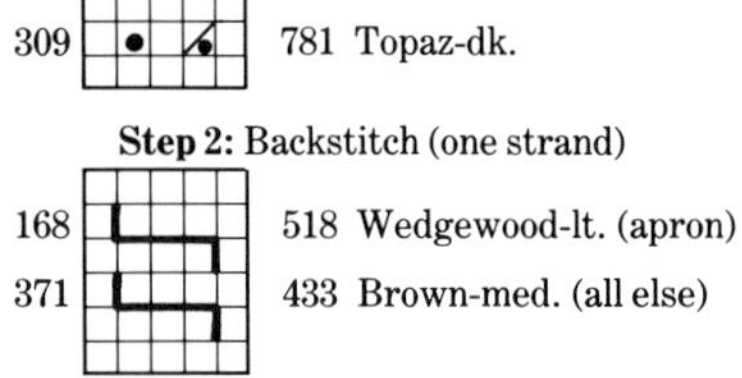

Bates	DMC (used for sample)	
168	518	Wedgewood-lt. (apron)
371	433	Brown-med. (all else)

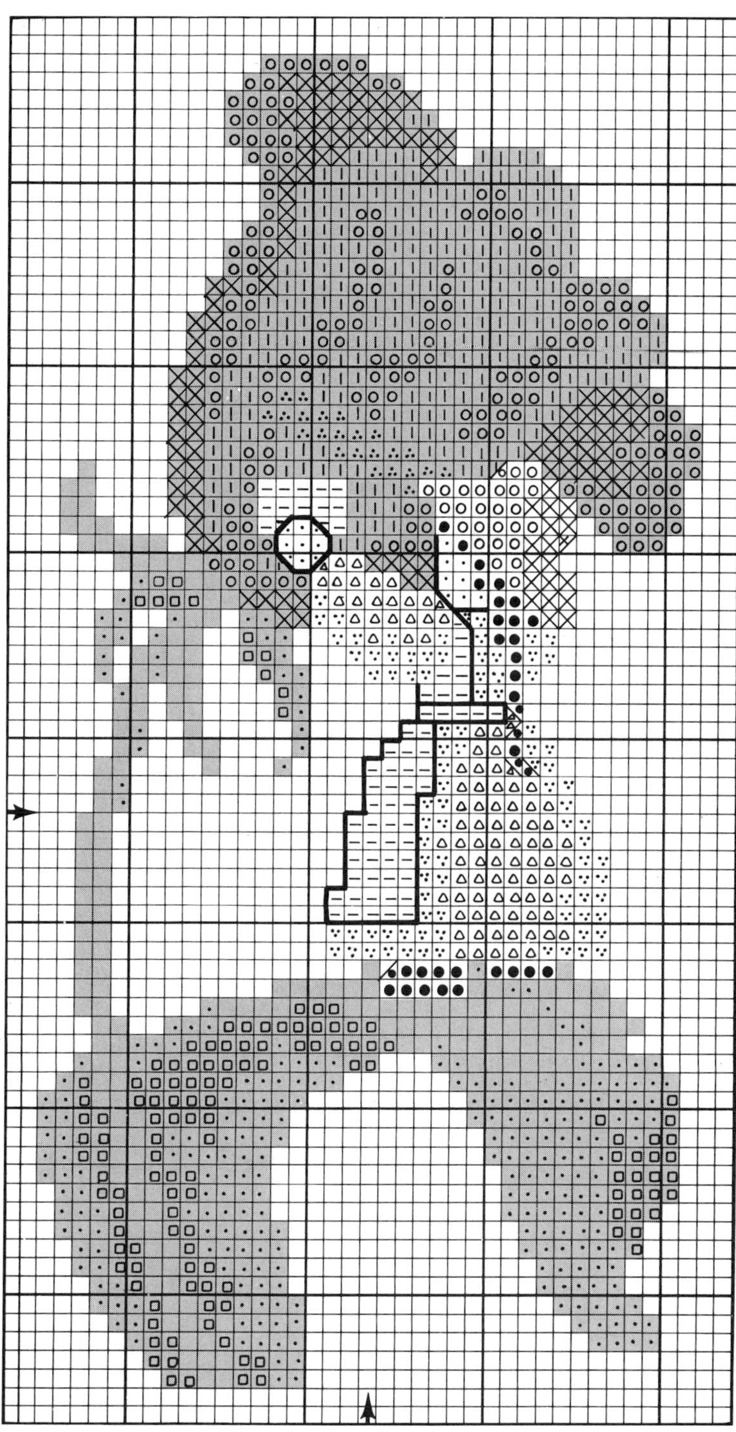

Stitch Count: 37 x 72

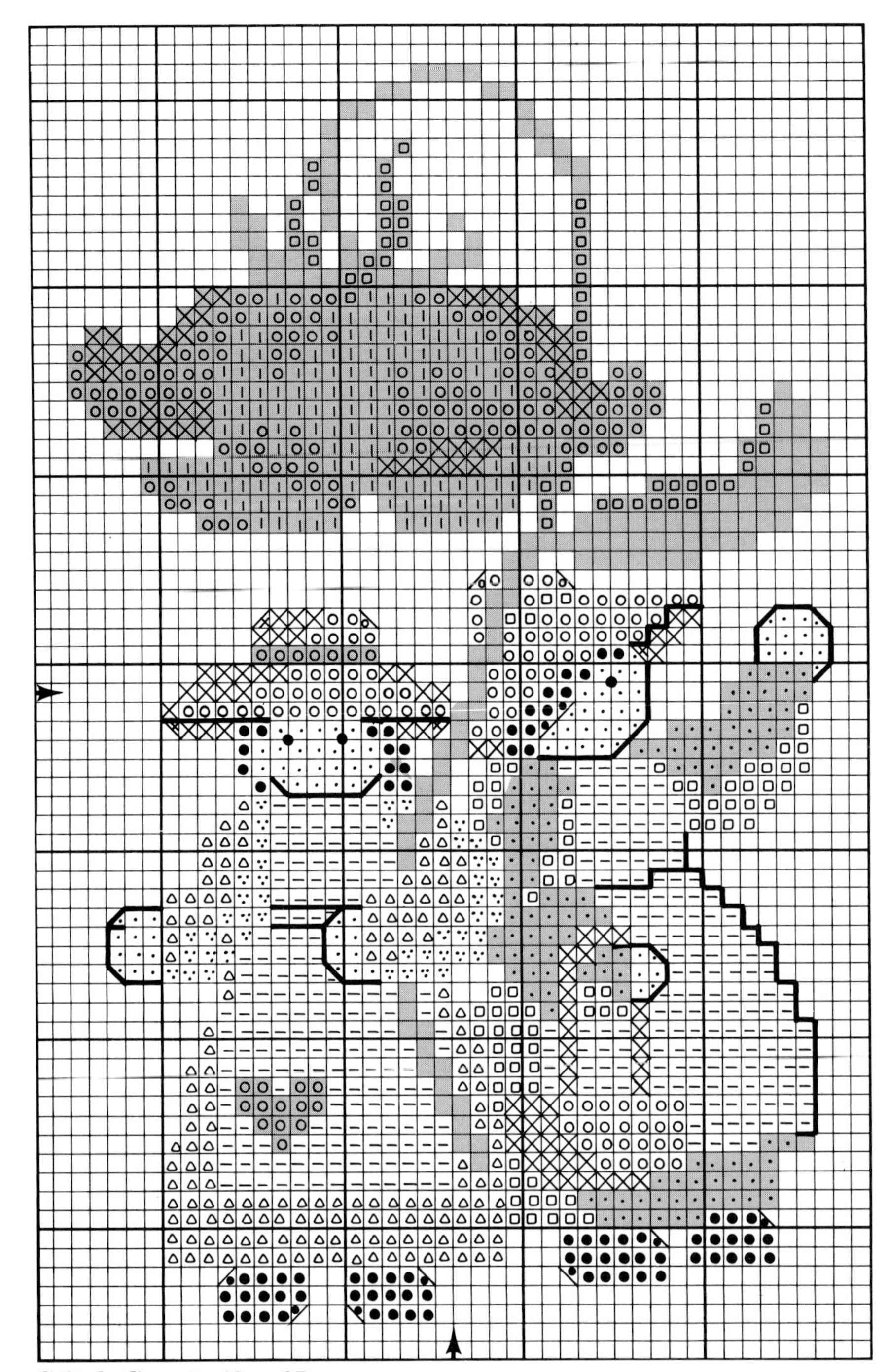

Stitch Count: 42 x 67

Poppy Card

SAMPLE

Stitched on white Perforated Paper 15, the finished design size is 2¾" x 4½". A 9" x 12" sheet of Perforated Paper was used. (Paper with this stitch count must be used so that the design will fit the card.)

Bates	DMC (used for sample)
Step 1: Cross-stitch (three strands)	
1	White
306	725 Topaz
778	948 Peach Flesh-vy. lt.
8	353 Peach Flesh
10	352 Coral-lt.
11	351 Coral
49	3689 Mauve-lt.
66	3688 Mauve-med.
167	519 Sky Blue
168	518 Wedgewood-lt.
203	954 Nile Green
209	913 Nile Green-med.
307	783 Christmas Gold
309	781 Topaz-dk.
Step 2: Backstitch (one strand)	
168	518 Wedgewood-lt. (aprons)
371	433 Brown-med. (all else)
Step 3: French Knots (one strand)	
371	433 Brown-med.

MATERIALS (for one card)

Completed cross-stitch on Perforated Paper 15; see sample information
Tracing paper
8" x 24" piece of heavy blue paper (available at art supply stores)
8" x 12" piece of decorative paper
Double-sided tape

DIRECTIONS

1. Trace the window pattern for the cross-stitch design.

2. Mark four 6″ intervals on the wrong side of the blue paper. Fold the paper on the marks, using the straight edge of a ruler as a guide (see Diagram). Trim ⅛″ from both outside ends.

6″	6″	6″	6″

3. Trace the window pattern on the wrong side of the second section from the left, centering it 1⅜″ from the bottom edge of the paper. Cut the window out.

4. Trim the perforated paper to 5½″ x 7½″ with the design centered. Place pieces of double-sided tape on the right side of the perforated paper near the edges. Center the design inside the opening and attach it to the blue paper.

5. Attach tape to the wrong side of the perforated paper near the edges. Fold first section of card over second and secure.

6. Attach tape to the wrong side of the fourth section of the card. Fold it in over the third section and secure.

7. Fold the decorative paper to measure 6″ x 8″. Trim ⅛″ from the edges so that the decorative paper is smaller on all sides than the blue paper card. Attach tape to back side of decorative paper near the fold. Insert it inside the card.

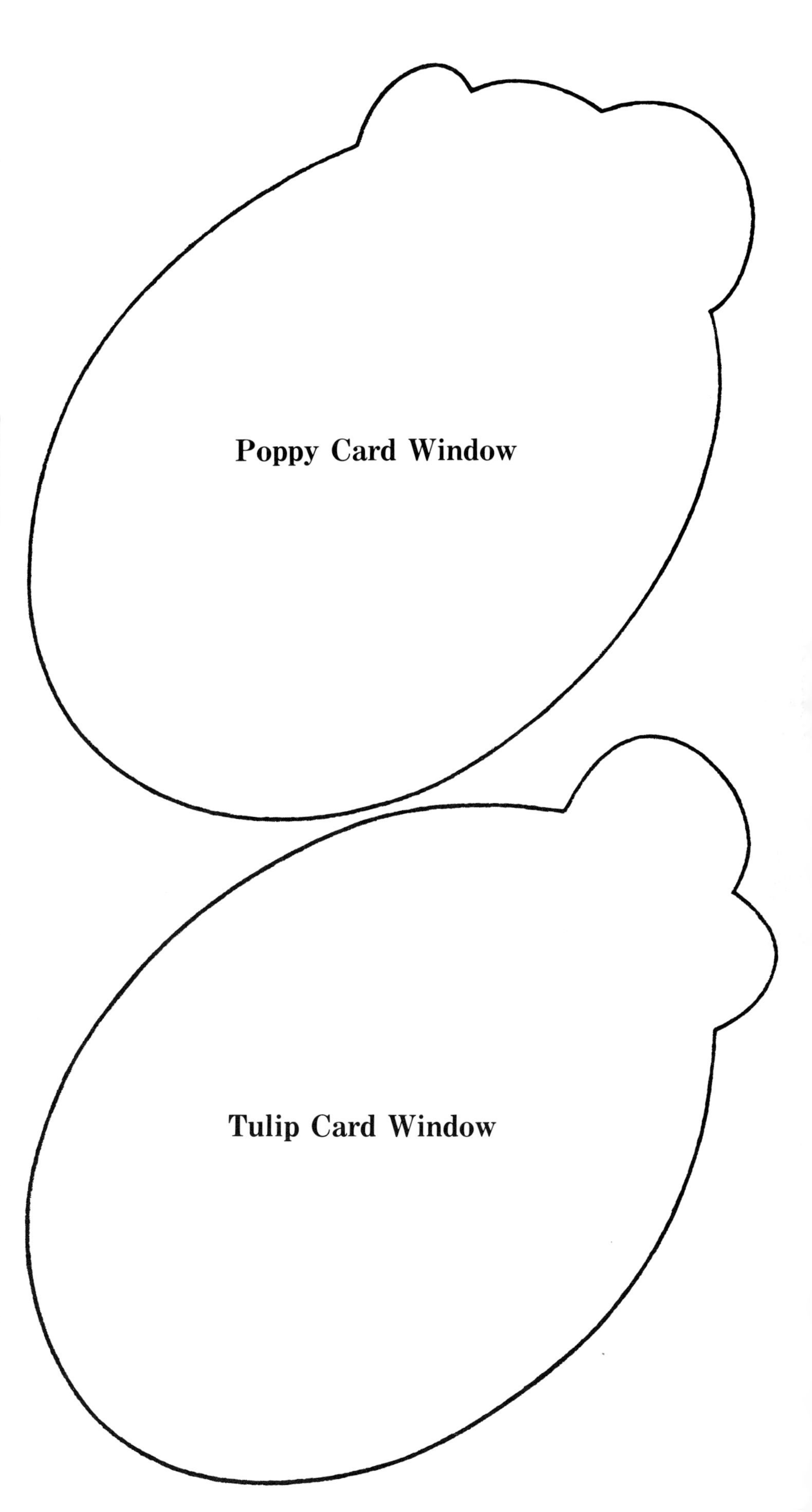

JUNE 21

Father's Day

Ever since the idea of Father's Day won the support of President Calvin Coolidge in 1924, the holiday has been imbued with warmth and dignity. These cross-stitch gifts, done just for Dad, exemplify the same masculine charm.

Ties & Box

SAMPLE
Neckties: Stitched on any purchased tie using waste canvas 14, the finished design size is ⅞″ x ⅞″. The waste canvas was cut 3″ x 3″.

SAMPLE
Box Lid: Stitched on grey Glenshee Linen 29 over two threads, the design was stitched three times. Place the lid of a 3″ box on the fabric to be stitched. Trace around the inside edge of the lid with a dressmakers' pen. Stitch the pattern as desired. (See Suppliers for information on ordering the wooden box.)

Navy Tie

Bates	Symbol	DMC (used for sample)
	Step 1:	Cross-stitch (two strands)
970	•	315 Antique Mauve-dk.
920	☒	932 Antique Blue-lt.
875	▫	503 Blue Green-med.

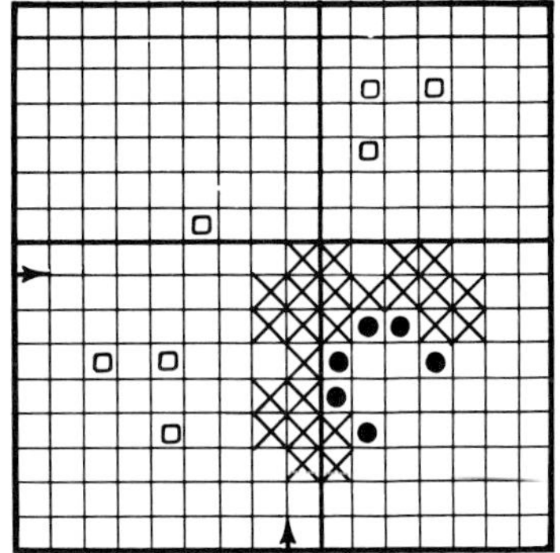

Stitch Count: 12 x 12

Grey Tie & Box

Step 1: Cross-stitch (two strands)

Bates	Symbol	DMC (used for sample)
970	X	315 Antique Mauve-dk.
922	o	930 Antique Blue-dk.
876	•	502 Blue Green

Initial Boxes

SAMPLE
Stitched on Glenshee Egyptian Cotton quality E (thread count 18), the finished design size varies, depending upon the letter. For each letter, the fabric was cut 6″ x 6″. (A fabric with this stitch count must be used so that the design will fit the box.) Place the lid of the box on the fabric and trace around the inside edge with a dressmakers' pen. Center one letter within the circle. Each letter fits the lid of a 4″ box. (See Suppliers for information on ordering the wooden boxes.) Two color schemes are given so that you can choose the one that best suits your dad's tastes.

Color Scheme 1

Step 1: Cross-stitch (two strands)

Bates	Symbol	DMC (used for sample)
970	· (shaded)	315 Antique Mauve-dk.
922	■	930 Antique Blue-dk.
875	–	503 Blue Green-med.
876	o	502 Blue Green
878	X	501 Blue Green-dk.

Step 2: Beadwork (sewn over cross-stitch)

Symbol	
■	Bright Blue

Color Scheme 2

Step 1: Cross-stitch (two strands)

Bates	Symbol	DMC (used for sample)
266	–	3347 Yellow Green-med.
257	o	3346 Hunter Green
246	X	319 Pistachio Green-vy. dk.
5968	■	355 Terra Cotta-dk.
355	· (shaded)	975 Golden Brown-dk.

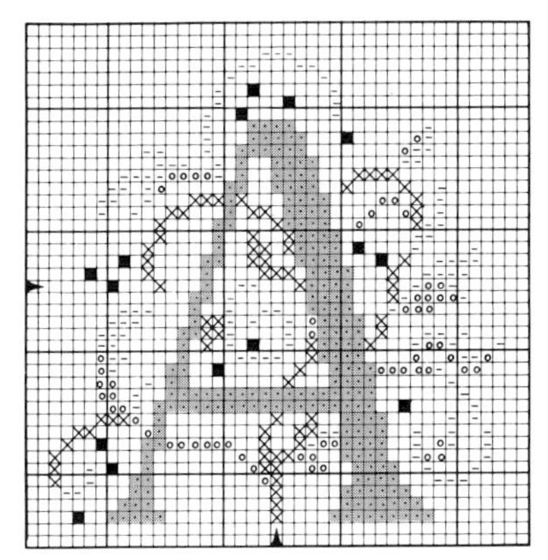

Stitch Count: 39 x 39

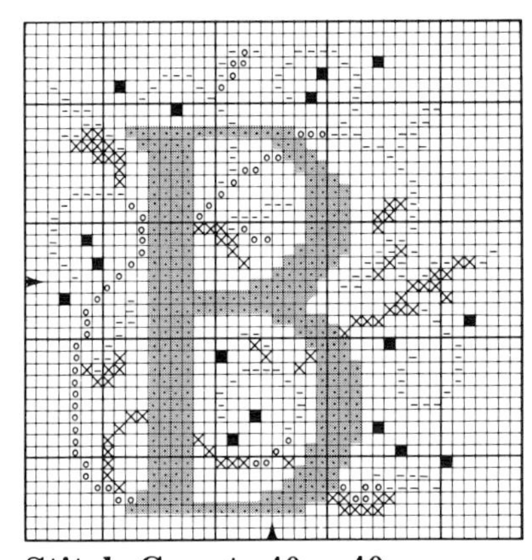

Stitch Count: 40 x 40

continued . . .

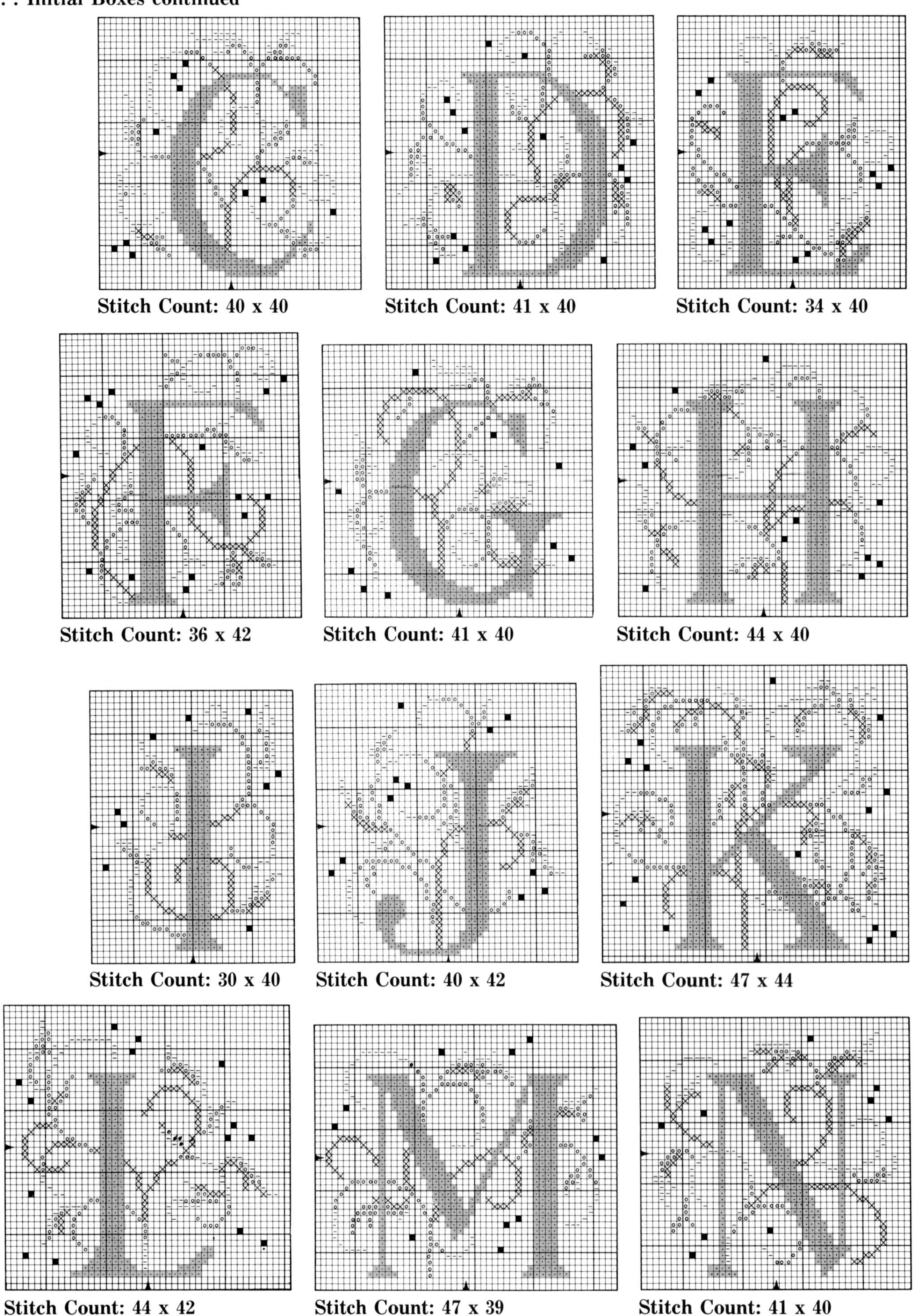

Stitch Count: 40 x 40

Stitch Count: 41 x 40

Stitch Count: 34 x 40

Stitch Count: 36 x 42

Stitch Count: 41 x 40

Stitch Count: 44 x 40

Stitch Count: 30 x 40

Stitch Count: 40 x 42

Stitch Count: 47 x 44

Stitch Count: 44 x 42

Stitch Count: 47 x 39

Stitch Count: 41 x 40

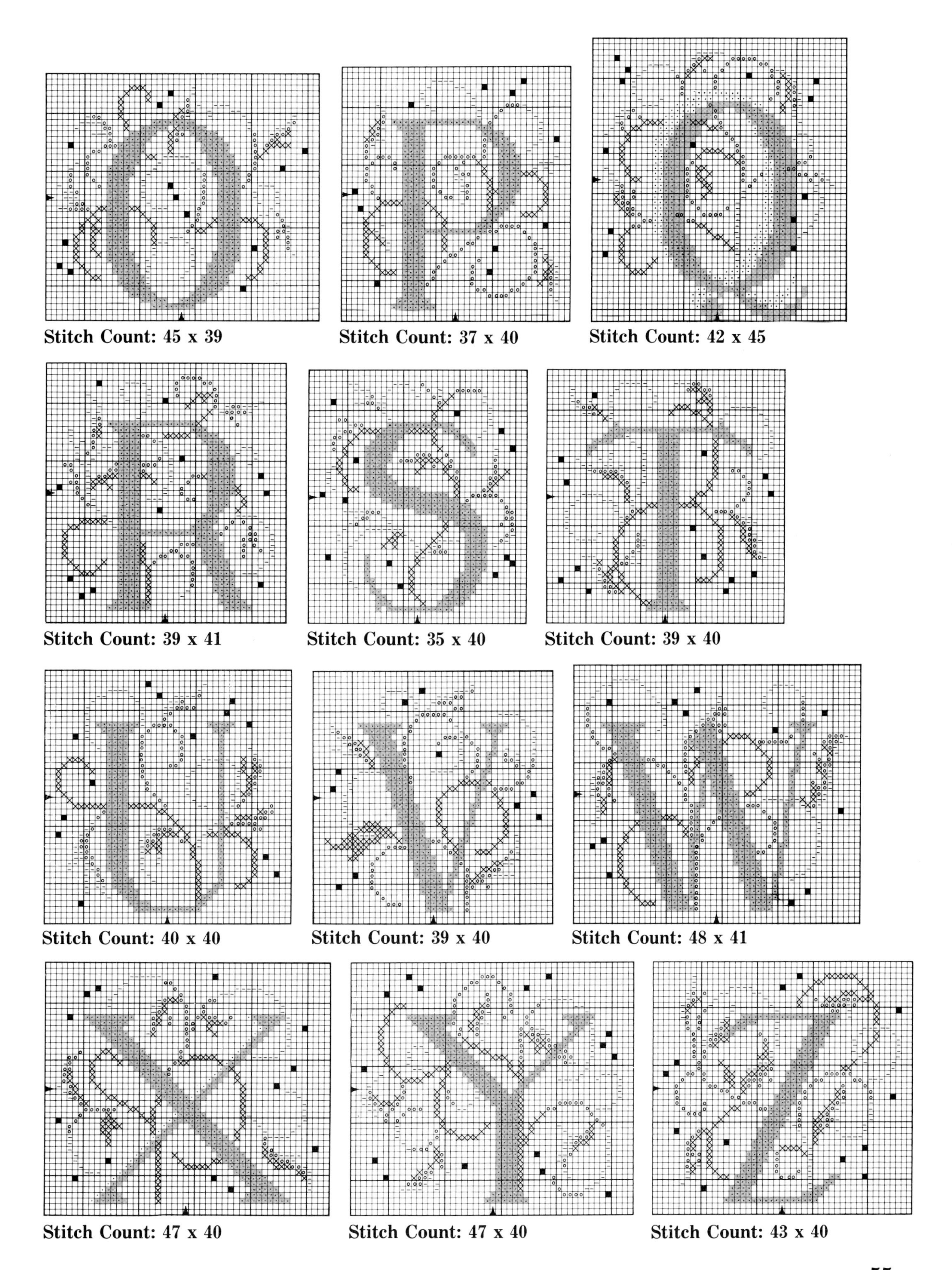

Stitch Count: 45 x 39

Stitch Count: 37 x 40

Stitch Count: 42 x 45

Stitch Count: 39 x 41

Stitch Count: 35 x 40

Stitch Count: 39 x 40

Stitch Count: 40 x 40

Stitch Count: 39 x 40

Stitch Count: 48 x 41

Stitch Count: 47 x 40

Stitch Count: 47 x 40

Stitch Count: 43 x 40

Woodland Sampler

SAMPLE
Stitched on Linaida 14, the finished design size is 7½" x 10⅝". The fabric was cut 14" x 17".

Bates	DMC (used for sample)	
Step 1: Cross-stitch (two strands)		
1		White
920	932	Antique Blue-lt.
266	3347	Yellow Green-med.
257	3346	Hunter Green
876	502	Blue Green
246	319	Pistachio Green-vy. dk.
307	977	Golden Brown-lt.
308	976	Golden Brown-med.
355	975	Golden Brown-dk.
387	822	Beige Grey-lt.
379	840	Beige Brown-med.
380	839	Beige Brown-dk.
380	838	Beige Brown-vy. dk.
309	435	Brown-vy. lt.
371	433	Brown-med.
357	801	Coffee Brown-dk.

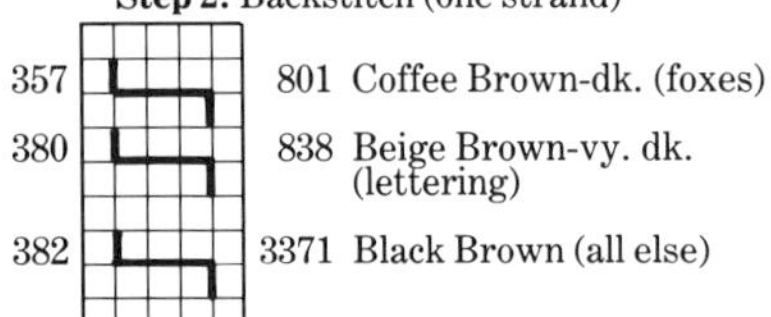

Bates	DMC	
Step 2: Backstitch (one strand)		
357	801	Coffee Brown-dk. (foxes)
380	838	Beige Brown-vy. dk. (lettering)
382	3371	Black Brown (all else)
Step 3: French Knots (one strand)		
380	838	Beige Brown-vy. dk.

FABRICS	DESIGN SIZES
Aida 11	9½" x 13⅝"
Aida 14	7½" x 10⅝"
Aida 18	5⅞" x 8¼"
Hardanger 22	4¾" x 6¾"

A·B·C·D·E·F·G·H·I
It is a
wise father
that knows his
own child.
SHAKESPEARE
For Dad
A.E.M.

It is a wise father that knows his own child.
SHAKESPEARE
for Dad
A.E.M.
1987

Stitch Count: 105 x 149

JULY 4

Independence Day

Since the signing of the Declaration of Independence in Philadelphia on this day in 1776, we have celebrated July 4 as the birthday of our country. Commemorating the birthday, this cross-stitch set focuses upon traditional patriotic symbols.

Patriotic Pair

SAMPLE
Home of the Brave: Stitched on white Belfast Linen 32 over two threads, finished design size is 4¾" x 3¾". Fabric was cut 11" x 10".

Bates	Symbol	DMC (used for sample)	
		Step 1: Cross-stitch (two strands)	
893	(shaded) /	224	Shell Pink-lt.
42	X	3350	Dusty Rose-vy. dk.
108	o	211	Lavender-lt.
159	–	3325	Baby Blue
131	· /	798	Delft-dk.
132	X	797	Royal Blue
885	·	739	Tan-ultra lt.
891	Δ	676	Old Gold-lt.
903	▲	640	Beige Grey-vy. dk.
397	| /	762	Pearl Grey-vy. lt.
398	+	415	Pearl Grey
400	●	317	Pewter Grey
		Step 2: Backstitch (one strand)	
382	(backstitch line)	3371	Black Brown

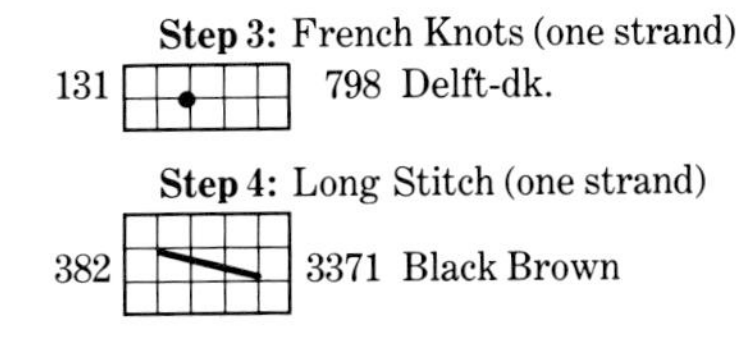

FABRICS	DESIGN SIZES
Aida 11	7″ x 5⅜″
Aida 14	5½″ x 4¼″
Aida 18	4¼″ x 3¼″
Hardanger 22	3½″ x 2⅝″

SAMPLE

Liberty: Stitched on white Belfast Linen 32 over two threads, the finished design size is 5″ x 3¾″. The fabric was cut 11″ x 10″.

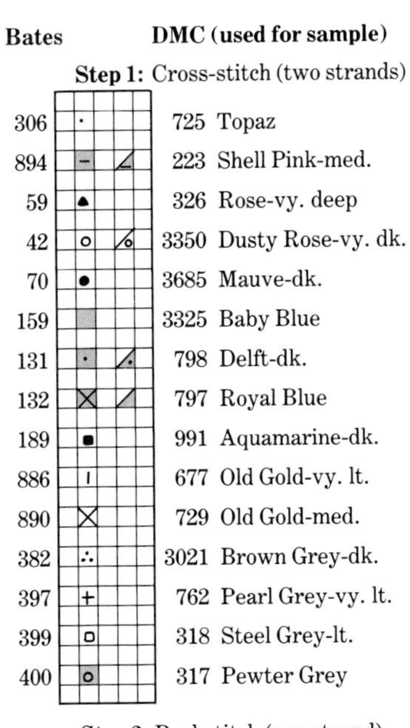

Bates **DMC (used for sample)**

Step 1: Cross-stitch (two strands)

Bates	DMC
306	725 Topaz
894	223 Shell Pink-med.
59	326 Rose-vy. deep
42	3350 Dusty Rose-vy. dk.
70	3685 Mauve-dk.
159	3325 Baby Blue
131	798 Delft-dk.
132	797 Royal Blue
189	991 Aquamarine-dk.
886	677 Old Gold-vy. lt.
890	729 Old Gold-med.
382	3021 Brown Grey-dk.
397	762 Pearl Grey-vy. lt.
399	318 Steel Grey-lt.
400	317 Pewter Grey

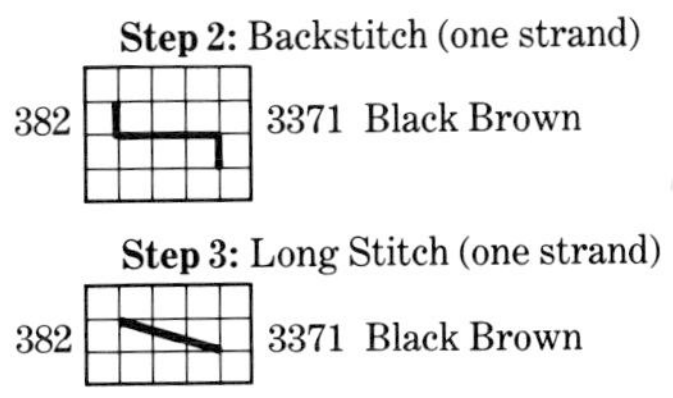

FABRICS	DESIGN SIZES
Aida 11	7⅜″ x 5½″
Aida 14	5¾″ x 4⅜″
Aida 18	4½″ x 3⅜″
Hardanger 22	3⅝″ x 2¾″

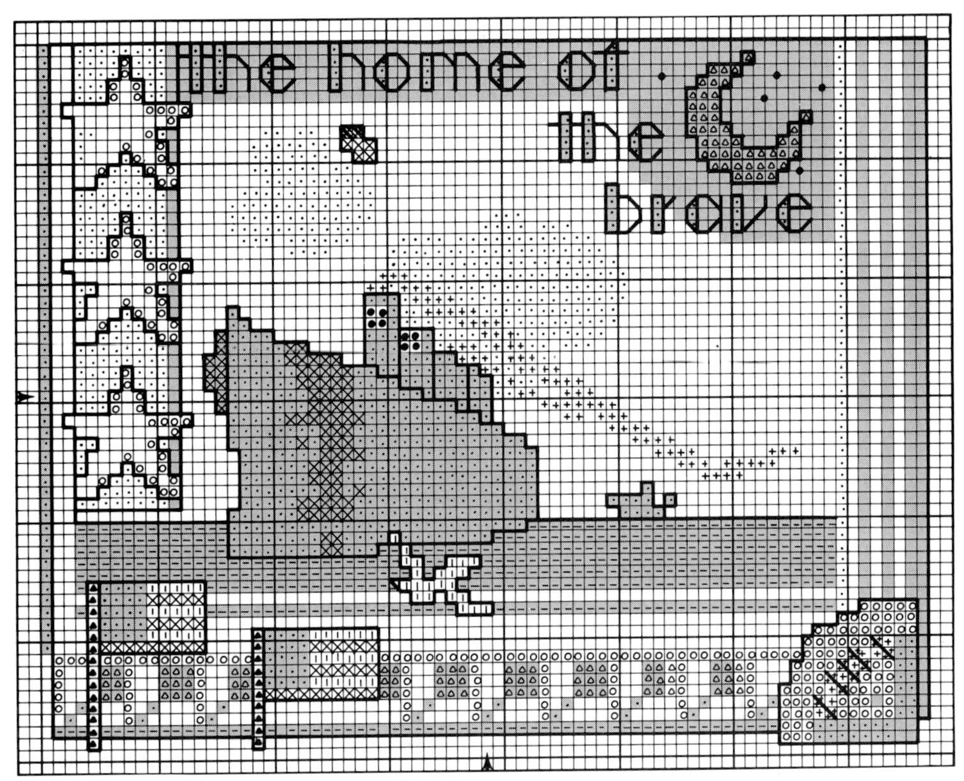

Stitch Count: 77 x 59

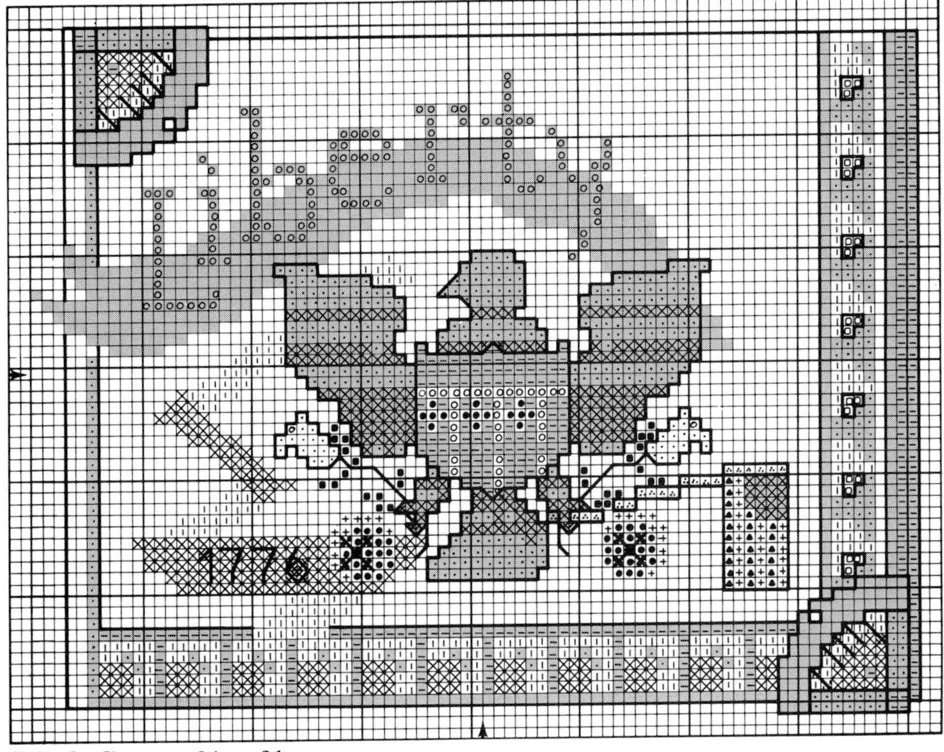

Stitch Count: 81 x 61

Stitch Count: 134 x 97

America

SAMPLE
Stitched on white Belfast Linen 32 over two threads, the finished design size is 8⅜" x 6". The fabric was cut 15" x 12".

Step 1: Cross-stitch (two strands)

Bates	DMC (used for sample)	
1		White
778	948	Peach Flesh-vy. lt.
8	761	Salmon-lt.
894	223	Shell Pink-med.
897	221	Shell Pink-dk.

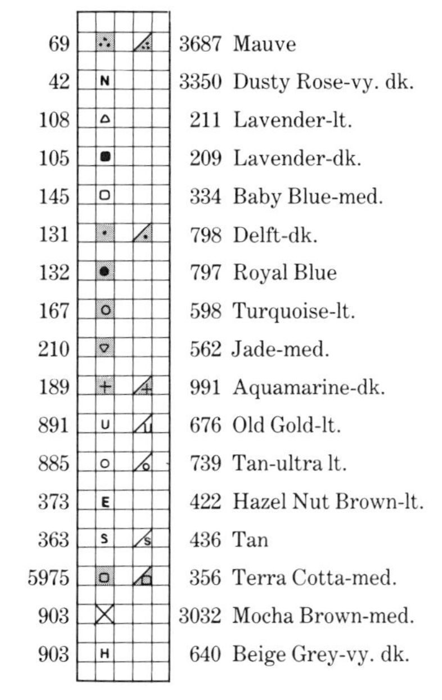

Bates	DMC	
69	3687	Mauve
42	3350	Dusty Rose-vy. dk.
108	211	Lavender-lt.
105	209	Lavender-dk.
145	334	Baby Blue-med.
131	798	Delft-dk.
132	797	Royal Blue
167	598	Turquoise-lt.
210	562	Jade-med.
189	991	Aquamarine-dk.
891	676	Old Gold-lt.
885	739	Tan-ultra lt.
373	422	Hazel Nut Brown-lt.
363	436	Tan
5975	356	Terra Cotta-med.
903	3032	Mocha Brown-med.
903	640	Beige Grey-vy. dk.
379	840	Beige Brown-med.
382	3021	Brown Grey-dk.
900	928	Grey Green-lt.
400	317	Pewter Grey

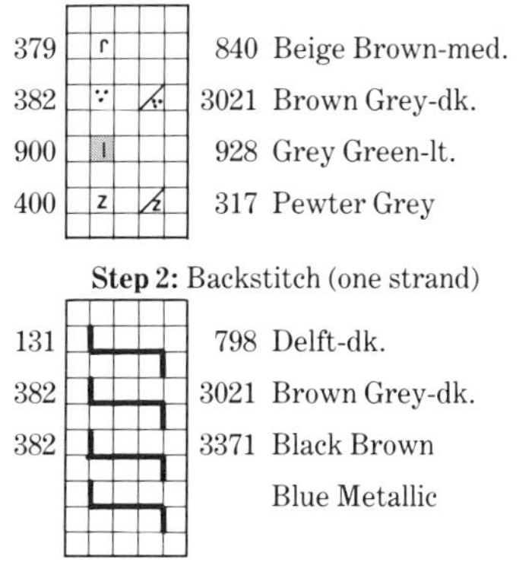

Step 2: Backstitch (one strand)

Bates	DMC	
131	798	Delft-dk.
382	3021	Brown Grey-dk.
382	3371	Black Brown
		Blue Metallic

FABRICS	DESIGN SIZES
Aida 11	12⅛" x 8⅞"
Aida 14	9⅝" x 6⅞"
Aida 18	7½" x 5⅜"
Hardanger 22	6⅛" x 4⅜"

JULY 12

National Ice Cream Day

The second Sunday in July, right in the middle of summer's hottest days, seems the perfect time to celebrate a holiday proclaiming the virtues of ice cream. The refreshing treat was first introduced in Europe by the Italians during the 1400s. But it wasn't until the mid-1800s and the invention of the hand-operated freezer that ice cream was made commercially in the United States. The perfections shown here are guaranteed not to melt, regardless of the heat, so you can enjoy them year-round.

Ice Cream Cones

SAMPLE

Stitched on white Aida 11, the design is stitched to fit the cone pattern. The fabric was cut 5" x 7". (A fabric with this stitch count must be used so that the design will fit the cone.) Position the stitching as desired, repeating the pattern to fill the cone area.

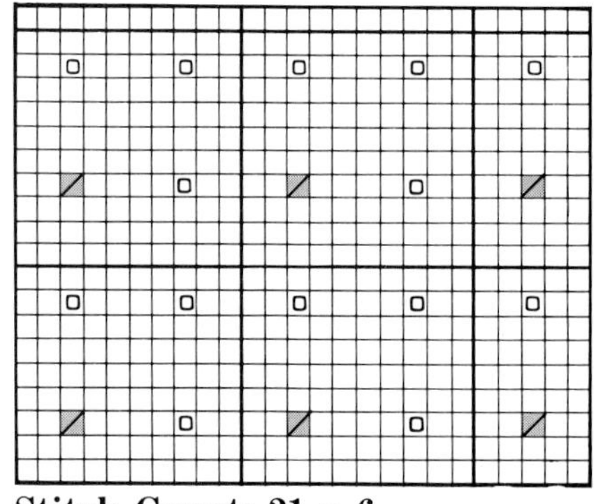

Stitch Count: 21 x 6

Bates		DMC (used for sample)
	Step 1: Cross-stitch (three strands)	
108	▫	211 Lavender-lt.
158	⁄	747 Sky Blue-vy. lt.

MATERIALS (for one cone)

Completed cross-stitch on white Aida 11 and matching thread; see sample information
7" x 7" piece of light green or lavender fabric for the ice cream; matching thread
7" x 7" piece of polyester fleece
2" Styrofoam ball
4½" x 4½" piece of fusible interfacing
¾ yard of ⅜"-wide light green or lavender satin ribbon
8 to 10 small lengths of ⅜"-wide satin ribbon to make ribbon flowers and leaves
White glue
Stuffing
Dressmakers' pen
Tracing paper for patterns

continued . . .

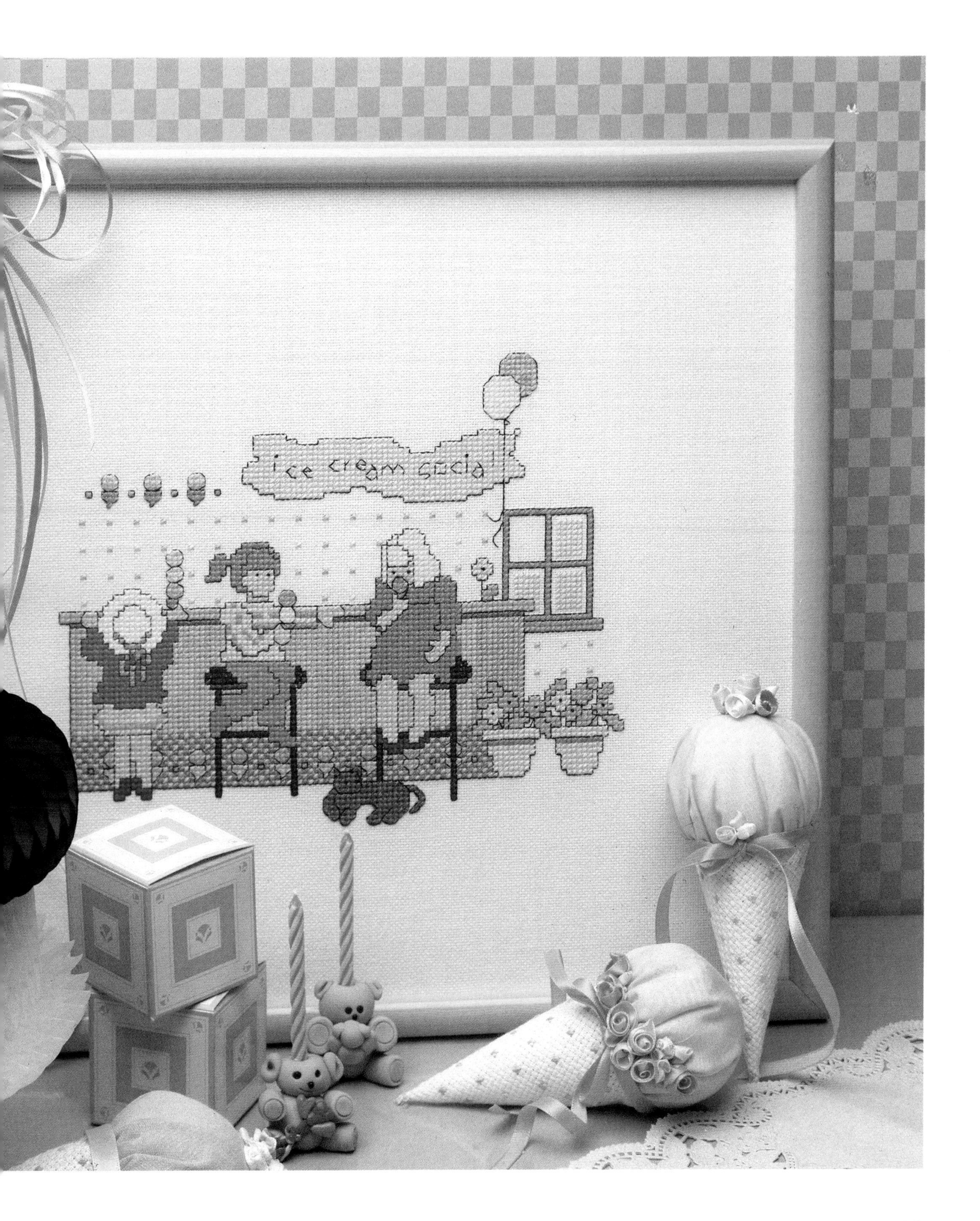
ice cream social

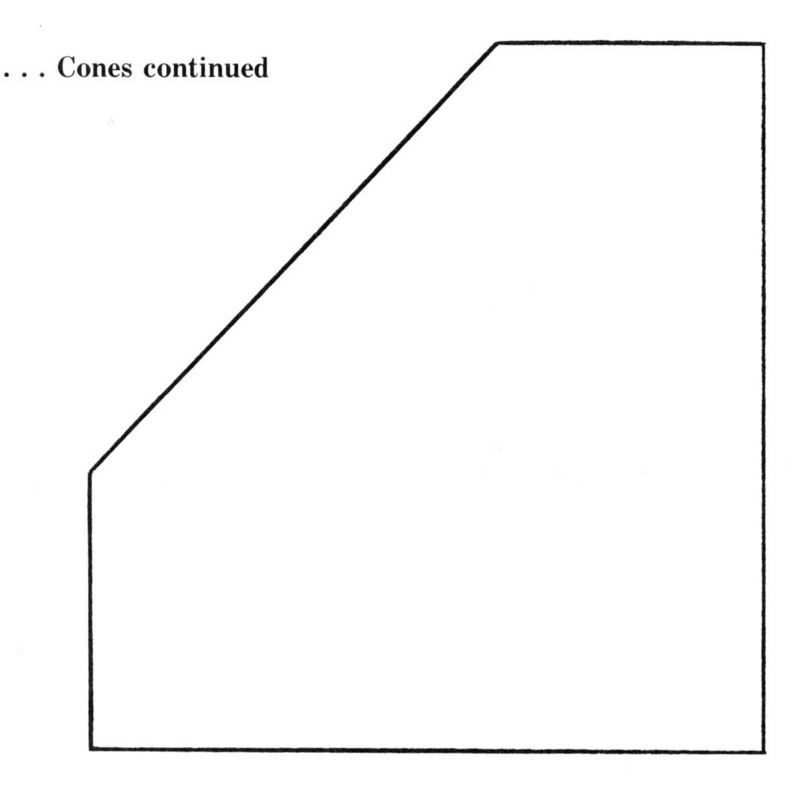

DIRECTIONS

1. Trace the pattern for the cone; then make a 6½″ circle pattern (see General Instructions).

2. Center the cone pattern over the stitched area of the Aida. Trace around the pattern, using a dressmakers' pen.

3. Fuse the interfacing to the wrong side of the stitched area of the Aida. Cut the cone from the Aida, handling carefully to avoid raveling.

4. Roll the Aida, stitched side out, to form a cone, overlapping the edges ⅛″. Glue or slipstitch the seam, beginning at the bottom of the cone.

5. Apply a small amount of glue to the bottom of the cone to control raveling. Fill the cone firmly with stuffing.

6. Cut a 6½″ circle from the fabric for the ice cream. Stitch gathering threads along the edge.

7. Cut one fleece circle, trimming ¼″ from the outside edge.

8. Place the fleece over the Styrofoam ball. Then cover the ball with the ice cream fabric. Pull the gathering thread so that the fabric fits tightly around the ball; secure the thread.

9. Place the ice cream on top of the cone with the gathered edges next to the stuffing. Slipstitch or glue together.

10. Tie the ⅜″-wide ribbon in a bow around the top of the cone to cover the seam. Tack in place. Trim the ends to desired lengths.

11. Make ribbon flowers and leaves (see General Instructions). Glue the flowers and leaves, as desired, to the ice cream or the cone.

Ice Cream Social

SAMPLE
Stitched on white Hardanger 22 over two threads, the finished design size is 9⅝″ x 7⅞″. The fabric was cut 18″ x 16″.

Step 1: Cross-stitch (three strands)

Bates	DMC (used for sample)	
1		White
288	445	Lemon-lt.
891	676	Old Gold-lt.
892	225	Shell Pink-vy. lt.
49	963	Dusty Rose-vy. lt.
25	3326	Rose-lt.
8	761	Salmon-lt.
108	211	Lavender-lt.
104	210	Lavender-med.
158	747	Sky Blue-vy. lt.
160	813	Blue-lt.
121	793	Cornflower Blue-med.
940	792	Cornflower Blue-dk.
168	597	Turquoise
208	563	Jade-lt.
885	739	Tan-ultra lt.
373	422	Hazel Nut Brown-lt.
379	840	Beige Brown-med.
380	839	Beige Brown-dk.
398	415	Pearl Grey
399	452	Shell Grey-med.
400	414	Steel Grey-dk.

Step 2: Backstitch (one strand)

Bates	DMC	
150	823	Navy Blue-dk.

Step 3: French Knots (one strand)

Bates	DMC	
150	823	Navy Blue-dk.

FABRICS	DESIGN SIZES
Aida 11	9⅝″ x 7⅞″
Aida 14	7⅝″ x 6¼″
Aida 18	5⅞″ x 4⅞″
Hardanger 22	4⅞″ x 4″

Stitch Count: 106 x 87

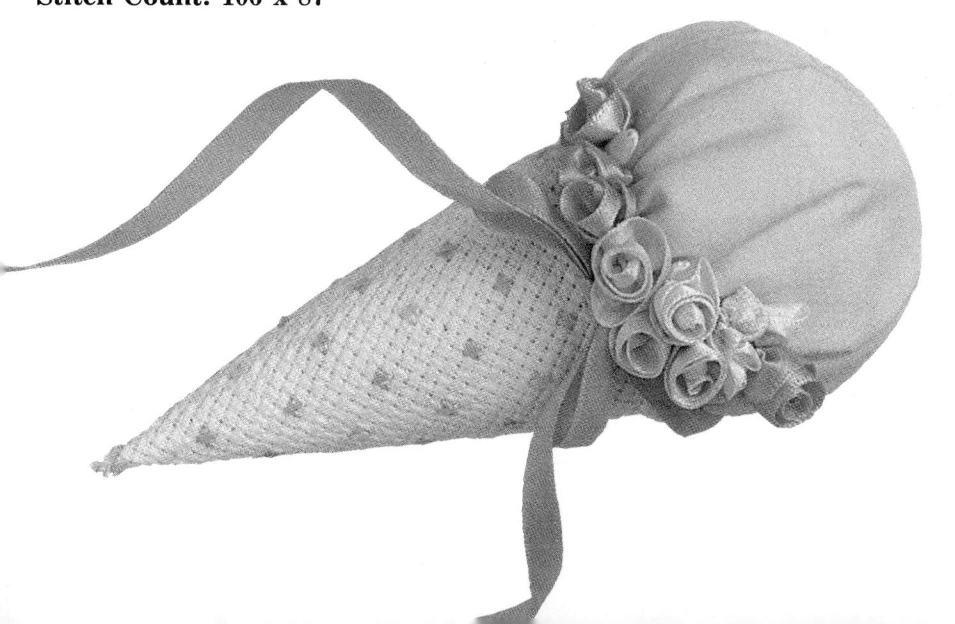

AUGUST 4

National Picnic Day

If you are in Australia on August 4, you will want to gather your family, friends, and picnic basket, and find an inviting spot to celebrate Australia's Picnic Day. If you find yourself closer to home, feel free to borrow the holiday. These small designs are favorite summer treats, whether you are picnicking here or "down under."

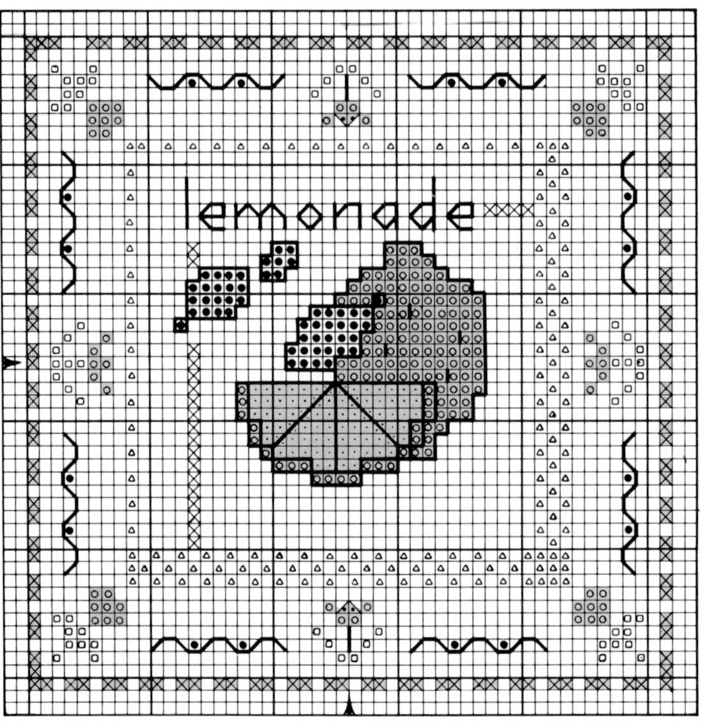

Stitch Count: 52 x 51 (29 x 29 for Picnic Cloth)

Lemonade

SAMPLE
Stitched on white Hardanger 22 over two threads, the finished design size is 4¾" x 4⅝". The fabric was cut 11" x 11".

Bates		DMC (used for sample)
	Step 1: Cross-stitch (three strands)	
300	·	745 Yellow-lt. pale
301	o ⁄o	744 Yellow-pale
47	△	321 Christmas Red
158	X	775 Baby Blue-lt.
206	▫	955 Nile Green-lt.
210	•	562 Jade-med.
	Step 2: Backstitch (one strand)	
206		955 Nile Green-lt. (two strands, light green stems)
210		562 Jade-med. (dark green stems)
149		336 Navy Blue (all else)

continued . . .

Stitch Count: 50 x 53 (27 x 29 for Picnic Cloth)

Stitch Count: 50 x 52 (28 x 29 for Picnic Cloth)

Ice Cream

SAMPLE
Stitched on white Hardanger 22 over two threads, the finished design size is 4½" x 4¾". The fabric was cut 11" x 11".

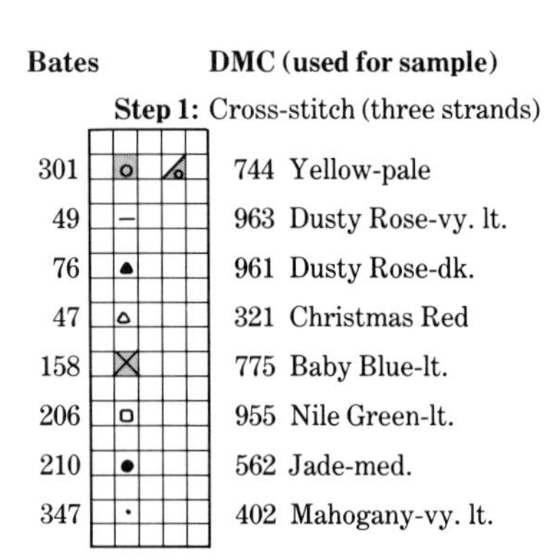

Bates	DMC (used for sample)
Step 1: Cross-stitch (three strands)	
301	744 Yellow-pale
49	963 Dusty Rose-vy. lt.
76	961 Dusty Rose-dk.
47	321 Christmas Red
158	775 Baby Blue-lt.
206	955 Nile Green-lt.
210	562 Jade-med.
347	402 Mahogany-vy. lt.

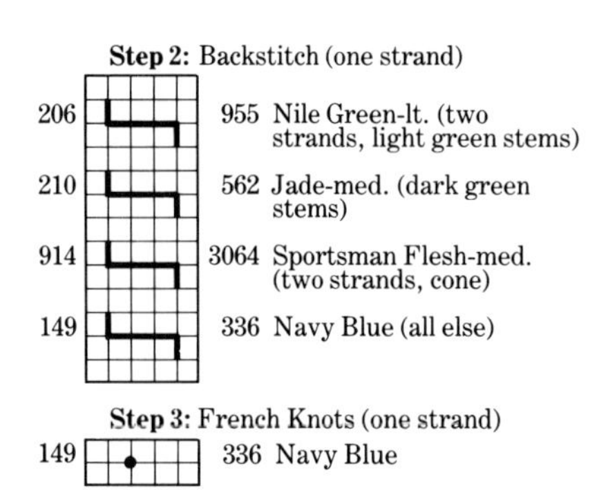

Bates	DMC
Step 2: Backstitch (one strand)	
206	955 Nile Green-lt. (two strands, light green stems)
210	562 Jade-med. (dark green stems)
914	3064 Sportsman Flesh-med. (two strands, cone)
149	336 Navy Blue (all else)
Step 3: French Knots (one strand)	
149	336 Navy Blue

Cherry Pie

SAMPLE
Stitched on white Hardanger 22 over two threads, the finished design size is 4½" x 4¾". The fabric was cut 11" x 11".

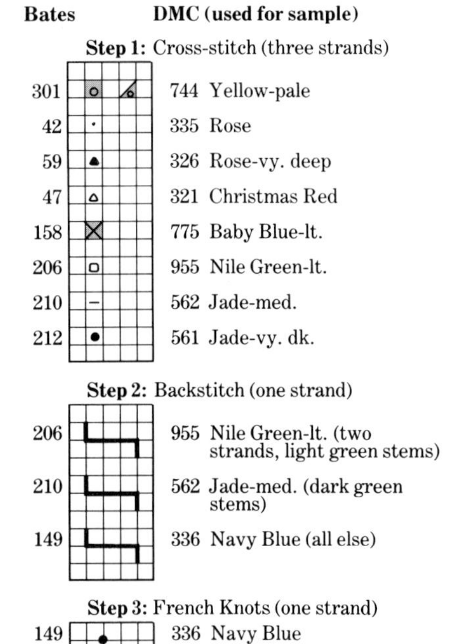

Bates	DMC (used for sample)
Step 1: Cross-stitch (three strands)	
301	744 Yellow-pale
42	335 Rose
59	326 Rose-vy. deep
47	321 Christmas Red
158	775 Baby Blue-lt.
206	955 Nile Green-lt.
210	562 Jade-med.
212	561 Jade-vy. dk.
Step 2: Backstitch (one strand)	
206	955 Nile Green-lt. (two strands, light green stems)
210	562 Jade-med. (dark green stems)
149	336 Navy Blue (all else)
Step 3: French Knots (one strand)	
149	336 Navy Blue

FABRICS	DESIGN SIZES
Aida 11	4½" x 4¾"
Aida 14	3⅝" x 3¾"
Aida 18	2¾" x 2⅞"
Hardanger 22	2¼" x 2⅜"

Picnic Cloth

SAMPLE

Stitched on red Kitchen Hardanger 22, finished design sizes are Lemonade—1⅜" x 1⅜"; Cherry Pie—1¼" x 1⅜"; Ice Cream—1¼" x 1⅜". (A fabric with this stitch count must be used so that the design will fit between the red threads of the Kitchen Hardanger.) The fabric was cut 19" x 19". Position the designs as desired between the red threads. Notice from the photograph that only a portion of each framed design is used for the picnic cloth. In addition, note that the designs for the picnic cloth are stitched using only *one* strand of floss.

MATERIALS

Completed cross-stitch on red Kitchen Hardanger 22; see sample information

⅜ yard of 45"-wide green fabric for binding; matching thread

DIRECTIONS

1. Trim the Hardanger on a colored thread to measure 18½" x 18½".

2. From the green fabric, cut a 2¼"-wide bias strip, piecing as needed, to equal 2¼ yards.

3. With the right sides of the bias strip and the Hardanger together, stitch ½" from the edge, stopping ½" from the corner; backstitch (Diagram A). Fold the bias strip at the edge of the fabric and turn the corner. Resume stitching with a backstitch ½" from the adjacent edge (Diagram B). Repeat at each corner.

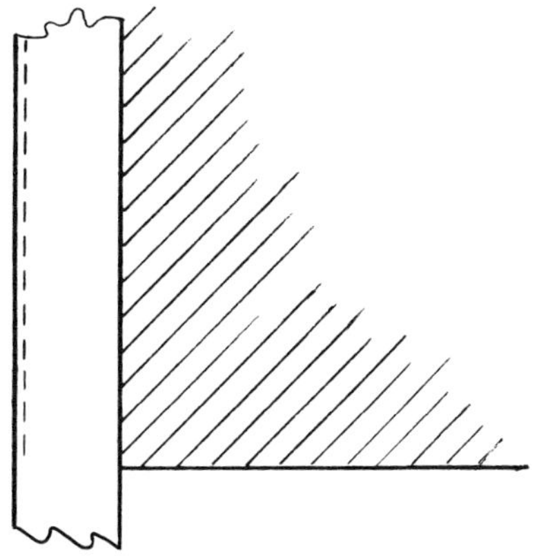

Diagram A

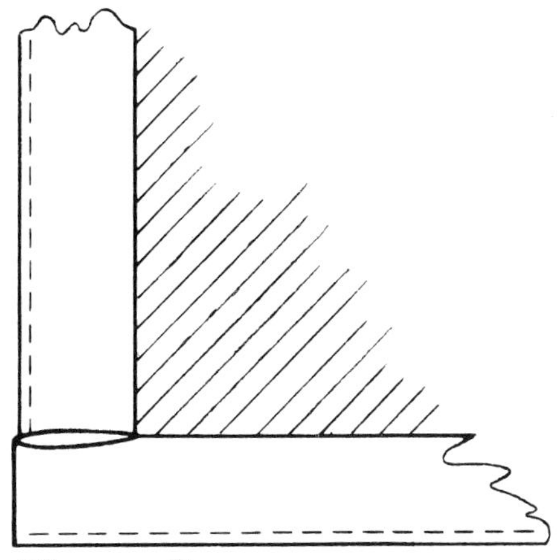

Diagram B

4. Double-fold the bias to the wrong side of the Hardanger and slipstitch, mitering each corner.

SEPTEMBER 8

First Day of School

In many parts of the country, the school bell rings the first day after Labor Day, tolling the end of summer vacation for thousands of children. The day doesn't seem like a holiday to the students, but parents celebrate it from coast to coast. Needleworkers can mark the day with cross-stitched apples and a charming doll dressed in her school-day best.

Schoolgirl Doll

SAMPLE
Stitched on white Belfast Linen 32 over two threads, the finished design size for one apple is ⅜" x ½". (A fabric with this stitch count must be used so that the design will fit the pinafore.) The fabric was cut 9" x 7". Trace the pinafore skirt front pattern onto the fabric with a dressmakers' pen (see General Instructions). Position the stitching as desired. Stitch the first three apples according to the graph and repeat the third apple across the width of the pinafore (see the photo).

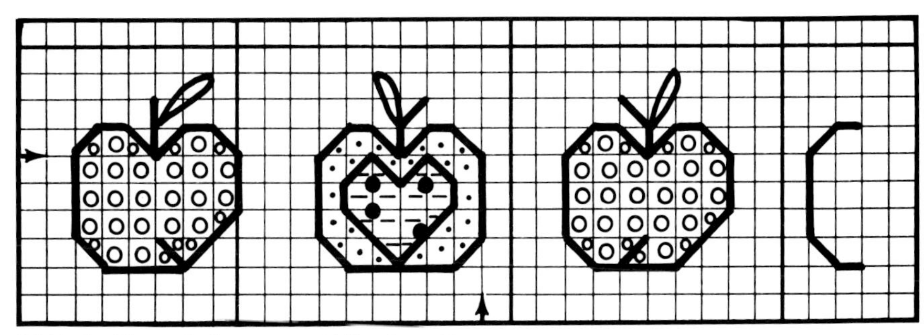

Stitch Count (one motif): 6 x 7

Bates		DMC (used for sample)
		Step 1: Cross-stitch (two strands)
386		746 Off-white
885		739 Tan-ultra lt.
13		349 Coral-dk.
		Step 2: Backstitch (one strand)
13		349 Coral-dk. (around apple)
357		801 Coffee Brown-dk. (all else)
		Step 3: French Knots (one strand)
357		801 Coffee Brown-dk.
		Step 4: Lazy Daisy Stitch (one strand)
923		699 Christmas Green

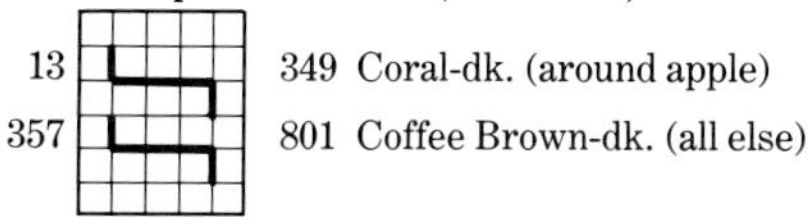

Alphabet Apples

SAMPLE

Stitched on Christmas green Hardanger 22, the finished design size varies. (A fabric with this stitch count must be used so that the design will fit the leaf.)

Bates		DMC (used for sample)
		Step 1: Cross-stitch (one strand)
293		727 Topaz-vy. lt. or
13		349 Coral-dk. or
130		799 Delft-med.

MATERIALS (for one apple)

Completed cross-stitch on Christmas green Hardanger 22 and matching thread; see sample information
Small piece of unstitched green Hardanger 22
Small pieces of matching green fabric
⅜ yard of 45″-wide red fabric; matching thread
¾ yard of ⅜″-wide blue satin ribbon; matching thread (optional)
Stuffing
Tracing paper for patterns
Dressmakers' pen or chalk

DIRECTIONS

1. Trace the leaf pattern. Also make a 10″ circle pattern for the apple (see General Instructions).

2. Center the leaf pattern over the stitched letter and cut out one leaf. Also cut one leaf from the unstitched piece of Hardanger.

3. Cut two leaves from the matching green fabric.

4. From the red fabric, cut one circle.

5. To make the apple, fold the edge of the circle under ¼″ and stitch gathering threads next to the fold. Gather and stuff firmly. Tightly pull the gathering thread and secure.

6. To make the leaf, place the right sides of the stitched and the plain Hardanger pieces together and stitch with a ¼″ seam, leaving the straight edge open. Clip the seam; turn. Stuff lightly. Turn the raw edge ¼″ to the inside and stitch gathering threads through all layers next to the fold. Gather the threads tightly; secure. Make a plain leaf in the same manner.

7. Tack the leaves to the apple over the gathered edge.

8. Optional: Tie the ribbon in a bow and tack it to the top of the apple.

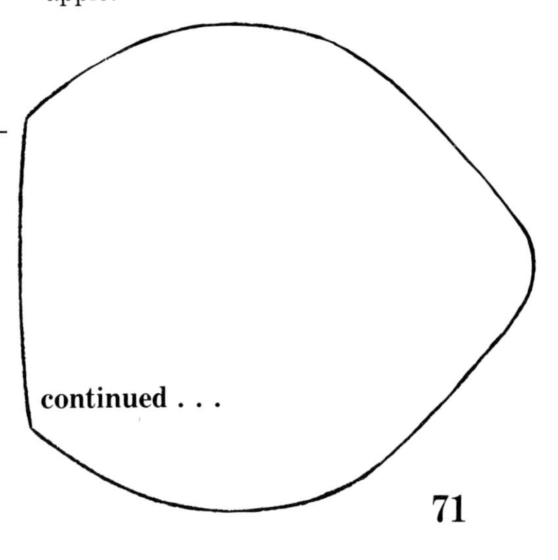

continued . . .

. . . Alphabet Apples continued

ABCDE
FGHIJ
KLMNO
PQRST
UVWXY
Z12345
67890

SEPTEMBER 13

Grandparents' Day

By presidential proclamation, the first Sunday following Labor Day is National Grandparents' Day. Why not spoil the people who have spoiled you for years—give them handmade gifts designed just for them.

Beaded Sachet Pillow

SAMPLE
Stitched on cream Aida 14, the finished design size is 5⅛" x 5⅛". The fabric was cut 9" x 9". For the best results, stitch this design only on Aida 14. (This design may also be worked in cross-stitch.)

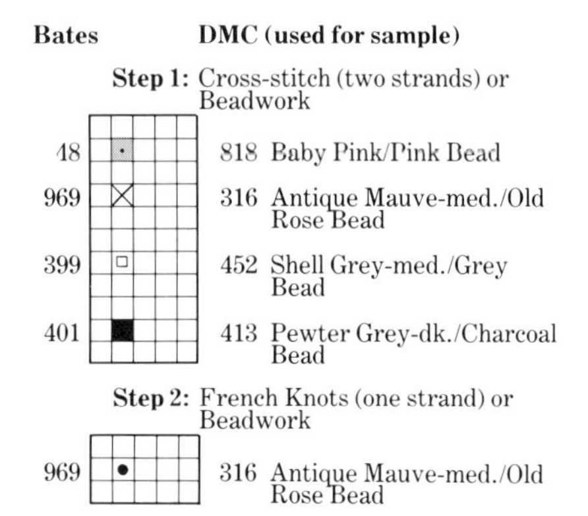

Bates
DMC (used for sample)
Step 1: Cross-stitch (two strands) or Beadwork
48
818 Baby Pink/Pink Bead
969
316 Antique Mauve-med./Old Rose Bead
399
452 Shell Grey-med./Grey Bead
401
413 Pewter Grey-dk./Charcoal Bead
Step 2: French Knots (one strand) or Beadwork
969
316 Antique Mauve-med./Old Rose Bead

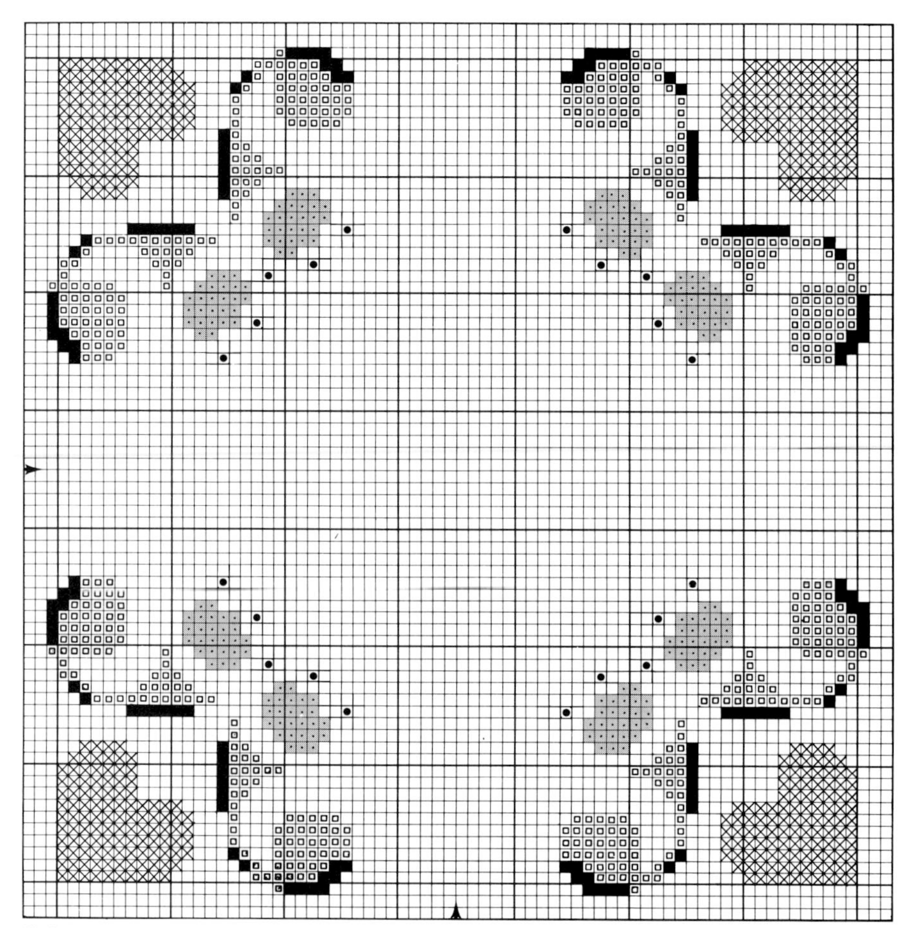

Stitch Count: 72 x 72

MATERIALS
Completed beadwork on cream Aida 14 and matching thread; see sample information
6¾" x 6¾" piece of pink print fabric for back
6¾" x 6¾" piece of muslin
⅜ yard of cream lace net
12" of ¼"-wide cream lace
2¾ yards of ¼"-wide pink satin ribbon
2¾ yards of ¹⁄₁₆"-wide silver satin ribbon
Two tablespoons of potpourri
Stuffing
Tracing paper for pattern
Dressmakers' pen

DIRECTIONS
All seam allowances are ¼".

1. Make a pattern for a 2½" square. Turn the pattern so that it is a diamond. Center it on the beaded Aida and trace around it.

2. Cut the Aida ¼" inside the traced line. Clip the corners to the line. Fold the edges under ¼" and press.

3. From the lace net, cut a bias strip 4½" wide, piecing as needed, to equal 2 yards. Also cut one 3½" square.

4. Center the 3½" square of lace net behind the opening in the Aida and baste in place.

5. Place the beaded Aida, right side up, on the muslin. Slipstitch the Aida to the muslin through the net on three sides of the diamond. Then insert the potpourri and close the fourth side.

6. Slipstitch the ¼"-wide lace over the lace net, placing the straight edge against the design piece and mitering the corners.

7. To make the ruffle, fold the lace net bias strip in half to measure 2¼" wide. Divide the strip into quarters and mark. Stitch gathering threads through both layers next to the raw edges. Gather to fit the pillow. Pin the ruffle to the pillow front, matching the quarter marks to the corners of the pillow, and stitch.

8. With right sides together and ruffle to the middle, place the print fabric over the design piece. Stitch together, leaving a 4″ opening on one side. Turn right side out. Stuff firmly and slipstitch the opening closed.

9. Cut both the pink ribbon and the silver ribbon into four equal lengths. Tie one of each color together to make four bows. At each corner of the pillow, pull the ruffle edge down to the corner and tack (see photo). Tack the bows in the same place.

Grandma's Music Box

SAMPLE
Stitched on white Hardanger 22, the finished design size is 1⅞″ x 1⅞″. The fabric was cut 4″ x 4″. (A fabric with this stitch count must be used so that the design will fit the box lid.) Center the lid of the music box over the stitched design and trace around the inside edge of the lid with a dressmakers' pen. Cut out the stitched design and insert into the lid. (See Suppliers for information on ordering the music box.)

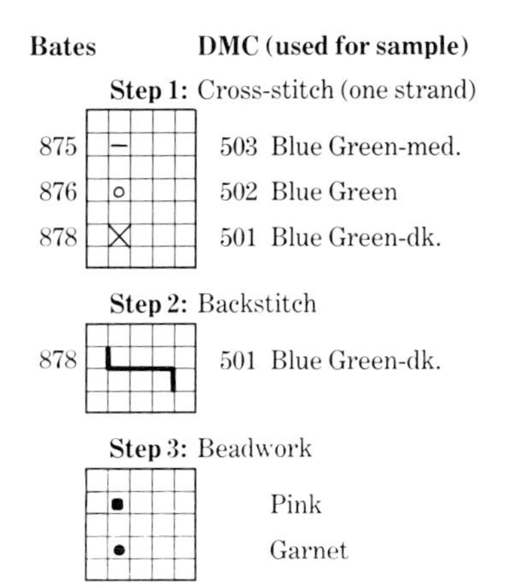

Bates
DMC (used for sample)
Step 1: Cross-stitch (one strand)
875
503 Blue Green-med.
876
502 Blue Green
878
501 Blue Green-dk.
Step 2: Backstitch
878
501 Blue Green-dk.
Step 3: Beadwork
Pink
Garnet

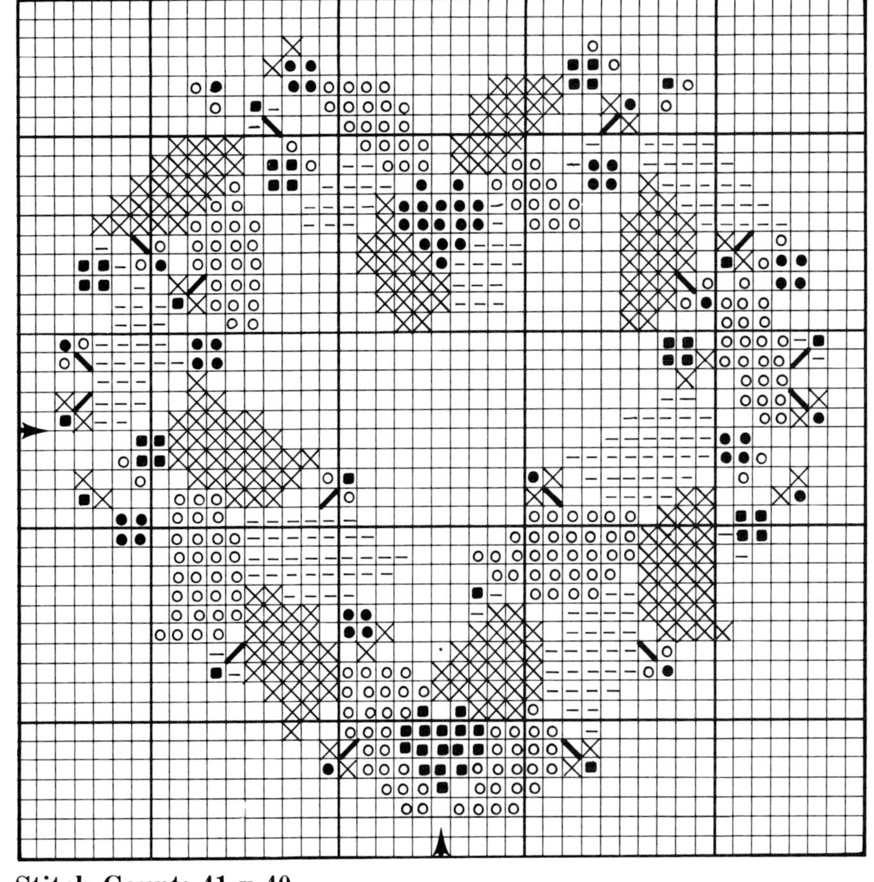

Stitch Count: 41 x 40

CIGARS
5¢

Stitch Count: 117 x 94

Grandpa's Cigar Tray

SAMPLE
Stitched on white Aida 14, the finished design size is 8⅜" x 6¾". The fabric was cut 15" x 13". (A fabric with this stitch count must be used so that the design will fit the tray.)

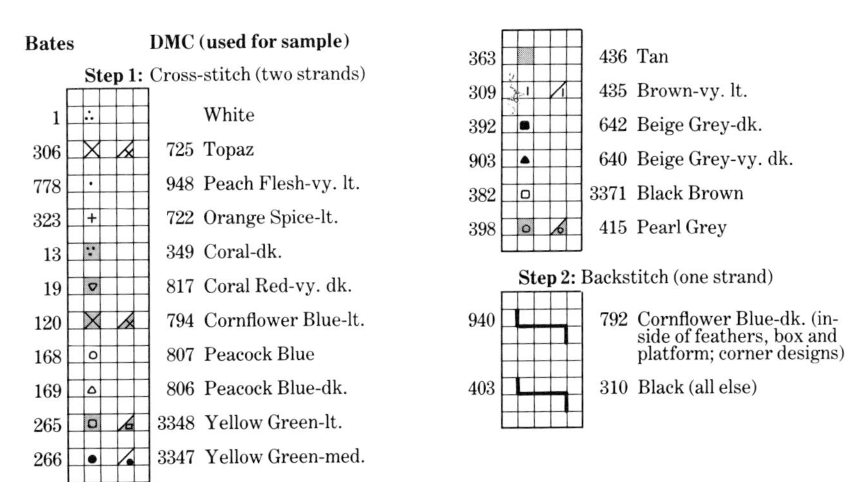

Step 1: Cross-stitch (two strands)

Bates	DMC (used for sample)
1	White
306	725 Topaz
778	948 Peach Flesh-vy. lt.
323	722 Orange Spice-lt.
13	349 Coral-dk.
19	817 Coral Red-vy. dk.
120	794 Cornflower Blue-lt.
168	807 Peacock Blue
169	806 Peacock Blue-dk.
265	3348 Yellow Green-lt.
266	3347 Yellow Green-med.
363	436 Tan
309	435 Brown-vy. lt.
392	642 Beige Grey-dk.
903	640 Beige Grey-vy. dk.
382	3371 Black Brown
398	415 Pearl Grey

Step 2: Backstitch (one strand)

Bates	DMC (used for sample)
940	792 Cornflower Blue-dk. (inside of feathers, box and platform; corner designs)
403	310 Black (all else)

We The People
of the United States, in order
to form a more perfect Union,
establish justice, insure domestic
tranquility, provide for the common
defense, promote the general
welfare, and secure the blessings
of liberty to ourselves and our
posterity, do ordain and establish
this Constitution for the
United States of America.
BURNS

SEPTEMBER 17

Bicentennial of the Constitution

On September 17, 1787, thirty-nine of our nation's founders signed what was called "the most wonderful work ever struck off at a given time by the brain and purpose of man." According to Thomas Jefferson, the men who penned the Constitution were "an assembly of demi-gods." Celebrate the anniversary of America's most important document with this dignified cross-stitch piece. The stirring first words of our Constitution swell from a backdrop of America's great treasures: the mountain ranges, the forest lands, the farms, and the big blue sky.

The Preamble

SAMPLE
Stitched on Glenshee Egyptian Cotton quality D over two threads, the finished design size is 10¼" x 8⅝". The fabric was cut 16" x 15".

FABRICS	DESIGN SIZES
Aida 11	12½" x 10¾"
Aida 14	9¾" x 8⅜"
Aida 18	7⅝" x 6½"
Hardanger 22	6¼" x 5⅜"

We the people
of the United States, in order
to form a more perfect Union,
establish justice, insure domestic
tranquility, provide for the common
defense, promote the general
welfare, and secure the blessings
of liberty to ourselves and our
posterity, do ordain and establish
this Constitution for the
United States of America

Stitch Count: 137 x 118

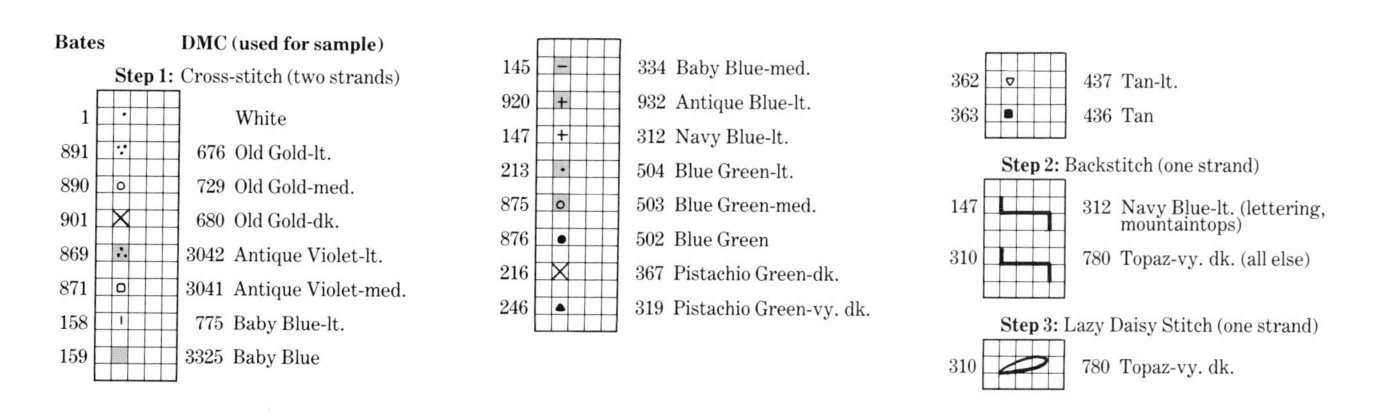

Step 1: Cross-stitch (two strands)

Bates	Symbol	DMC (used for sample)
1	·	White
891	∵	676 Old Gold-lt.
890	o	729 Old Gold-med.
901	X	680 Old Gold-dk.
869	∴ (shaded)	3042 Antique Violet-lt.
871	▫	3041 Antique Violet-med.
158	ı	775 Baby Blue-lt.
159	(shaded)	3325 Baby Blue
145	– (shaded)	334 Baby Blue-med.
920	+ (shaded)	932 Antique Blue-lt.
147	+	312 Navy Blue-lt.
213	· (shaded)	504 Blue Green-lt.
875	o (shaded)	503 Blue Green-med.
876	●	502 Blue Green
216	X	367 Pistachio Green-dk.
246	▲	319 Pistachio Green-vy. dk.
362	▽	437 Tan-lt.
363	■	436 Tan

Step 2: Backstitch (one strand)

Bates	DMC
147	312 Navy Blue-lt. (lettering, mountaintops)
310	780 Topaz-vy. dk. (all else)

Step 3: Lazy Daisy Stitch (one strand)

Bates	DMC
310	780 Topaz-vy. dk.

OCTOBER 31

Halloween

With the moon watching over the ghosts and goblins, little spooks gather their goodies on All Hallows' Eve. This occasion has been celebrated for centuries, but today most children know it as the night of tricks and treats. There's nothing tricky about these Halloween projects though. Stitch a black cat, a bat, and other scary creatures you might see lurking around on Halloween night.

Halloween Doll

SAMPLE
Stitched on black Hardanger 22, the finished design size is 3″ x 2¾″. (A fabric with this stitch count must be used so that the design will fit the pinafore.) The fabric was cut 9″ x 7″. Trace the pinafore skirt front pattern onto the fabric with a dressmakers' pen or chalk (see General Instructions). Position the stitching as desired (see the photo).

Step 1: Cross-stitch (one strand)

Bates	Symbol	DMC (used for sample)
297	–	743 Yellow-med.
316	X	740 Tangerine
256	○	704 Chartreuse-bright
258	●	904 Parrot Green-vy. dk.

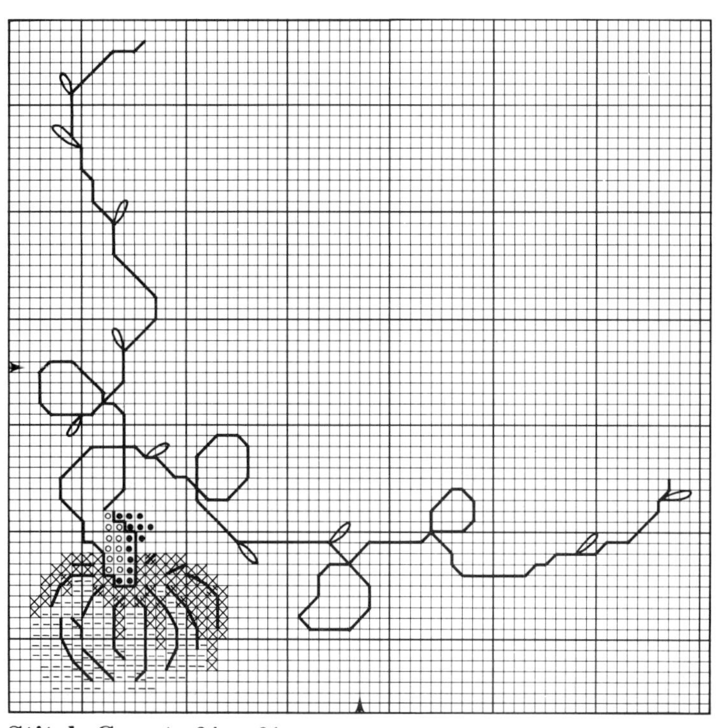

Stitch Count: 64 x 61

Step 2: Backstitch (two strands)

258		904 Parrot Green-vy. dk. (vines)
403		310 Black (all else)

Step 3: Lazy Daisy Stitch (one strand)

258		904 Parrot Green-vy. dk.

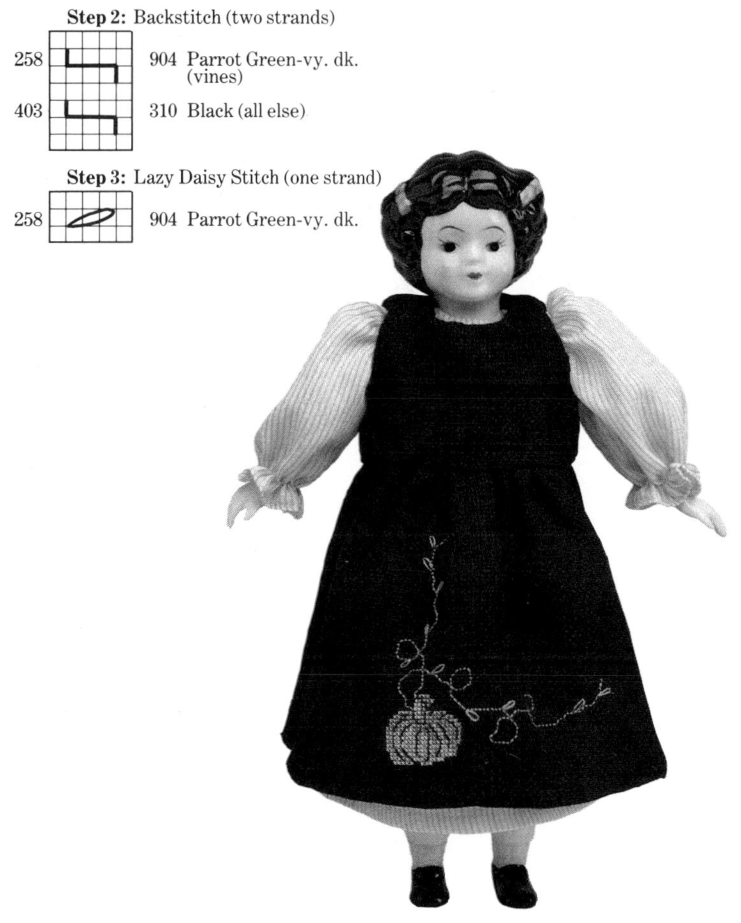

Trick or Treat Bag

SAMPLE

Stitched on white Aida 14, the finished design size is 10⅜" x 8¾". The fabric was cut 17" x 17". Begin stitching the lower left corner of the design 3¼" from the left and 4¼" from the bottom edge of the fabric. (A fabric with this stitch count must be used so that the design will fit the bag.)

Step 1: Cross-stitch (two strands)

Bates	Symbol	DMC (used for sample)
1	·	White
886	–	677 Old Gold-vy. lt.
303	X	742 Tangerine-lt.
316	+	971 Pumpkin
330	o	947 Burnt Orange
26	△	957 Geranium-pale
130	∴	799 Delft-med.
131	□	798 Delft-dk.
256	|	704 Chartreuse-bright
258	●	904 Parrot Green-vy. dk.
398	♥	415 Pearl Grey
400	▒	317 Pewter Grey
403	■	310 Black

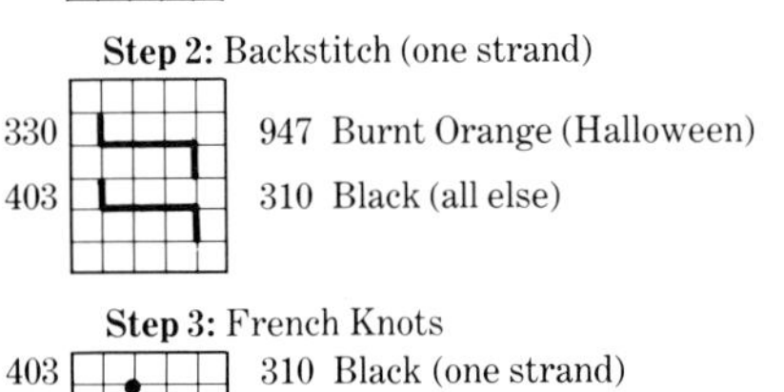

Step 2: Backstitch (one strand)

Bates	DMC
330	947 Burnt Orange (Halloween)
403	310 Black (all else)

Step 3: French Knots

Bates	DMC
403	310 Black (one strand)

MATERIALS

- Completed cross-stitch on white Aida 14; matching thread; see sample information
- 15" x 15½" piece of unstitched Aida 14
- ½ yard of 45"-wide black print fabric; matching thread
- 1¼ yards of 1"-wide white webbing
- ½ yard of 45"-wide polyester fleece

DIRECTIONS

All seam allowances are ½".

1. Cut the stitched Aida 15" x 15½" so that the design is centered horizontally. The top margin is 3¾" and the bottom margin is 3¼".

2. Cut two 15" x 15½" pieces from the black print lining fabric.

3. Cut two 15" x 15½" pieces from the fleece.

4. Layer the stitched design, right side up, over one piece of fleece. Baste together. Baste the unstitched Aida to the remaining fleece.

5. With right sides together, stitch the outside front and back pieces together along the sides and bottom.

continued . . .

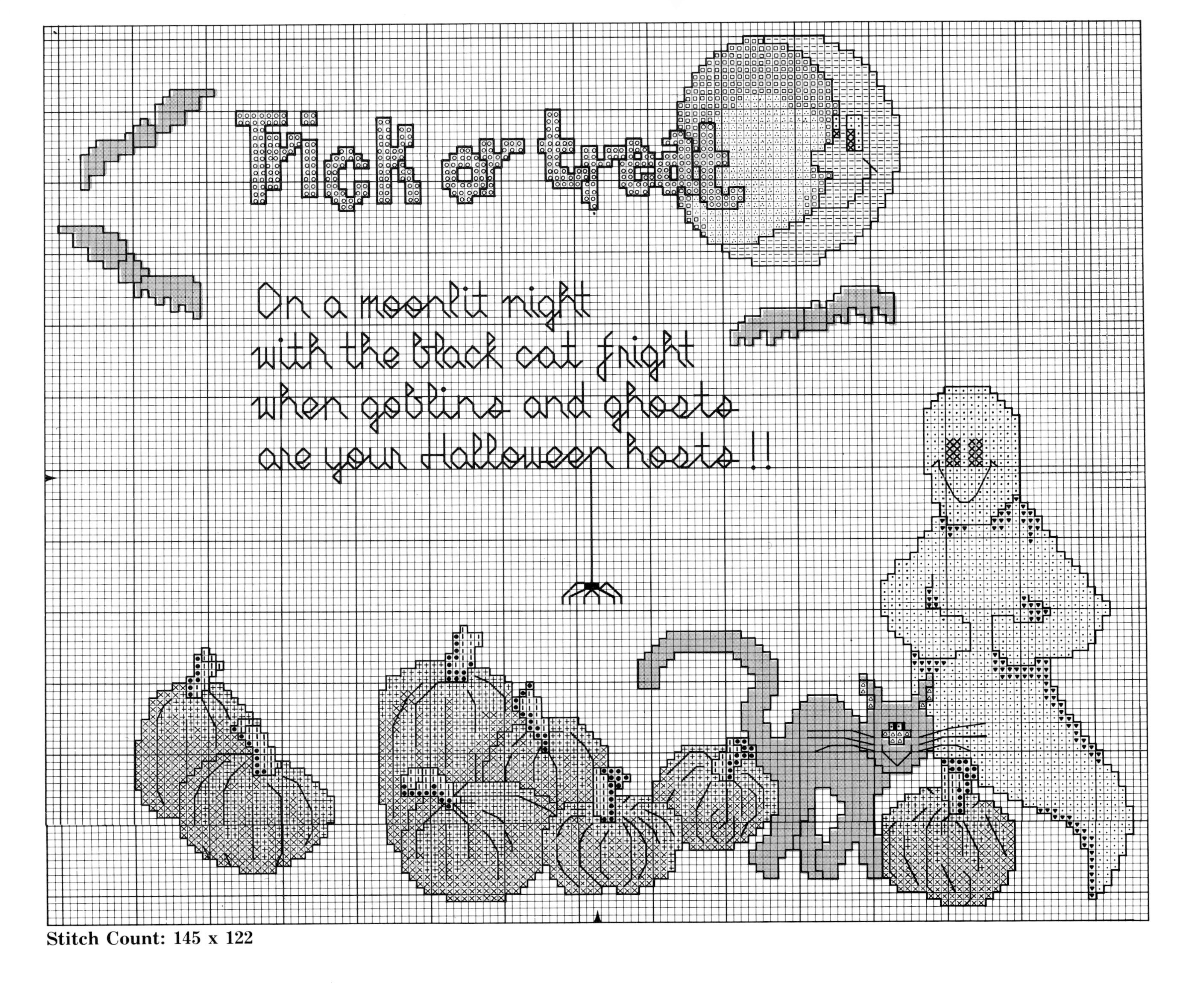

Stitch Count: 145 x 122

... **Bag continued**

6. With the bag still inside out, and the side seam and bottom seam aligned, stitch across the corner (Diagram A). Repeat with the second corner. Trim seam allowance to ½″. Turn the bag right side out.

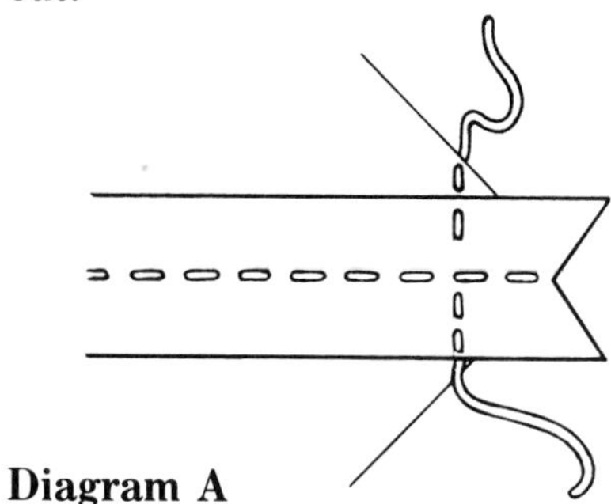

Diagram A

7. Repeat Steps 5 and 6 for the lining, leaving a 5″ opening in the bottom edge. Do not turn right side out.

8. Cut two 19″ pieces of webbing for the handles. Pin the raw ends of the webbing to the right sides of the Aida (Diagram B).

9. With right sides together and side seams matching, slide the lining over the Aida. Stitch the top edges of the lining and the tote bag together. Turn the bag right side out through the opening in the lining, and then slipstitch the opening closed.

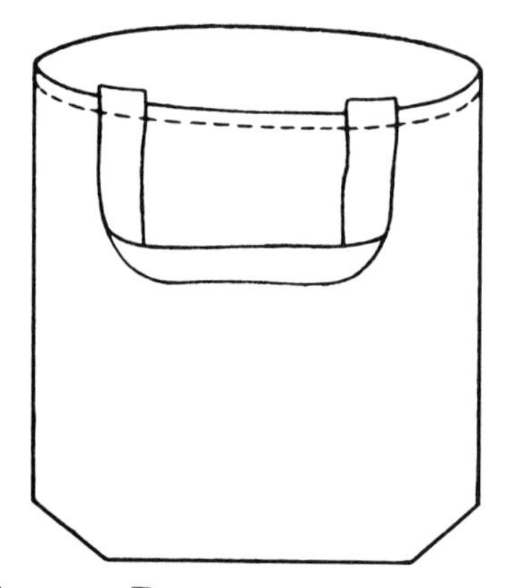

Diagram B

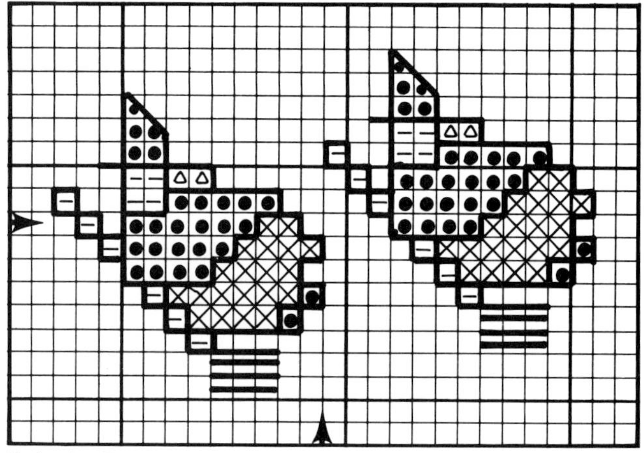

Stitch Count: 24 x 15

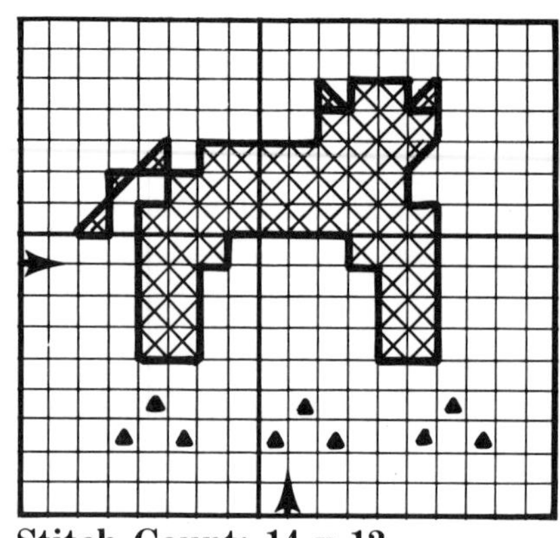

Stitch Count: 14 x 12

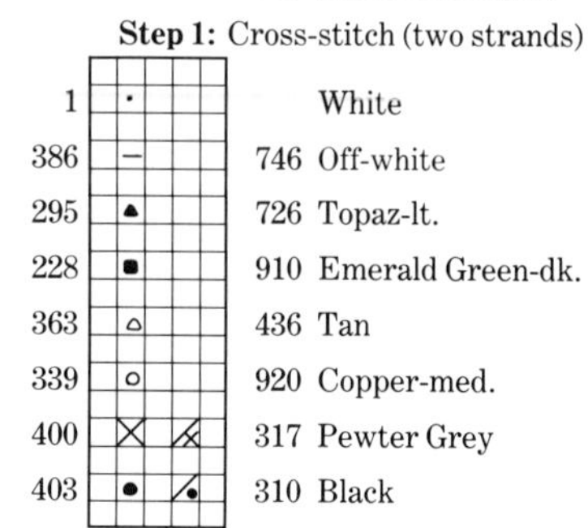

Bates	DMC (used for sample)
Step 1: Cross-stitch (two strands)	
1	White
386	746 Off-white
295	726 Topaz-lt.
228	910 Emerald Green-dk.
363	436 Tan
339	920 Copper-med.
400	317 Pewter Grey
403	310 Black
Step 2: Backstitch (one strand)	
403	310 Black
Step 3: French Knots (one strand)	
403	310 Black

Treat Bags

SAMPLES
The designs are stitched on brown paper, using waste canvas 14 over two threads. (The designs are suitable only for waste canvas with a thread count of 14.) Also needed: one small piece of fusible interfacing for each design. Fuse the interfacing to the back of the paper before stitching.

Ghost and Pumpkin: The finished design size is 2″ x 1⅞″. The paper was cut 4″ x 4″.

Cat: The finished design size is 2″ x 1¾″. The paper was cut 4″ x 4″.

Witches: Finished design size is 3⅜″ x 1⅛″. Paper was cut 5″ x 4″.

MATERIALS
Completed cross-stitch on brown paper with fusible interfacing and waste canvas; see sample information
Purchased colored-paper gift bag
Crayons
Glue

DIRECTIONS
1. Color the unstitched portions of the designs with crayons; see the photograph for colors.

2. Cut the single motifs into 2½″ x 2½″ pieces. Glue onto the gift bags.

3. Cut the witch motif 2¼″ x 3¾″. Glue onto the gift bag at an angle (see the photo).

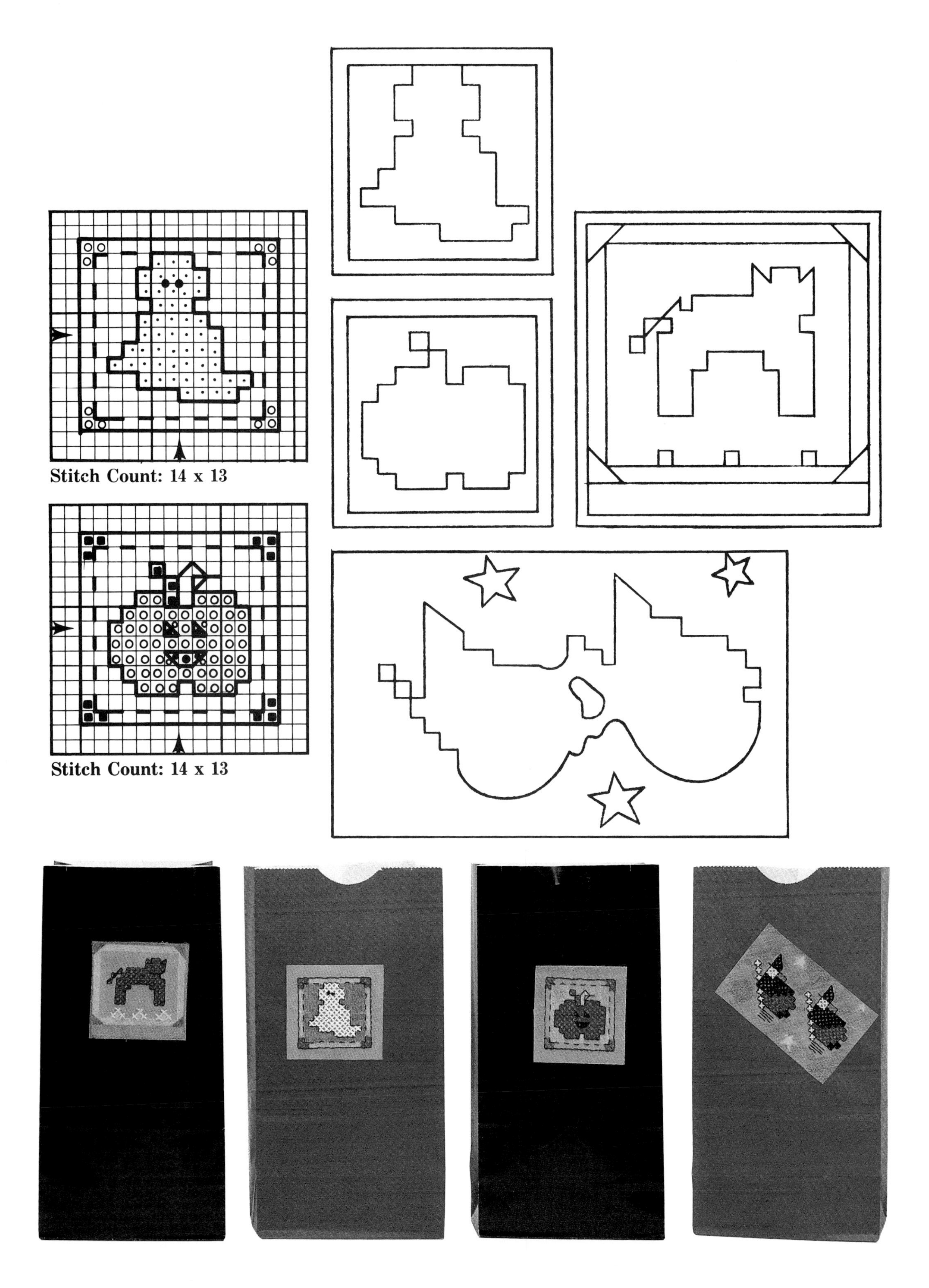
Stitch Count: 14 x 13
Stitch Count: 14 x 13

NOVEMBER 26

Thanksgiving

After the hardships of the first winter in the New World, the Pilgrims greeted their first harvest with rejoicing and thanksgiving. Today, we continue to give thanks on this holiday for the bounty bestowed on our country.

Stitch Count: 83 x 83

Village

SAMPLE
Stitched on driftwood Dublin 25 over two threads, the finished design size is 6⅝″ x 6⅝″. The fabric was cut 13″ x 13″.

FABRICS	DESIGN SIZES
Aida 11	7½″ x 7½″
Aida 14	5⅞″ x 5⅞″
Aida 18	4⅝″ x 4⅝″
Hardanger 22	3¾″ x 3¾″

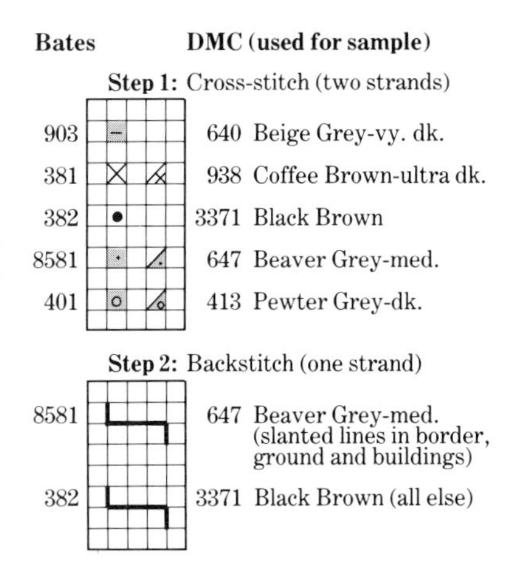

Bates	DMC (used for sample)
	Step 1: Cross-stitch (two strands)
903	640 Beige Grey-vy. dk.
381	938 Coffee Brown-ultra dk.
382	3371 Black Brown
8581	647 Beaver Grey-med.
401	413 Pewter Grey-dk.
	Step 2: Backstitch (one strand)
8581	647 Beaver Grey-med. (slanted lines in border, ground and buildings)
382	3371 Black Brown (all else)

Stitch Count: 83 x 83

House

SAMPLE
Stitched on driftwood Dublin 25 over two threads, the finished design size is 6⅝" x 6⅝". The fabric was cut 13" x 13".

FABRICS	DESIGN SIZES
Aida 11	7½" x 7½"
Aida 14	5⅞" x 5⅞"
Aida 18	4⅝" x 4⅝"
Hardanger 22	3¾" x 3¾"

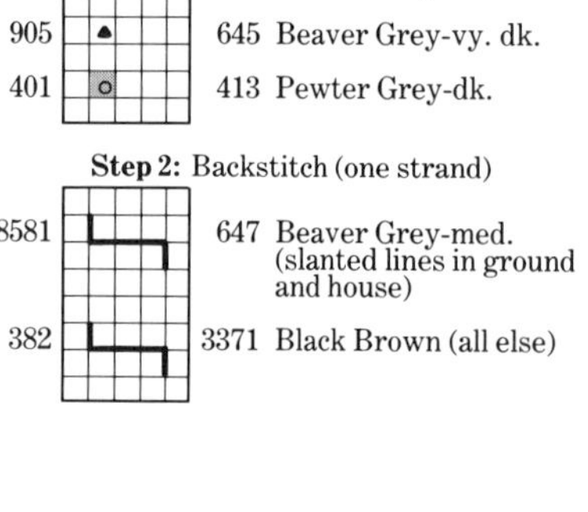

Bates	DMC (used for sample)
	Step 1: Cross-stitch (two strands)
903	640 Beige Grey-vy. dk.
380	839 Beige Brown-dk.
381	938 Coffee Brown-ultra dk.
382	3371 Black Brown
8581	647 Beaver Grey-med.
905	645 Beaver Grey-vy. dk.
401	413 Pewter Grey-dk.
	Step 2: Backstitch (one strand)
8581	647 Beaver Grey-med. (slanted lines in ground and house)
382	3371 Black Brown (all else)

Heart of the Home Sampler

SAMPLE
Stitched on light brown Linen 32 over two threads, the finished design size is 10½″ x 14¾″. The fabric was cut 17″ x 21″.

continued . . .

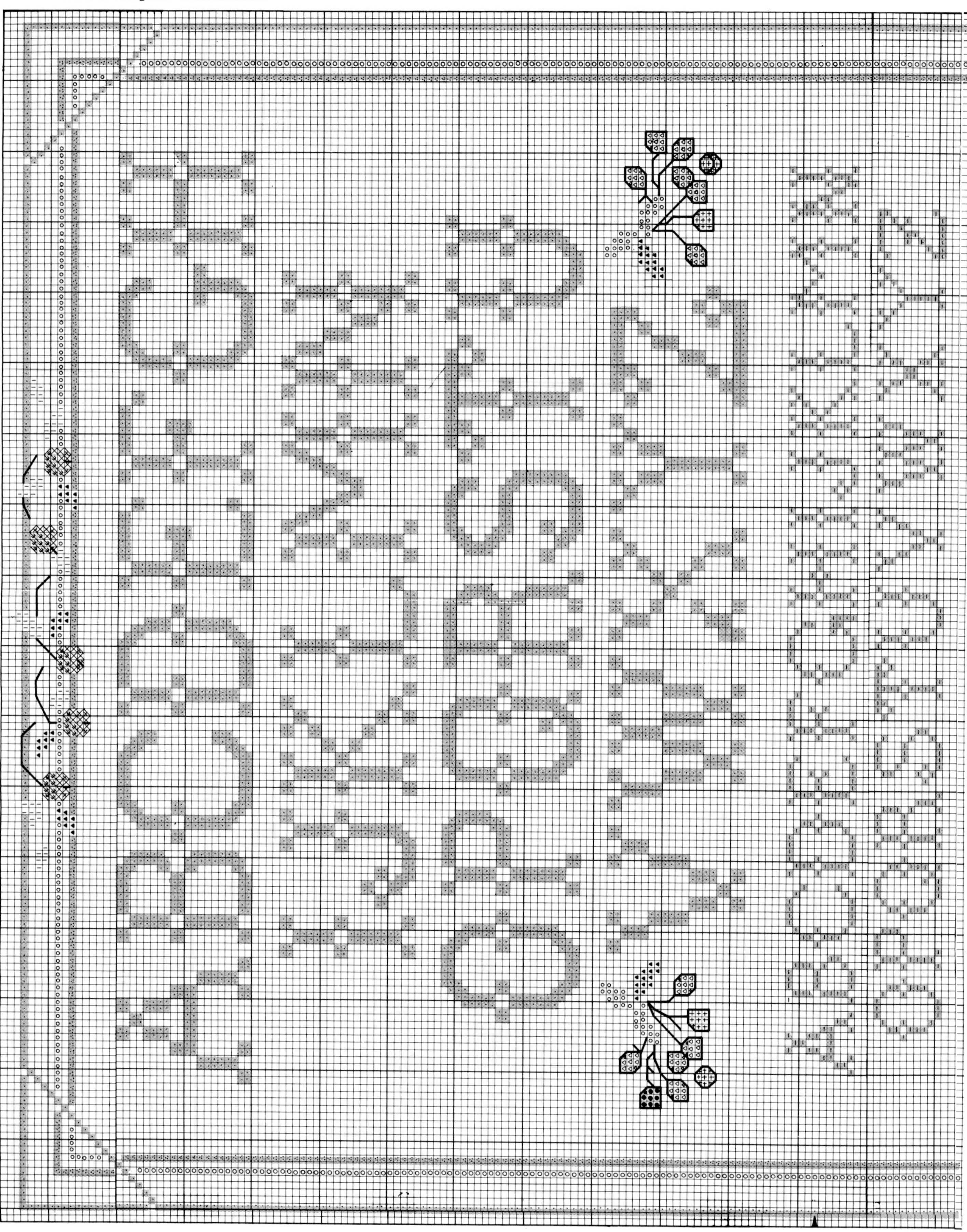

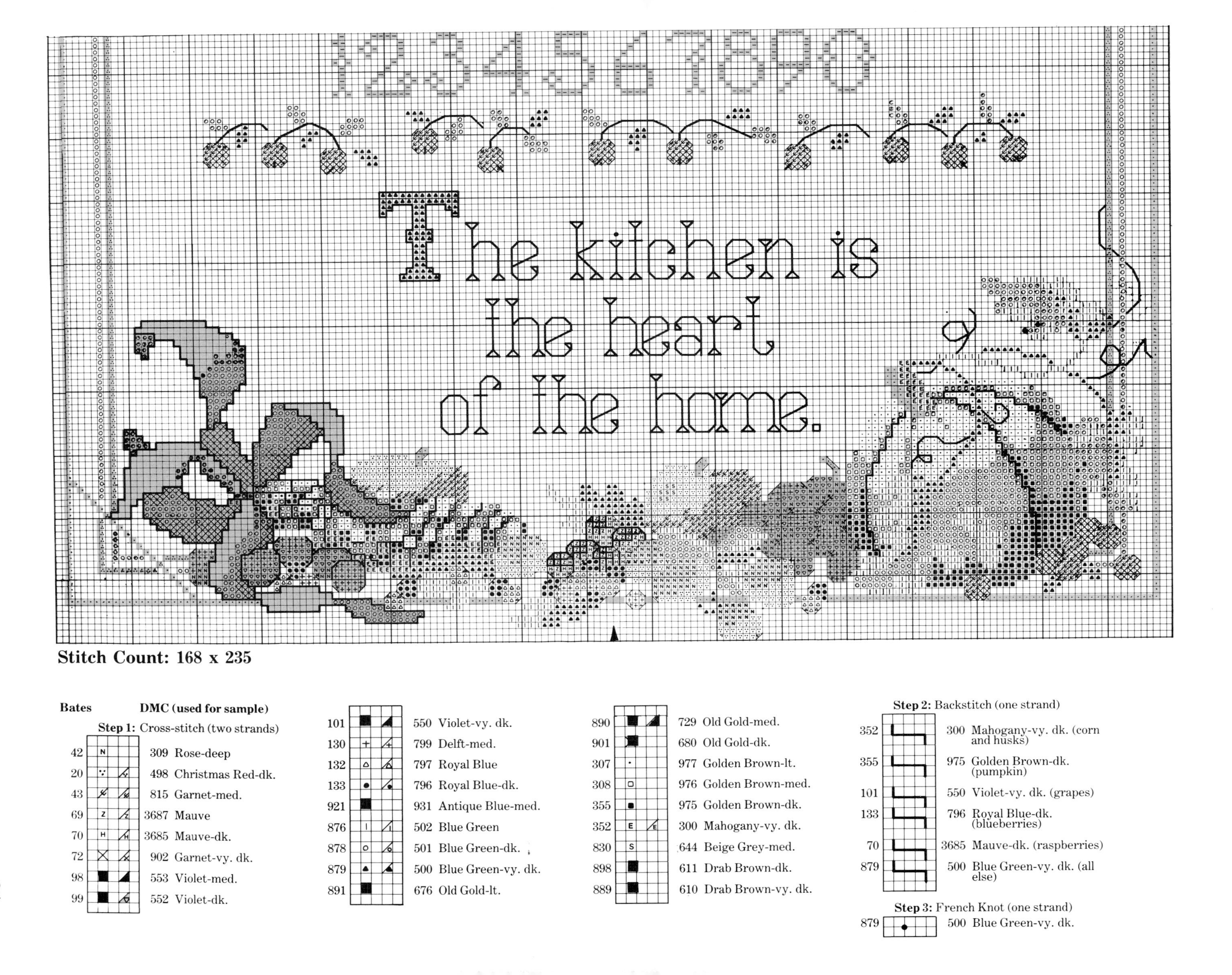

Stitch Count: 168 x 235

Step 1: Cross-stitch (two strands)

Bates	DMC (used for sample)	
42	309	Rose-deep
20	498	Christmas Red-dk.
43	815	Garnet-med.
69	3687	Mauve
70	3685	Mauve-dk.
72	902	Garnet-vy. dk.
98	553	Violet-med.
99	552	Violet-dk.
101	550	Violet-vy. dk.
130	799	Delft-med.
132	797	Royal Blue
133	796	Royal Blue-dk.
921	931	Antique Blue-med.
876	502	Blue Green
878	501	Blue Green-dk.
879	500	Blue Green-vy. dk.
891	676	Old Gold-lt.
890	729	Old Gold-med.
901	680	Old Gold-dk.
307	977	Golden Brown-lt.
308	976	Golden Brown-med.
355	975	Golden Brown-dk.
352	300	Mahogany-vy. dk.
830	644	Beige Grey-med.
898	611	Drab Brown-dk.
889	610	Drab Brown-vy. dk.

Step 2: Backstitch (one strand)

Bates	DMC	
352	300	Mahogany-vy. dk. (corn and husks)
355	975	Golden Brown-dk. (pumpkin)
101	550	Violet-vy. dk. (grapes)
133	796	Royal Blue-dk. (blueberries)
70	3685	Mauve-dk. (raspberries)
879	500	Blue Green-vy. dk. (all else)

Step 3: French Knot (one strand)

Bates	DMC	
879	500	Blue Green-vy. dk.

DECEMBER 6

St. Nicholas' Day

The details of the life of St. Nicholas, a fourth-century saint, are shrouded in mystery, but this hasn't kept him from being one of the most popular saints in both the eastern and western Christian churches. As Bishop of Myra, he was noted for his charity, and it is thought that Santa Claus and his custom of giving gifts stem from this legend. Whether we call him by his German name, St. Nicholas, his Dutch name, Kris Kringle, or his Russian name, Father Ice, this fatherly Santa Claus figure continues to be popular worldwide.

St. Nicholas
Kris Kringle

St. Nicholas

SAMPLE
Stitched on white Belfast Linen 32 over two threads, the finished design size is 8¼" x 10¾". The fabric was cut 15" x 17".

Bates	Symbol	DMC (used for sample)
		Step 1: Cross-stitch (two strands)
1	∴	White
778	z	948 Peach Flesh-vy. lt.
778	K	754 Peach Flesh-lt.
4146	V	950 Sportsman Flesh-lt.
43	o	815 Garnet-med.
44	◙	814 Garnet-dk.
72	•	902 Garnet-vy. dk.
900	(shaded)	928 Grey Green-lt.
849	▫	927 Grey Green-med.
920	ш	932 Antique Blue-lt.
921	ø	931 Antique Blue-med.
875	·	503 Blue Green-med.
876	o	502 Blue Green
878	■	501 Blue Green-dk.
229	W	909 Emerald Green-vy. dk.
376	⁘	842 Beige Brown-vy. lt.
378	I	841 Beige Brown-lt.
379	X	840 Beige Brown-med.
380	▽	839 Beige Brown-dk.
380	•	838 Beige Brown-vy. dk.
375	S	420 Hazel Nut Brown-dk.
371	□	433 Brown-med.
357	▲	801 Coffee Brown-dk.
397	+	762 Pearl Grey-vy. lt.
398	△	415 Pearl Grey
		Step 2: Filet Cross-stitch (one strand)
900	·	928 Grey Green-lt.
849	–	927 Grey Green-med.
876	X	502 Blue Green
		Step 3: Backstitch (one strand)
72		902 Garnet-vy. dk. (gown, hat)
849		927 Grey Green-med. (border)
922		930 Antique Blue-dk. (snowflakes)
876		502 Blue Green (lettering)
382		3371 Black Brown (bag, bear)
400		317 Pewter Grey (all else)

Step 4: Beadwork

Symbol	
■	White

FABRICS	DESIGN SIZES
Aida 11	11⅞" x 15¾"
Aida 14	9⅜" x 12⅜"
Aida 18	7¼" x 9⅝"
Hardanger 22	6" x 7⅞"

Stitch Count: 131 x 173

Kris Kringle

SAMPLE
Stitched on white Belfast Linen 32 over two threads, the finished design size is 8¼″ x 10¾″. The fabric was cut 15″ x 17″.

Step 1: Cross-stitch (two strands)

Bates	DMC (used for sample)	
1		White
778	948	Peach Flesh-vy. lt.
4146	950	Sportsman Flesh-lt.
778	754	Peach Flesh-lt.
306	725	Topaz
307	783	Christmas Gold
43	815	Garnet-med.
72	902	Garnet-vy. dk.
101	327	Antique Violet-dk.
160	813	Blue-lt.
900	928	Grey Green-lt.
849	927	Grey Green-med.
851	924	Grey Green-vy. dk.
876	502	Blue Green
878	501	Blue Green-dk.
879	500	Blue Green-vy. dk.
307	977	Golden Brown-lt.
378	841	Beige Brown-lt.
379	840	Beige Brown-med.
380	839	Beige Brown-dk.
375	420	Hazel Nut Brown-dk.
371	433	Brown-med.
357	801	Coffee Brown-dk.
397	762	Pearl Grey-vy. lt.
398	415	Pearl Grey

Step 2: Filet Cross-stitch (one strand)

Bates	DMC	
900	928	Grey Green-lt.
849	927	Grey Green-med.
876	502	Blue Green

Step 3: Backstitch (one strand)

Bates	DMC	
849	927	Grey Green-med. (border)
379	840	Beige Brown-med. (lettering)
380	839	Beige Brown-dk. (rabbits)
382	3371	Black Brown (baskets, sleeve)
400	317	Pewter Grey (all else)

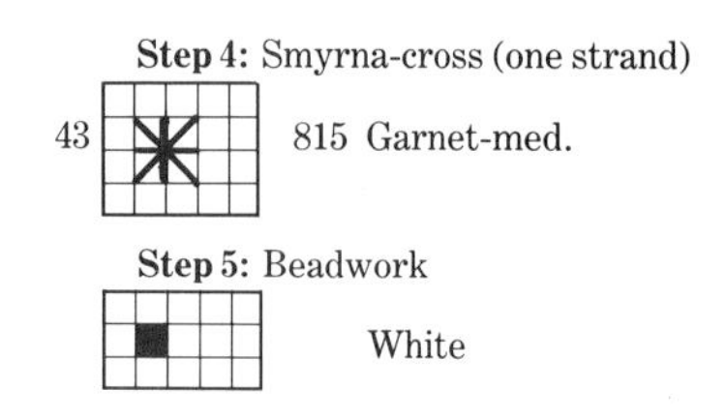

Step 4: Smyrna-cross (one strand)

Bates	DMC	
43	815	Garnet-med.

Step 5: Beadwork

White

FABRICS	DESIGN SIZES
Aida 11	11⅞″ x 15¾″
Aida 14	9⅜″ x 12⅜″
Aida 18	7¼″ x 9⅝″
Hardanger 22	6″ x 7⅞″

Stitch Count: 131 x 173

Father Ice

SAMPLE
Stitched on white Belfast Linen 32 over two threads, the finished design size is 8¼" x 10¾". The fabric was cut 15" x 17".

Step 1: Cross-stitch (two strands)

Bates	Symbol	DMC (used for sample)	Color
1	•		White
778	+	948	Peach Flesh-vy. lt.
4146	S	950	Sportsman Flesh-lt.
778	∵	754	Peach Flesh-lt.
306	Z	725	Topaz
19	◬	817	Coral Red-vy. dk.
20	✓	498	Christmas Red-dk.
43	●	815	Garnet-med.
130	R	809	Delft
920	O	932	Antique Blue-lt.
921	E	931	Antique Blue-med.
900	△	928	Grey Green-lt.
849	□	927	Grey Green-med.
876	┌	502	Blue Green
878	N	501	Blue Green-dk.
882	◘	407	Sportsman Flesh-dk.
891	H	676	Old Gold-lt.
898	K	611	Drab Brown-dk.
375	▒	420	Hazel Nut Brown-dk.
371	+	433	Brown-med.
357	∴	801	Coffee Brown-dk.
397	I	762	Pearl Grey-vy. lt.
399	O	318	Steel Grey-lt.
400	╳	414	Steel Grey-dk.
400	▲	317	Pewter Grey

Step 2: Filet Cross-stitch (one strand)

Bates	Symbol	DMC	Color
900	•	928	Grey Green-lt.
849	–	927	Grey Green-med.
876	╳	502	Blue Green

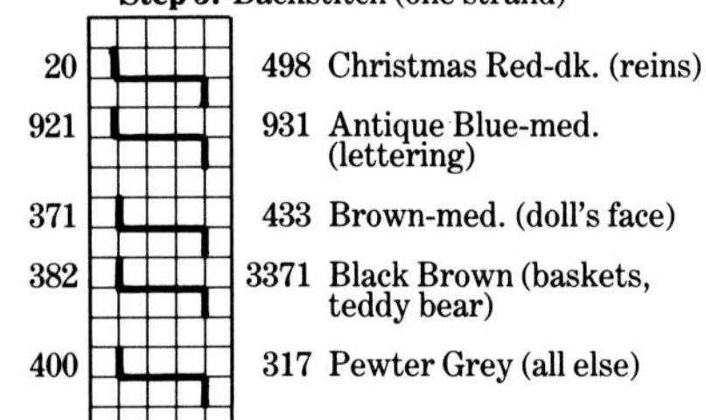

Step 3: Backstitch (one strand)

Bates	DMC	Color
20	498	Christmas Red-dk. (reins)
921	931	Antique Blue-med. (lettering)
371	433	Brown-med. (doll's face)
382	3371	Black Brown (baskets, teddy bear)
400	317	Pewter Grey (all else)

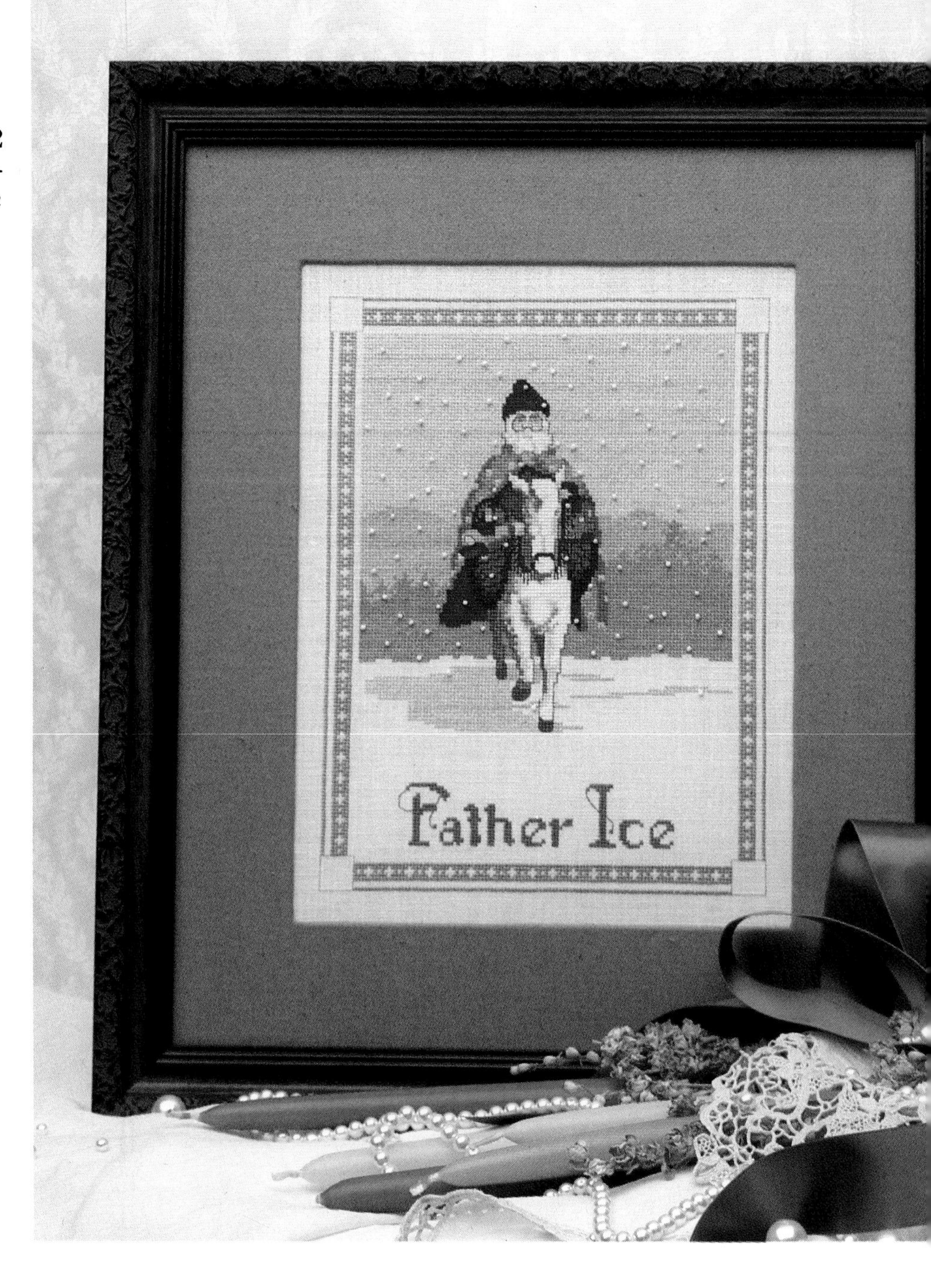

Step 4: French Knots (one strand)

357 — 801 Coffee Brown-dk.

Step 5: Smyrna-cross (one strand)

891 — 676 Old Gold-lt.

Step 6: Beadwork

White

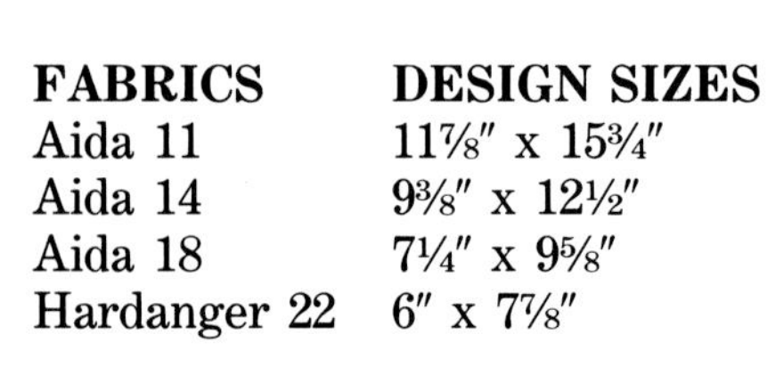

FABRICS	DESIGN SIZES
Aida 11	11⅞" x 15¾"
Aida 14	9⅜" x 12½"
Aida 18	7¼" x 9⅝"
Hardanger 22	6" x 7⅞"

Stitch Count: 131 x 173

DECEMBER 21

Snow White's 50th Anniversary

Snow White has been a favorite since the Grimm brothers' story in the 1800s. But it was Walt Disney who made her a star 50 years ago when he premiered the first full-length animated movie.

Snow White

SAMPLE
Stitched on ash rose Lugana 25 over two threads, the finished design size is 8½" x 12". The fabric was cut 15" x 18".

Bates — **DMC (used for sample)**

Step 1: Cross-stitch (two strands)

Bates	Symbol	DMC	Color
1	•		White
386	•	746	Off-white
885	–	739	Tan-ultra lt.
886	S	677	Old Gold-vy. lt.
891	K	676	Old Gold-lt.
892	U	819	Baby Pink-lt.
49	△	963	Dusty Rose-vy. lt.
893	O	224	Shell Pink-lt.
894	I	223	Shell Pink-med.
897	⊠	221	Shell Pink-dk.
72	▲	902	Garnet-vy. dk.
5968	▢	355	Terra Cotta-dk.
970	X	315	Antique Mauve-dk.
869	–	3042	Antique Violet-lt.
101	E	327	Antique Violet-dk.
128	O	800	Delft-pale
117	∴	341	Blue Violet-lt.
940		792	Delft-dk.
921	+	931	Antique Blue-med.
150	+	823	Navy Blue-dk.
168	r	597	Turquoise
851	∵	924	Grey Green-vy. dk.
187	▢	958	Seagreen-dk.
187	▽	992	Aquamarine
189	■	991	Aquamarine-dk.
876	X	502	Blue Green
215	I	368	Pistachio Green-lt.
373	R	3045	Yellow Beige-dk.
375	⊥	420	Hazel Nut Brown-dk.
903	/	640	Beige Grey-vy. dk.
403	•	310	Black

Step 2: Backstitch (one strand)

Bates	DMC	Color
150	823	Navy Blue-dk.

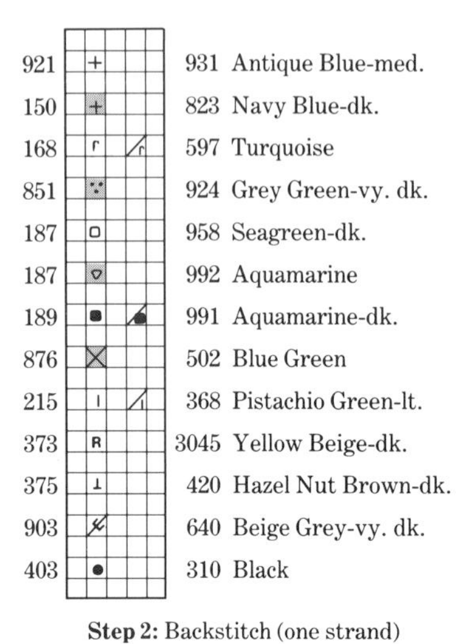

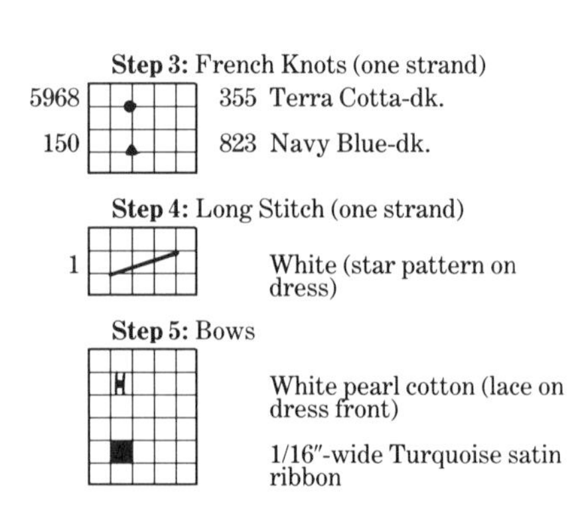

Step 3: French Knots (one strand)

Bates	DMC	Color
5968	355	Terra Cotta-dk.
150	823	Navy Blue-dk.

Step 4: Long Stitch (one strand)

Bates	Color
1	White (star pattern on dress)

Step 5: Bows

White pearl cotton (lace on dress front)

1/16"-wide Turquoise satin ribbon

FABRICS	DESIGN SIZES
Aida 11	9¾" x 14¼"
Aida 14	7⅝" x 11¼"
Aida 18	6" x 8¾"
Hardanger 22	4⅞" x 7⅛"

Stitch Count: 107 x 157

DECEMBER 25

Christmas

Just about everyone's favorite holiday, Christmas is a time when families are reunited, and the story of the birth of Jesus is retold throughout the world. This holiday of holidays fills our hearts and minds with visions of sugar plums, roast turkeys, and special gifts. And what could be more special than a gift you made yourself? This year choose from the myriad cross-stitch designs shown here and stitch a gift for someone you love.

Snowflake Doll

SAMPLE
Stitched on blue Belfast Linen 32 over two threads, the finished design size for one motif is ½" x ½". (A fabric with this stitch count must be used so that the design will fit the pinafore.) The fabric was cut 9" x 7" for skirt and 3¾" x 2½" for bodice. Trace the patterns for the pinafore bodice front and the pinafore skirt front onto the fabric with a dressmakers' pen (see General Instsructions). Repeat the motif randomly as desired (see the photo). For a unique effect, make a few of the lines one or two thread units longer than indicated on the graph.

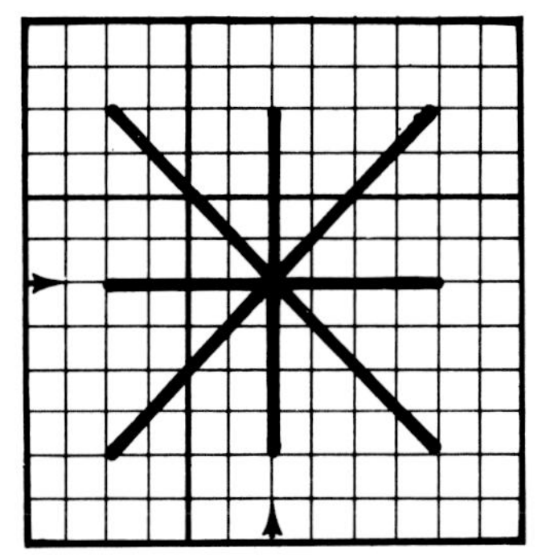

Stitch Count: 8 x 8

Step 1: Smyrna-cross (one strand)

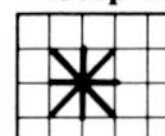

Silver Metallic and one strand pearl Balger Blending Filament

A Holiday Welcome

SAMPLE

Stitched on teal Jobelan 28 over three threads, the finished design size is 14⅞" x 8⅜". (A fabric with this stitch count must be used so that the design will fit the finished piece.) The fabric for the background design was cut 28" x 22". The finished design size for one house is 2½" x 3⅝". The fabric for each house was cut 9" x 10". As an option, the houses may be stitched on the same piece of fabric as the Welcome Friends design, following the placement indicated on the graph.

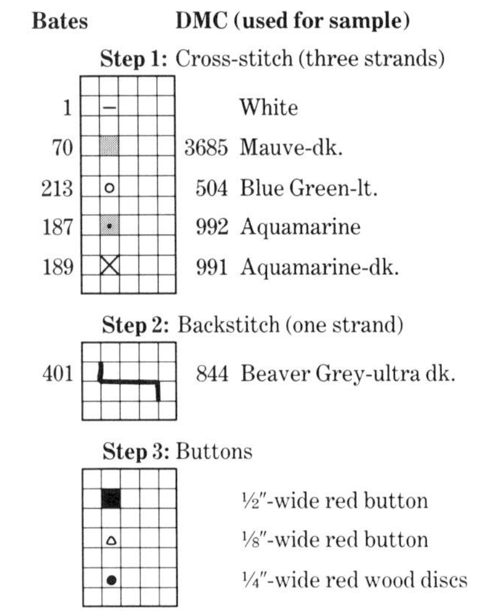

Bates	DMC (used for sample)
Step 1: Cross-stitch (three strands)	
1	White
70	3685 Mauve-dk.
213	504 Blue Green-lt.
187	992 Aquamarine
189	991 Aquamarine-dk.
Step 2: Backstitch (one strand)	
401	844 Beaver Grey-ultra dk.
Step 3: Buttons	
	½"-wide red button
	⅛"-wide red button
	¼"-wide red wood discs

MATERIALS

Completed cross-stitch for Welcome Friends design on teal Jobelan 28; three cross-stitch houses on separate pieces of teal Jobelan 28; see sample information
One 11" x 20" piece of foam-core board
Three 3" x 4½" pieces of foam-core board for houses
11" x 20" piece of polyester fleece
11" x 20" paper for backing
Craft knife
White craft glue
Tracing paper for patterns

DIRECTIONS

1. Trace the house pattern. To make a pattern for the plaque, place tracing paper on top of the Welcome Friends stitched piece and mark 1¼" above the O, M, E, F, R, and I and 2¼" above the W and S. Connect the marks to form an arc. Mark 2¾" below the W and S and draw a straight line across the bottom, connecting these marks. Fold paper in half at vertical center and cut pattern so that sides are symmetrical.

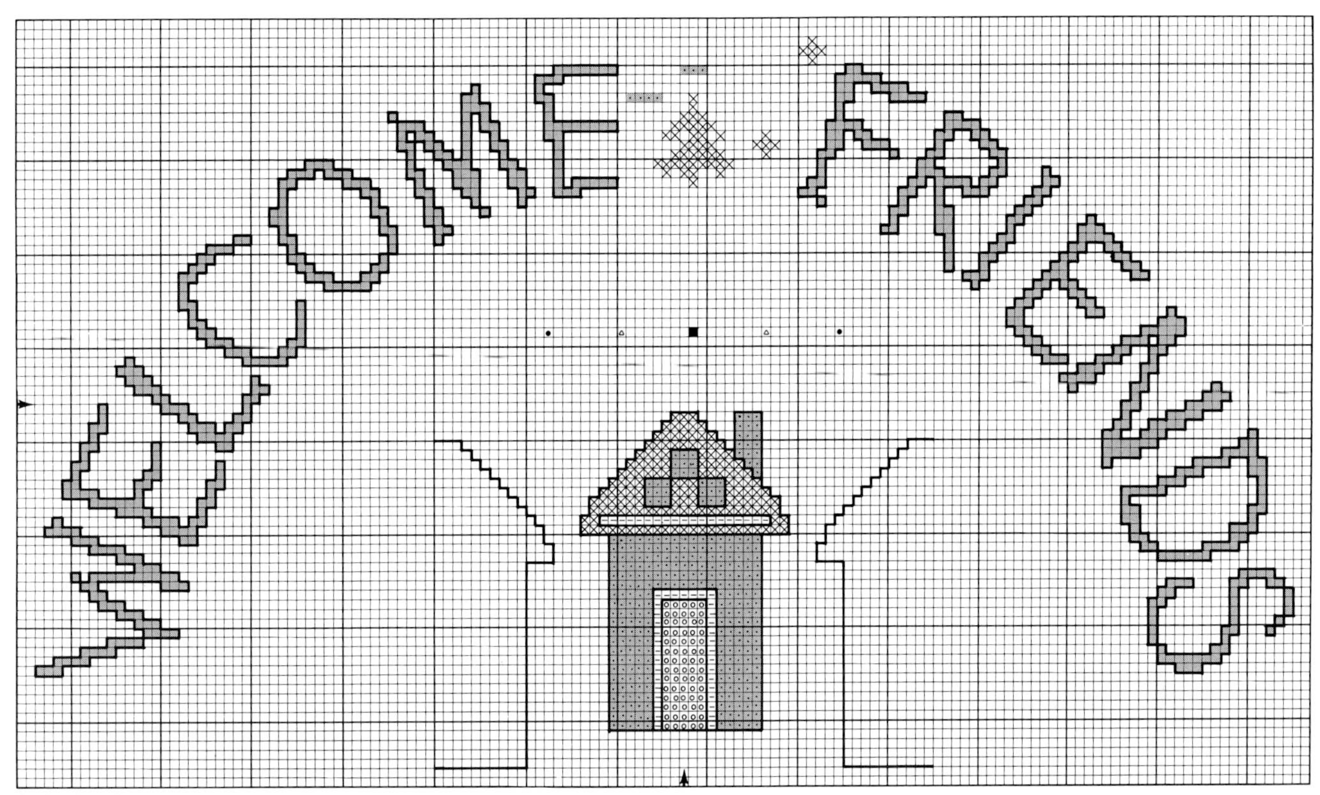

Stitch Count: 139 x 78
Stitch Count for one house: 23 x 34

2. Trace the plaque and house patterns onto foam-core board. Cut them out with a craft knife.

3. From polyester fleece, cut one plaque shape. Glue lightly to the foam-core board.

4. Mark the vertical center of the fabric with the Welcome Friends design. Mark the vertical center of the plaque on the back of the foam-core board. Place the design over the fleece, matching vertical centers; pin.

5. Trim fabric 2″ larger all around than the plaque. Fold bottom edge of fabric to back of foam-core board and glue. Continue to wrap the remaining fabric to the back of the foam-core board and glue in place.

6. Center a stitched house over a foam-core house. Cut the fabric 1½″ larger all around than the foam-core house. Fold carefully to the back and glue, clipping the corners to avoid unnecessary fullness. Allow glue to seal the raw edges of the fabric at the corners, especially near the chimney.

7. Glue the houses in place as indicated on the graph.

8. To finish, cut the plaque shape from the 11″ x 20″ paper and glue to the back of the plaque.

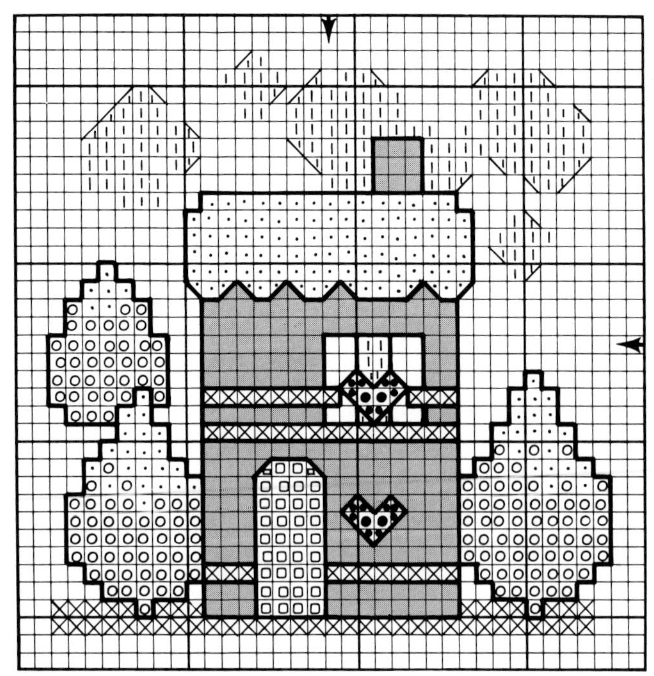

Stitch Count: 33 x 33

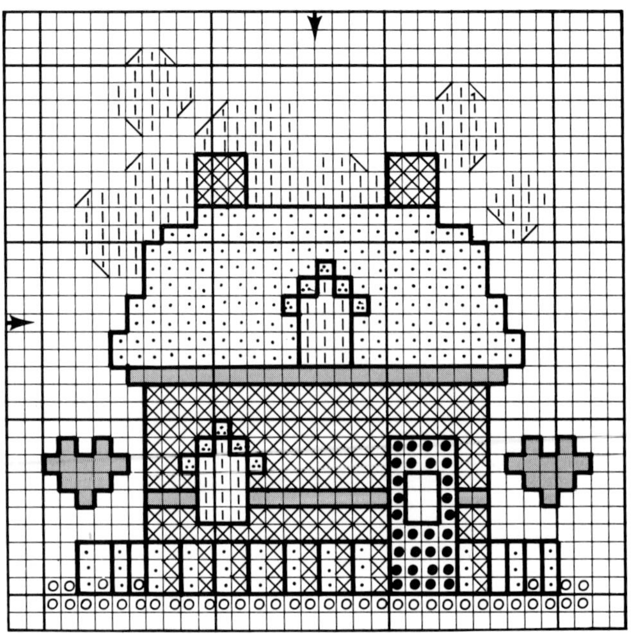

Stitch Count: 32 x 31

Christmas Ornaments

SAMPLES
The designs are stitched on white Aida 18. The fabric for each design was cut 6″ x 6″. (A fabric with this stitch count must be used so that the design will fit the ornament.)

Pink House: The finished design size is 1⅞″ x 1⅞″.

Brown House: The finished design size is 1¾″ x 1¾″.

Purple House: The finished design size is 1¾″ x 1½″.

Snowman: The finished design size is 1⅞″ x 1¾″.

Bates		DMC (used for sample)
	Step 1: Cross-stitch (two strands)	
1	· /	White
76	(shaded)	962 Dusty Rose-med.
42	●	309 Rose-deep
108	+	211 Lavender-lt.
110	◘	208 Lavender-vy. dk.
158	I	828 Blue-ultra lt.
168	■	518 Wedgewood-lt.
266	o	471 Avocado Green-vy. lt.
216	▵	320 Pistachio Green-med.
882	X	407 Sportsman Flesh-dk.
936	∴	632 Negro Flesh
400	▲	317 Pewter Grey
	Step 2: Backstitch (one strand)	
149		336 Navy Blue
	Step 3: French Knots (one strand)	
149		336 Navy Blue

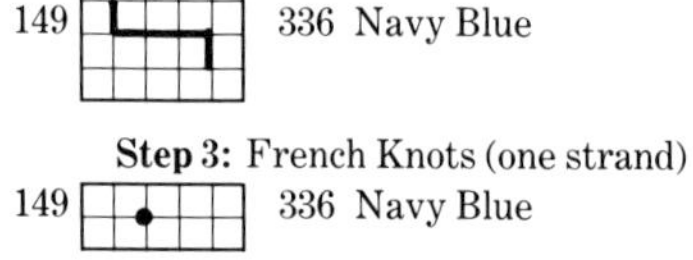

MATERIALS (for one large ornament)
Completed cross-stitch on white Aida 18; see sample information
6″ Styrofoam ball
Two 11″ x 11″ pieces of contrasting print fabric
Scrap of third print fabric; contrasting thread
⅝ yard of ⅛″-wide satin ribbon; matching thread
1 yard of ⅛″-wide contrasting ribbon for hanger; matching thread
Glue

DIRECTIONS
1. Fold under ¼″ on one edge of the third fabric. Place the folded edge on the cross-stitched piece, ⅛″ below the design, right side up. Sew a running stitch through all the layers with a contrasting thread.

2. Make a pattern for a 4″ circle, adding a ¼″ seam allowance. Cut one circle from the Aida with the design centered and the folded edge of the third fabric 1½″ from the edge of the circle.

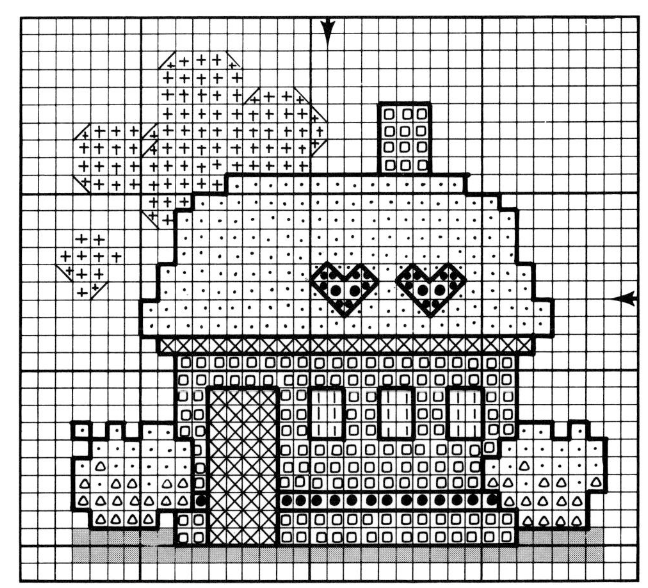

Stitch Count: 32 x 28

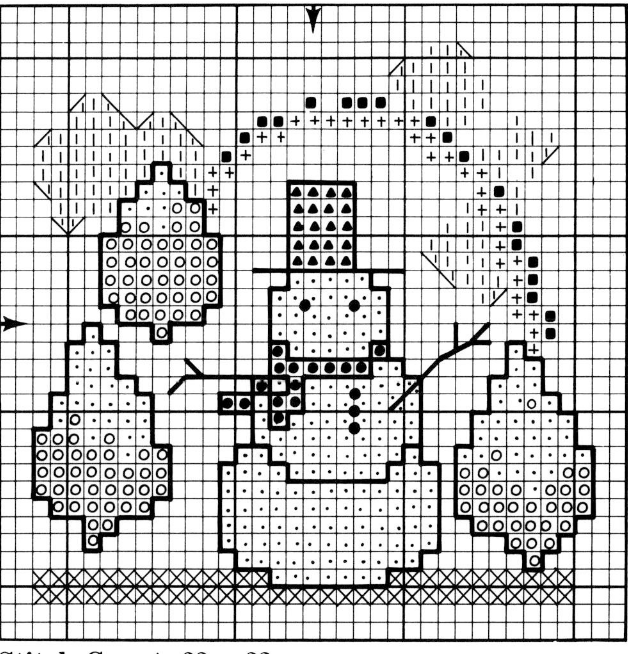

Stitch Count: 33 x 32

3. Center the Aida over one 11″ print fabric square. Fold under the 1/4″ seam allowance on the circle and slipstitch the Aida in place.

4. From the 5/8-yard length of ribbon, cut one 9″ piece. Knot one end and tack it to the left side of the design (see the photo). Twisting the ribbon, continue to tack it to the Aida to make an arc over the design. Fold the remaining ribbon into 1″ loops, leaving 2″ and 3″ ends. Tack the loops to the Aida. Knot and trim the ribbon ends.

5. Score around the center of the ball to make an indentation. Center the second 11″ fabric square over the back and tuck it into the indentation. Do not trim the fabric. Center the design piece over the front of the ball. Tuck it into the indentation. Do not trim.

6. Holding the edges of both fabric pieces together, trim them 3/8″ from the ball.

7. Mark the center of the 1-yard length of ribbon. Place the center at the bottom of the front of the ornament, 1/4″ in front of the indentation. Glue in place and knot at the center top. With ribbon ends, make a loop for hanging. Knot and trim the ends.

continued . . .

. . . **Ornaments continued**

MATERIALS (for one small ornament)
Completed cross-stitch on white Aida 18; see sample information
Two 8″ x 8″ pieces of contrasting print fabric
Scrap of third fabric
Yellow and bright blue thread
1 yard of ⅛″-wide satin ribbon; matching thread
4½″ Styrofoam ball

DIRECTIONS

1. Fold under ¼″ on one edge of the third fabric. Follow Step 1 directions for the large ornament.

2. Make a pattern for a 3″ circle and follow Step 2 directions for the large ornament, but place folded edge of third fabric ¾″ from edge of circle.

3. Center the Aida over one 8″ square of fabric. Using yellow thread, machine-satin-stitch the edge of the Aida with the widest stitch.

4. Score around the center of the ball. Center the second 8″ fabric square over the back and follow the Step 5 and Step 6 directions for the large ornament.

5. Cut an 8″ length of ribbon. Fold the remaining ribbon into 1½″ loops, leaving 8″ ends. Secure the loops with the 8″ length of ribbon. Attach the bow as desired. Knot and trim the ribbon ends.

NOEL

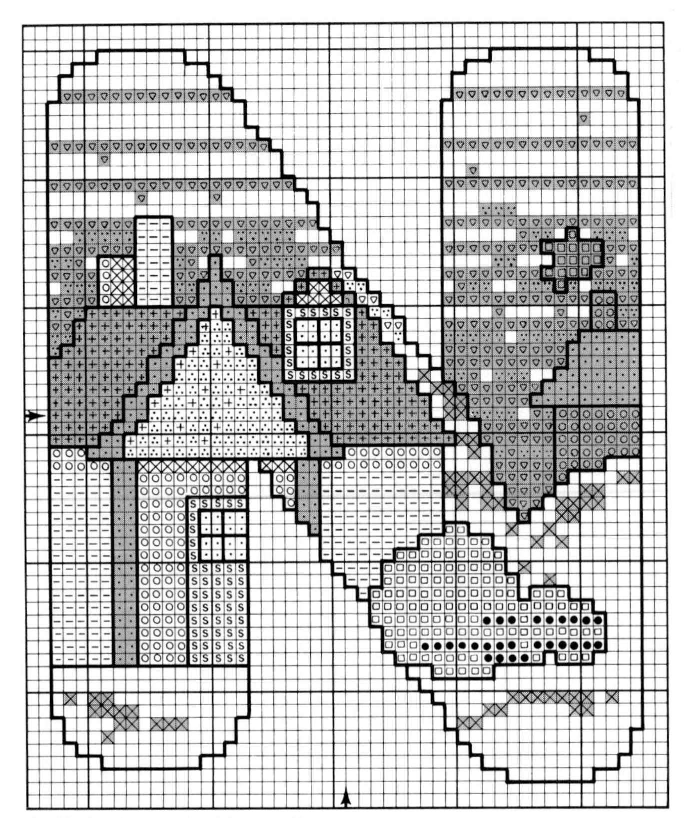

Stitch Count: 48 x 57

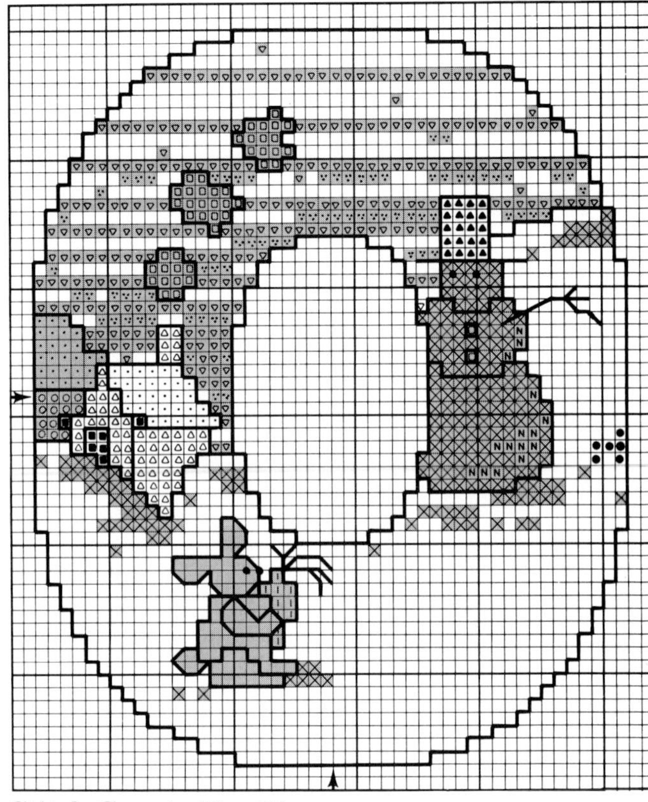

Stitch Count: 48 x 57

Noel Garland & Pillow

SAMPLES

Garland: Stitched on white Perforated Paper 15, each letter is 3¾" high and about 3¼" wide. A 12" x 18" sheet of perforated paper was used. Allow at least eight thread units between letters for cutting. Use three strands of embroidery floss for cross-stitch.

Pillow: Stitched on white Linda 27 over two threads, the finished design size is 15¾" x 4¼". The fabric was cut 20" x 9". (A fabric with this stitch count must be used so that the design will fit the pillow.) Leave eight thread units between letters. Use two strands of embroidery floss for cross-stitch.

Step 1: Cross-stitch (three strands)

Bates	Symbol	DMC (used for sample)
892	·	819 Baby Pink-lt.
893	▒ /	224 Shell Pink-lt.
8	| /	353 Peach Flesh
9	△	760 Salmon
11	○	3328 Salmon-med.
108	∵	211 Lavender-lt.
104	S	210 Lavender-med.
110	+	208 Lavender-vy. dk.
118	∴	340 Blue Violet-med.
158	X	828 Blue-ultra lt.
159	N	827 Blue-vy. lt.
158	▽	775 Baby Blue-lt.
978	+	322 Navy Blue-vy. lt.
922	▲	930 Antique Blue-dk.
875	□	503 Blue Green-med.
878	●	501 Blue Green-dk.
8581	▢	3023 Brown Grey-lt.
933	·	543 Beige Brown-ultra lt.
376	–	842 Beige Brown-vy. lt.
378	○	841 Beige Brown-lt.
379	X	840 Beige Brown-med.
371	■	433 Brown-med.

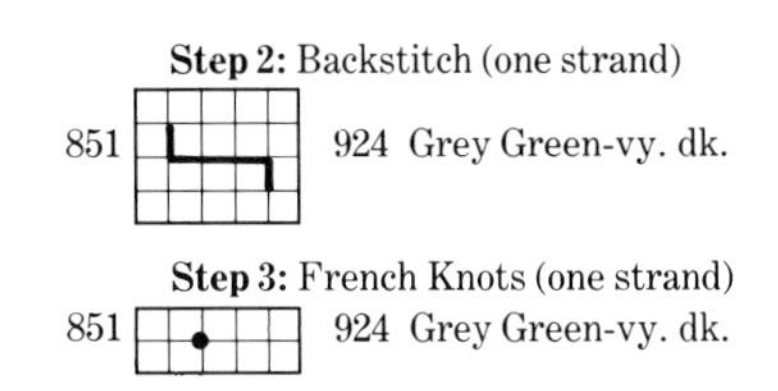

Step 2: Backstitch (one strand)

851 — 924 Grey Green-vy. dk.

Step 3: French Knots (one strand)

851 — 924 Grey Green-vy. dk.

MATERIALS (for garland)

Completed cross-stitch on Perforated Paper 15; see sample information
1½ yards of 1/16"-wide light blue satin ribbon
Large-eyed needle

DIRECTIONS

Cut around the outside of each design, three holes away from the backstitching. Thread the ribbon through the needle. Stitch the ribbon through each letter, two rows below the top row of backstitching (see the photo). With equal lengths of ribbon at each end of the garland, tie a loop for hanging.

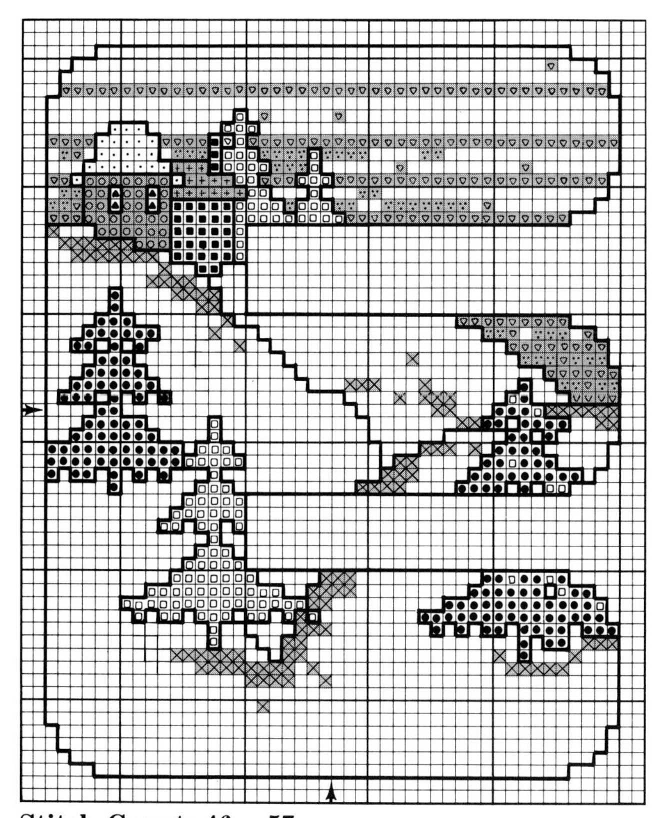

Stitch Count: 46 x 57

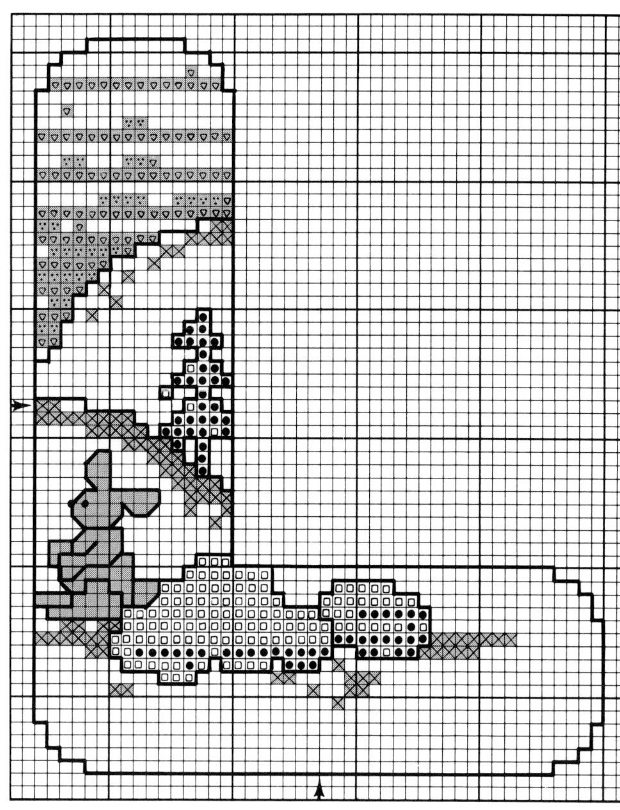

Stitch Count: 46 x 57

MATERIALS (for pillow)

Completed cross-stitch on white Linda 27; see sample information
1 yard of 45"-wide gold fabric; matching thread
Pink thread for quilting
11" x 22½" piece of muslin
Polyester fleece
Stuffing

DIRECTIONS

All seam allowances are ½".

1. Cut the Linda 18½" x 7", with the design centered.

2. From the gold fabric, cut one 11" x 22½" piece for the back, two 3" x 24½" pieces and two 3" x 12" pieces for the border. For ruffle, cut a 3"-wide bias strip, piecing as needed, to equal 4½ yards.

3. Cut one 11" x 22½" piece of fleece.

4. Mark centers on both edges of all strips of gold fabric and on each edge of Linda. With right sides together and center marks matching, sew one long gold strip to one long edge of Linda, stopping ½" from corner; backstitch. Press seam toward gold fabric. Repeat for remaining strips.

5. To miter corners, fold right sides of two adjacent strips together and sew at a 45-degree angle (see Diagram). Trim seam to ½". Repeat for remaining corners.

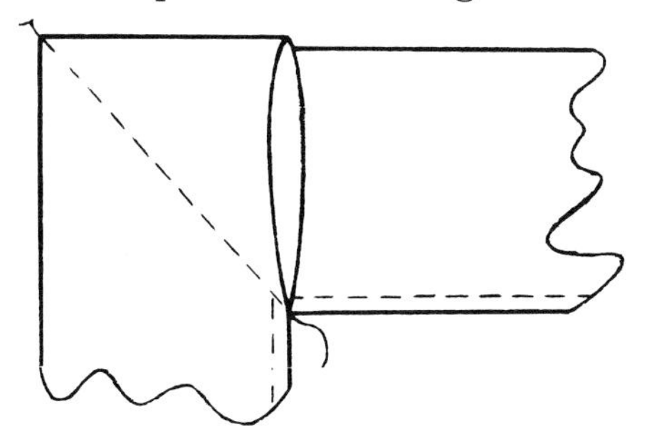

6. Layer the pillow front, right side up, over the fleece and muslin; baste together. With pink thread, quilt around each letter.

7. With right sides together, stitch short ends of bias strip together to make one continuous piece. With wrong sides together, fold bias strip in half lengthwise; press. Stitch gathering threads through both layers next to raw edges. Divide ruffle into fourths; mark. Mark centers of outside edges of pillow front.

8. Gather and pin the ruffle to the right side of the pillow front, matching the marks and allowing extra fullness at the corners. Stitch around all sides.

9. With right sides together, stitch pillow front to back, leaving a 6" opening. Turn and stuff. Slipstitch opening closed.

Christmas Gift Tags

SAMPLES

Joy: Stitched on pink Hardanger 22 over two threads, the finished design size is 2⅜″ x 3″. The fabric was cut 6″ x 6″.

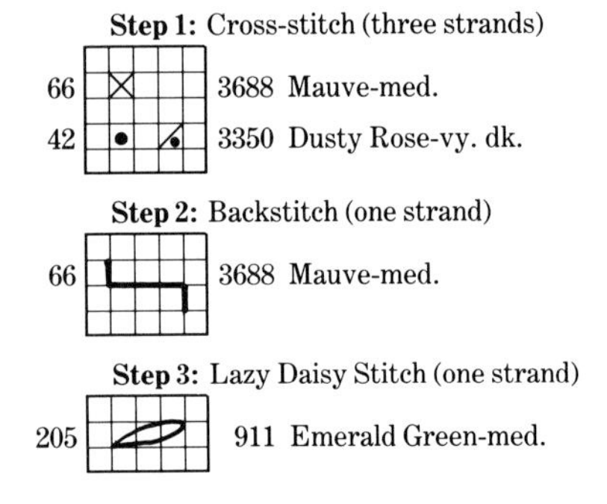

Bates	DMC (used for sample)
	Step 1: Cross-stitch (three strands)
66	3688 Mauve-med.
42	3350 Dusty Rose-vy. dk.
	Step 2: Backstitch (one strand)
66	3688 Mauve-med.
	Step 3: Lazy Daisy Stitch (one strand)
205	911 Emerald Green-med.

To Dad From Lisa: Stitched on white Aida 14, the finished design size is 2¾″ x 2¼″. The fabric was cut 6″ x 6″.

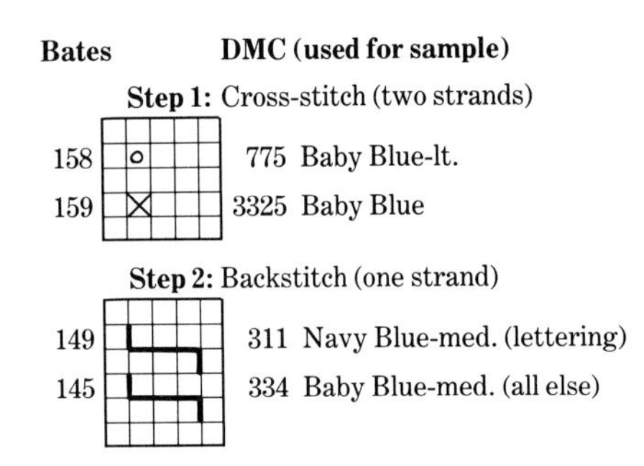

Bates	DMC (used for sample)
	Step 1: Cross-stitch (two strands)
158	775 Baby Blue-lt.
159	3325 Baby Blue
	Step 2: Backstitch (one strand)
149	311 Navy Blue-med. (lettering)
145	334 Baby Blue-med. (all else)

Rejoice: Stitched on cream Hardanger 22 over two threads, the finished design size is 3⅛″ x 2½″. The fabric was cut 6″ x 6″.

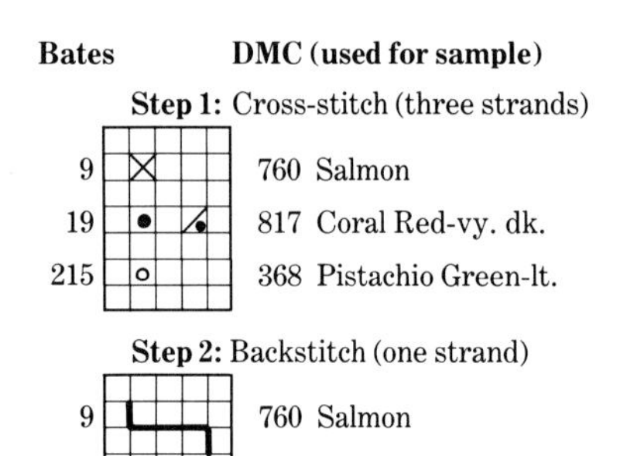

Bates	DMC (used for sample)
	Step 1: Cross-stitch (three strands)
9	760 Salmon
19	817 Coral Red-vy. dk.
215	368 Pistachio Green-lt.
	Step 2: Backstitch (one strand)
9	760 Salmon

Surprise!: Stitched on cream Aida 14, the finished design size is 2¼″ x 2¾″. The fabric was cut 6″ x 6″.

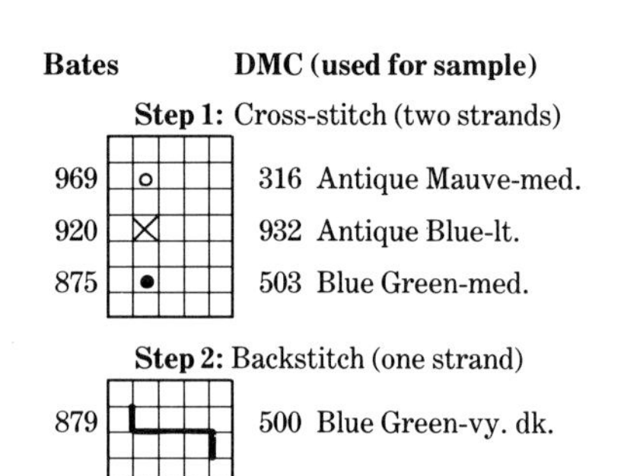

Bates	DMC (used for sample)
	Step 1: Cross-stitch (two strands)
969	316 Antique Mauve-med.
920	932 Antique Blue-lt.
875	503 Blue Green-med.
	Step 2: Backstitch (one strand)
879	500 Blue Green-vy. dk.

Noel: Stitched on white Aida 14, the finished design size is 2½″ x 2⅞″. The fabric was cut 6″ x 6″.

Bates	DMC (used for sample)
	Step 1: Cross-stitch (two strands)
50	605 Cranberry-vy. lt.
410	995 Electric Blue-dk.
239	702 Kelly Green

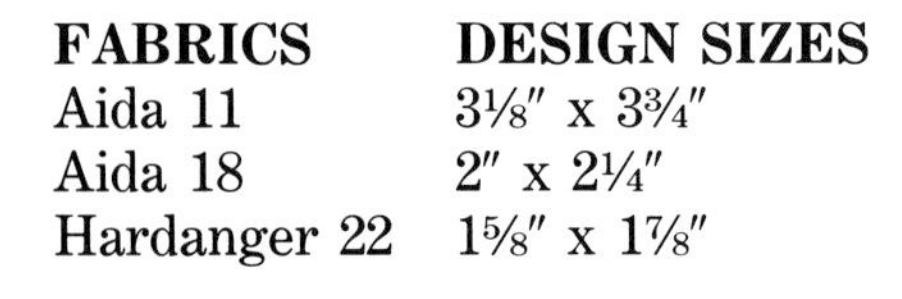

FABRICS	DESIGN SIZES
Aida 11	3⅛″ x 3¾″
Aida 18	2″ x 2¼″
Hardanger 22	1⅝″ x 1⅞″

continued . . .

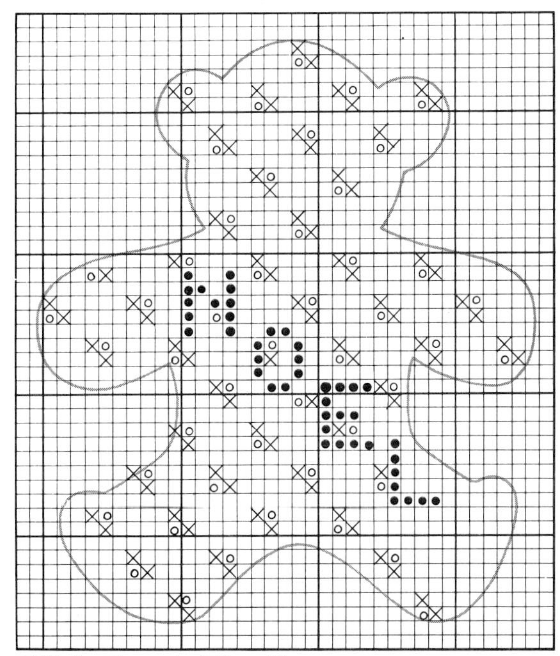

Stitch Count: 35 x 41

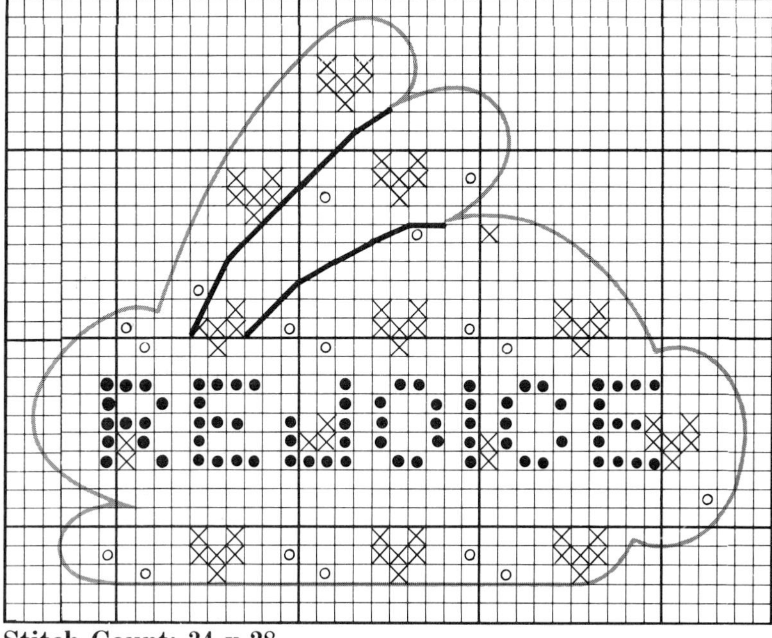

Stitch Count: 34 x 28

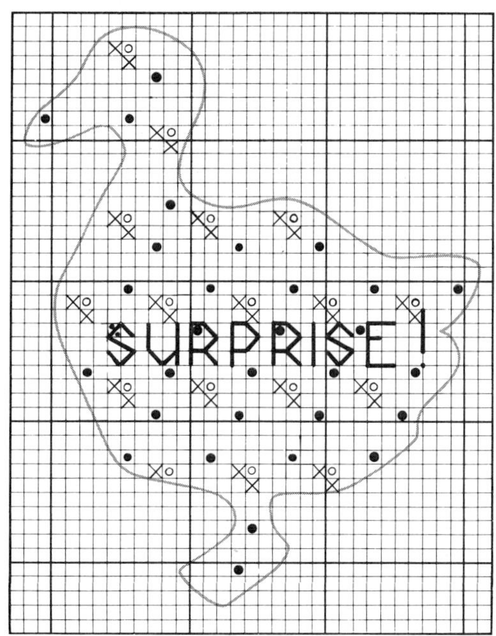

Stitch Count: 31 x 35

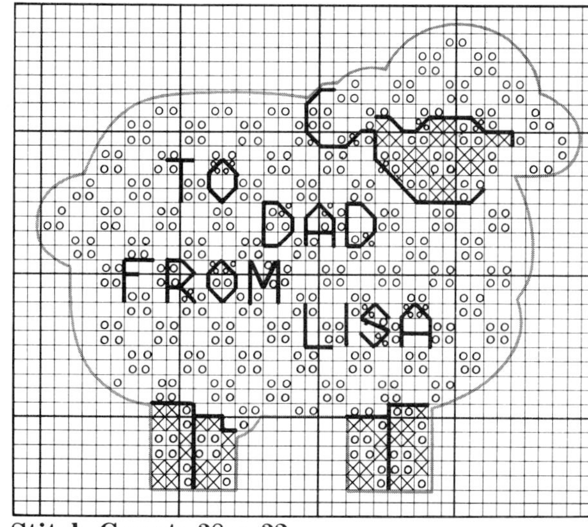

Stitch Count: 38 x 32

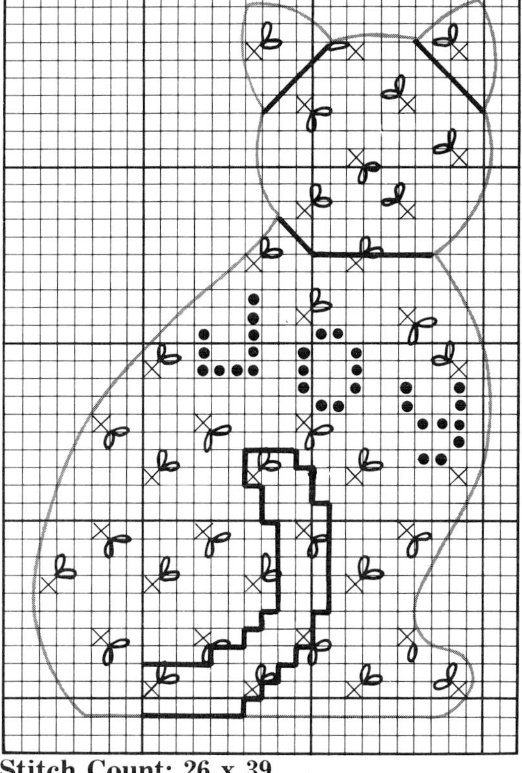

Stitch Count: 26 x 39

. . . **Gift Tags continued**

MATERIALS

Completed cross-stitch; see individual sample information
Small piece of print fabric for back
½ yard of 1/16"-wide matching satin ribbon
Small piece of a manila folder
Small piece of fusing material
Dressmakers' pen
Tracing paper for patterns
Glue

DIRECTIONS

1. Trace the gift tag pattern onto tracing paper and cut out. Position the pattern over the stitching and trace around it with the dressmakers' pen.

2. Cut two pieces of fusing material, one piece of manila paper, and one piece of print fabric, all slightly larger than the pattern.

3. With one piece of fusing material between the print fabric and the manila paper, fuse according to the manufacturer's directions. Place the other piece of fusing material between the stitched design and the manila paper and fuse.

4. Trim the tag, cutting on the pen lines through all four layers.

5. Knot the ribbon in the center and at both ends. Glue center knot to back of the tag. Tie the tag onto a gift or use it as an ornament.

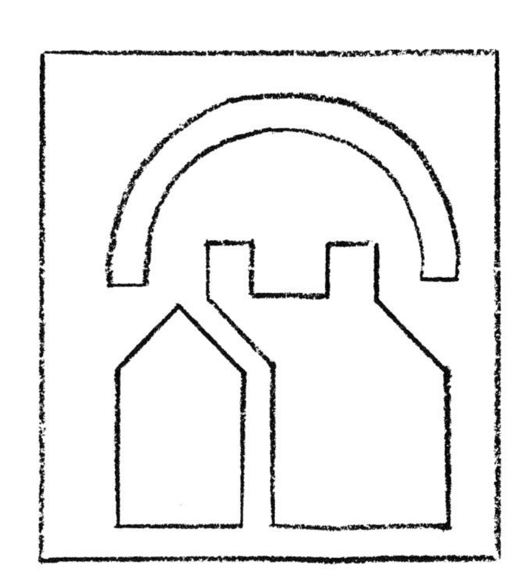

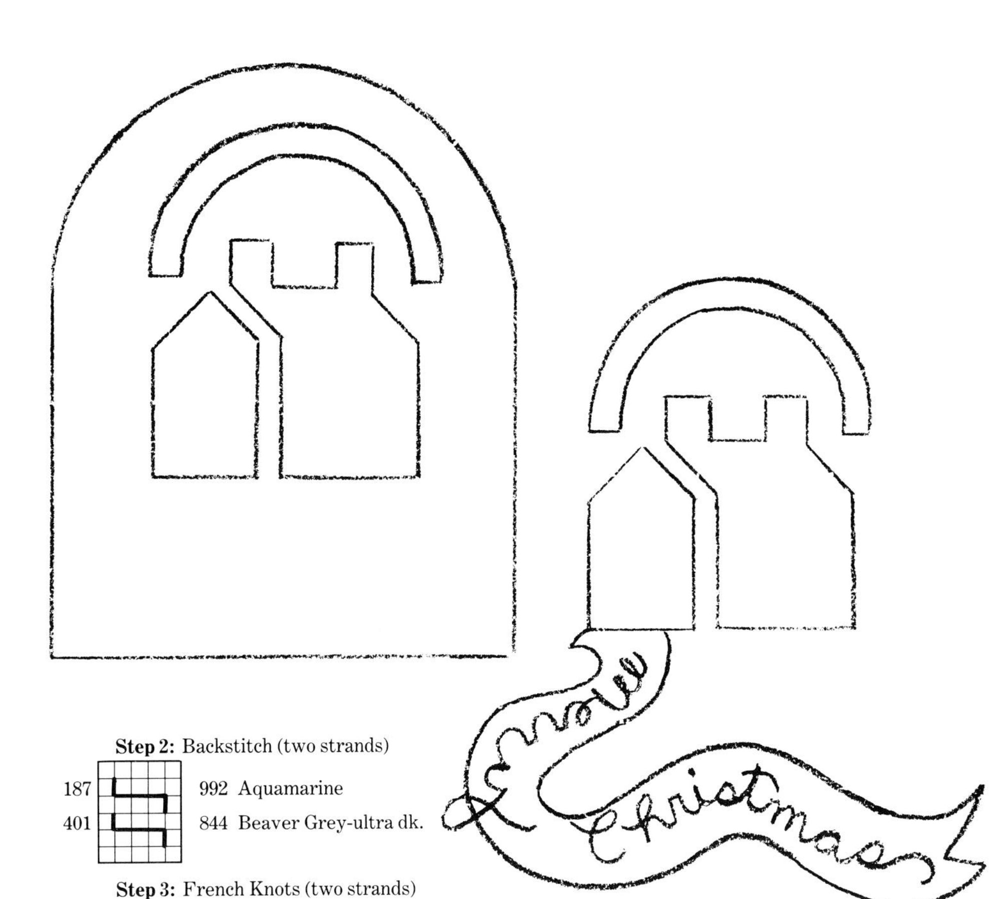

Paper Gift Bags

SAMPLE
The designs are stitched on brown paper, using waste canvas 14 over two threads. (The designs are suitable only for waste canvas with a thread count of 14.) Also needed: one small piece of fusible interfacing for each design. Fuse the interfacing to the back of the paper before stitching.

Welcome Friends: The finished design size is 2½″ x 3″. The paper was cut 5″ x 5″.

Flowers: The finished design size, including stenciling, is 2½″ x 3½″. The paper was cut 5″ x 6″.

Merry Christmas: The finished design size is 4½″ x 4½″. The paper was cut 7″ x 7″.

Bates **DMC (used for sample)**

Step 1: Cross-stitch (three strands)

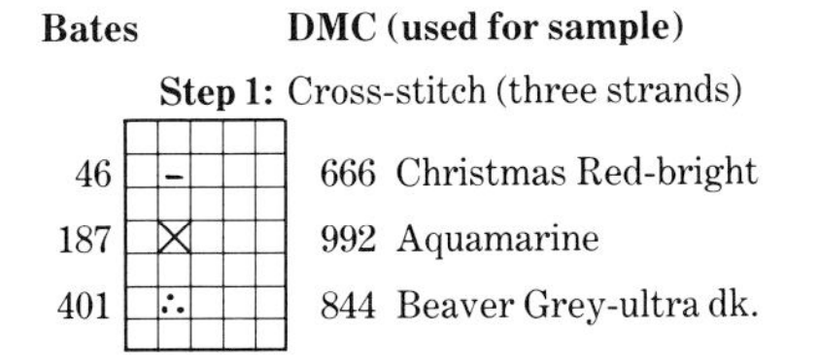

Bates	DMC
46	666 Christmas Red-bright
187	992 Aquamarine
401	844 Beaver Grey-ultra dk.

Step 2: Backstitch (two strands)

Bates	DMC
187	992 Aquamarine
401	844 Beaver Grey-ultra dk.

Step 3: French Knots (two strands)

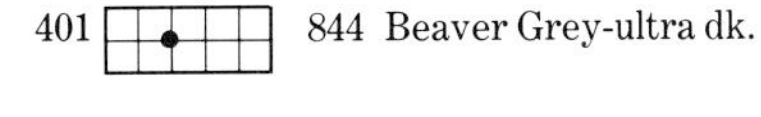

Bates	DMC
401	844 Beaver Grey-ultra dk.

MATERIALS
Completed cross-stitch on brown paper and fusible interfacing with waste canvas; see sample information
Small brown paper bags
Crayons
Black felt-tip pen for *Merry Christmas*
Glue

DIRECTIONS
1. Make the stencil for the house (see General Instructions). Stencil house onto stitched paper. Refer to pattern for placement.

2. For *Merry Christmas,* write the words with the felt-tip pen. Color around the designs with crayons (see the photo).

3. Cut each design ¼″ outside the widest part of the design. Glue onto the paper bags.

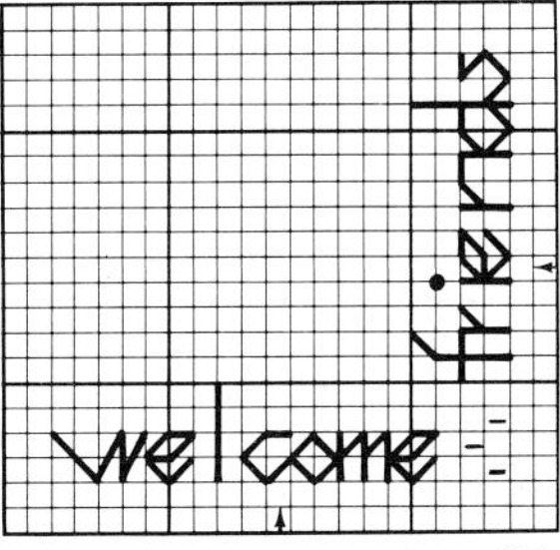

Stitch Count: 19 x 17

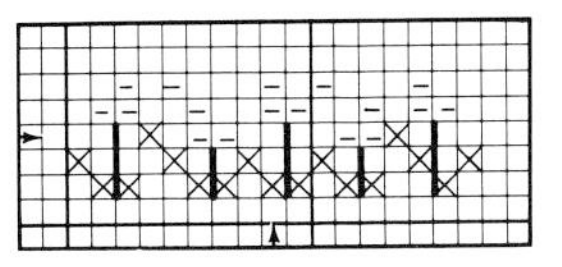

Stitch Count: 17 x 5

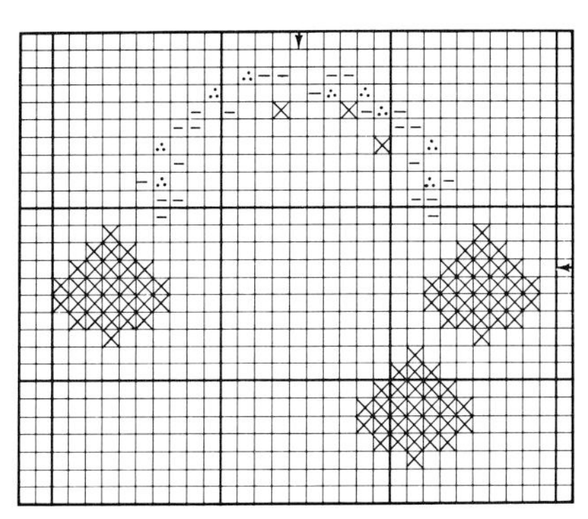

Stitch Count: 29 x 23

Drummer Boy

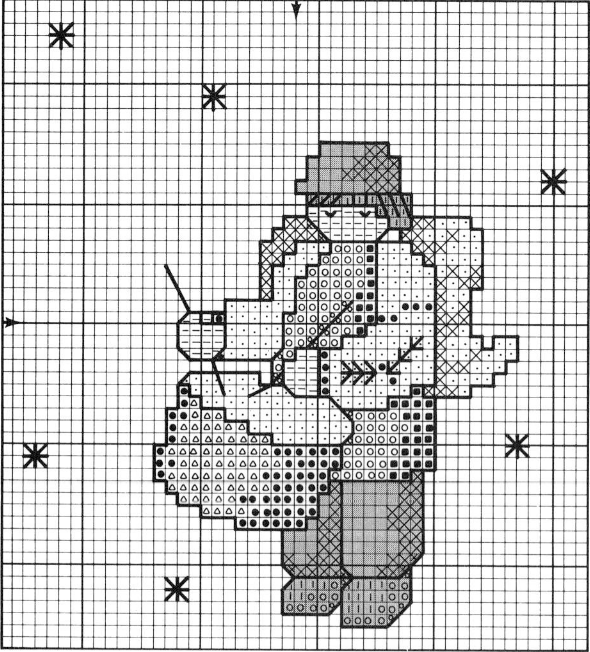

Stitch Count: 46 x 50

SAMPLE
Stitched on white Jobelan 28 over two threads, the finished design size is 3¼" x 3⅝". The fabric was cut 8" x 8". (A fabric with this stitch count must be used so that the design will fit the music box.)

Bates **DMC (used for sample)**

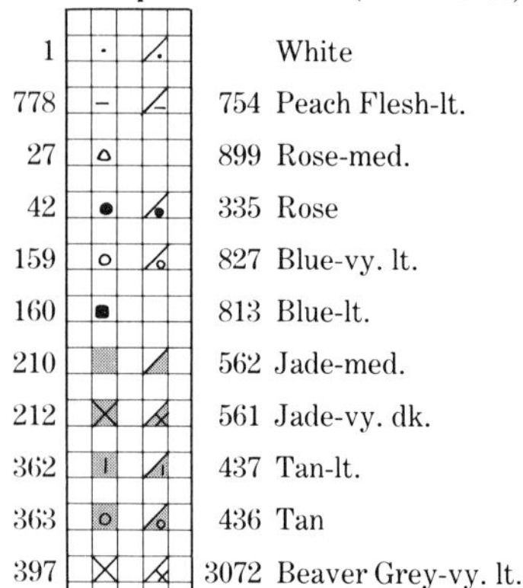

Step 1: Cross-stitch (two strands)

Bates	DMC	Color
1		White
778	754	Peach Flesh-lt.
27	899	Rose-med.
42	335	Rose
159	827	Blue-vy. lt.
160	813	Blue-lt.
210	562	Jade-med.
212	561	Jade-vy. dk.
362	437	Tan-lt.
363	436	Tan
397	3072	Beaver Grey-vy. lt.

Step 2: Backstitch (one strand)

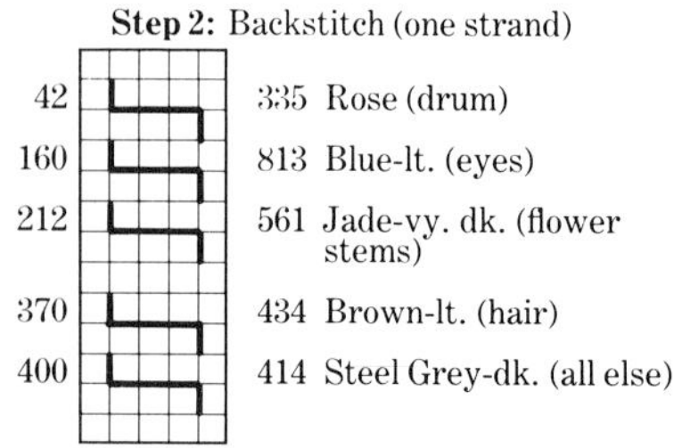

Bates	DMC	Color
42	335	Rose (drum)
160	813	Blue-lt. (eyes)
212	561	Jade-vy. dk. (flower stems)
370	434	Brown-lt. (hair)
400	414	Steel Grey-dk. (all else)

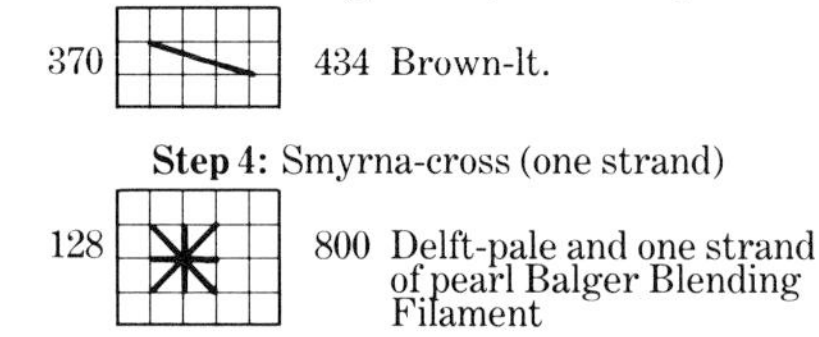

Step 3: Long Stitch (one strand)

Bates	DMC	Color
370	434	Brown-lt.

Step 4: Smyrna-cross (one strand)

Bates	DMC	Color
128	800	Delft-pale and one strand of pearl Balger Blending Filament

MATERIALS
Completed cross-stitch on white Jobelan 28 and matching thread; see sample information
Small pieces of green print fabric; matching thread
Small pieces of green fabric for cording
¾ yard of 1/16"-wide green satin ribbon
½ yard of 1/16"-wide grey satin ribbon
⅝ yard of small cording
Stuffing
2" x 2½" music box (see Suppliers)
Two small snaps

DIRECTIONS
All seam allowances are ½".

1. Cut the white Jobelan 5½" x 6" with the design centered.

2. From the print fabric, cut two pieces for the backing, one 3¼" x 5½" and one 5¾" x 5½".

3. From the green fabric, cut a 1¼"-wide bias strip, piecing as needed, to equal 20". Cover the cording.

4. Matching raw edges, stitch cording to front of the Jobelan.

5. Fold one edge of both green print backing pieces under ¼", then under ¾". Hem by hand or machine. Place pieces side by side, with the 5½" edges overlapping.

6. Sew a buttonhole 2" from the hem on the larger print piece for the key of the music box. Attach snaps so that the hem of the small piece overlaps the hem of the large piece. Snap the pieces together.

7. With right sides together, stitch the front to the back, sewing on the stitching line of the cording. Turn right side out and unsnap.

8. Cut one 10″ length of green ribbon and one 10″ length of grey ribbon. Form a loop and knot the ends together. Tack the knot to the center of the top edge, just behind the cording. Handling the remaining lengths as a single unit, tie a bow with 2″ loops and tack the ribbon ends to the center top edge, using matching thread (see the photo).

9. Lightly stuff the front of the fabric cover. Insert the music box, with the windup key through the buttonhole. Stuff around the music box to fill out the cover. Snap closed. Cover may be easily removed to be washed.

Christmas Collars

These designs can be used as desired to decorate collars and other clothing. Purchase a pattern and construct the collar from the fabrics specified in the sample information, or from any evenweave fabric. The samples illustrate some ways to use lace and ribbon for additional decoration.

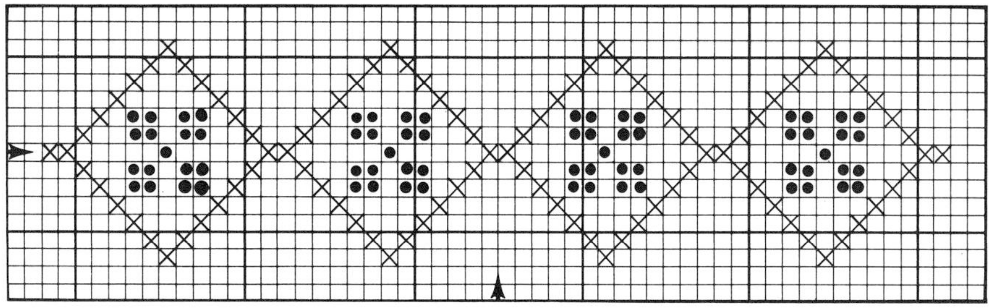

Stitch Count (one motif): 13 x 13

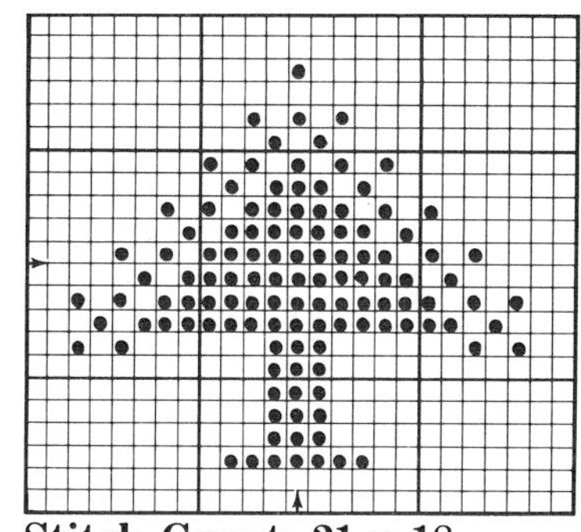

Stitch Count: 21 x 18

SAMPLE
Green tree motif: Stitched on white Jobelan 28 over two threads, the finished design size for one tree is 1½″ x 1¼″. The fabric was cut to fit the purchased collar pattern.

Bates		DMC (used for sample)
	Step 1: Cross-stitch (two strands)	
875	•	503 Blue Green-med.

FABRICS	DESIGN SIZES
Aida 11	1⅞″ x 1⅝″
Aida 14	1½″ x 1¼″
Aida 18	1⅛″ x 1″
Hardanger 22	1″ x ⅞″

SAMPLE
Pink diamond motif: Stitched on white Jobelan 28 over two threads, the finished design size for one diamond is ⅞″ x ⅞″. Fabric was cut to fit the purchased collar pattern.

Bates		DMC (used for sample)
	Step 1: Cross-stitch (two strands)	
968	X	778 Antique Mauve-lt.
969	•	316 Antique Mauve-med.

FABRICS	DESIGN SIZES
Aida 11	1⅛″ x 1⅛″
Aida 14	⅞″ x ⅞″
Aida 18	¾″ x ¾″
Hardanger 22	⅝″ x ⅝″

Quilt Block Wall Hanging

SAMPLE
The fabric was cut 6″ x 6″ for each design. (A fabric with this stitch count must be used so that the designs will fit the quilt.)

Design 1: Stitched on 20 pieces of light pink Hardanger 22 over two threads, the finished design size is 1⅜″ x 1⅜″.

Bates		DMC (used for sample)
		Step 1: Cross-stitch (three strands)
893	o	224 Shell Pink-lt.
878	•	501 Blue Green-dk.

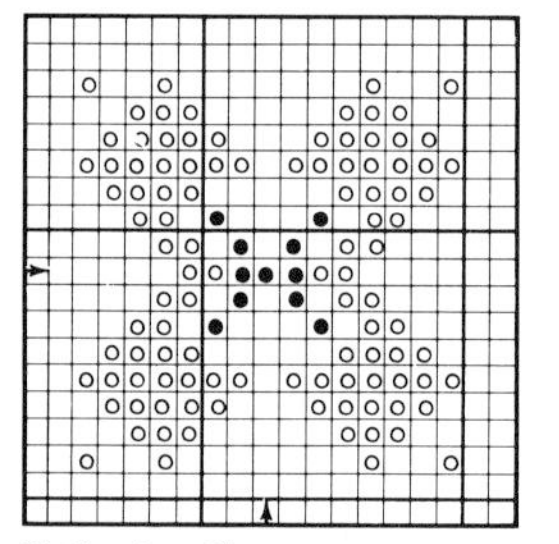

Stitch Count: 15 x 15

Design 2: Stitched on 8 pieces of evening rose Hardanger 22 over two threads, the finished design size is 1⅛" x 1¼".

Bates		DMC (used for sample)
	Step 1: Cross-stitch (three strands)	
893	○	224 Shell Pink-lt.
878	●	501 Blue Green-dk.

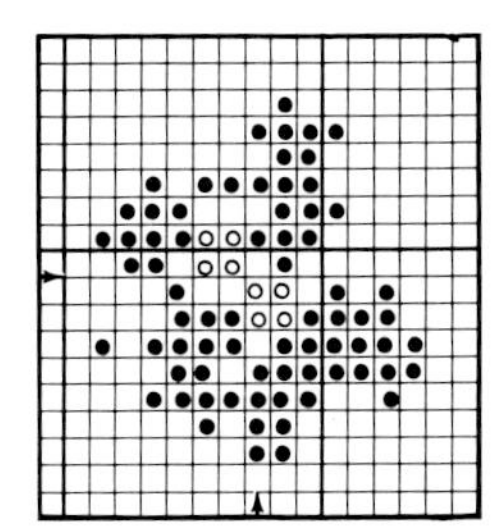

Stitch Count: 13 x 14

Design 3: Stitched on 8 pieces of light pink Hardanger 22 over two threads, the finished design size is 1½" x 1¾".

Bates		DMC (used for sample)
	Step 1: Cross-stitch (three strands)	
893	○	224 Shell Pink-lt.
920	–	932 Antique Blue-lt.
878	●	501 Blue Green-dk.
399	X	451 Shell Grey-dk.
	Step 2: Backstitch (one strand)	
878	(backstitch)	501 Blue Green-dk.

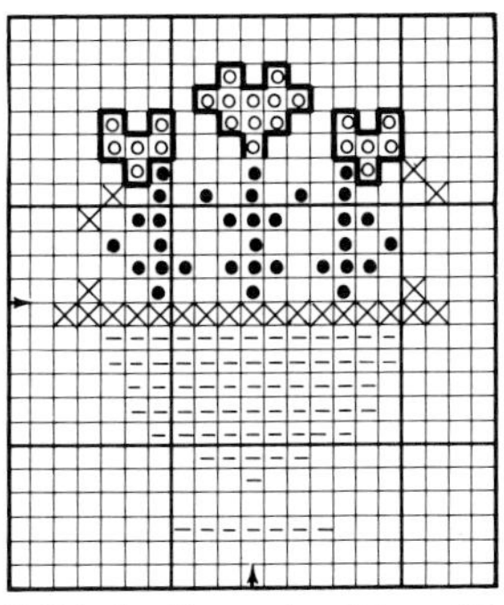

Stitch Count: 17 x 20

Design 4: Stitched on 5 pieces of evening rose Hardanger 22 over two threads, the finished design size is 1¾" x 1¾".

Bates		DMC (used for sample)
	Step 1: Cross-stitch (three strands)	
70	■	3685 Mauve-dk.
203	△	564 Jade-vy. lt.
878	●	501 Blue Green-dk.

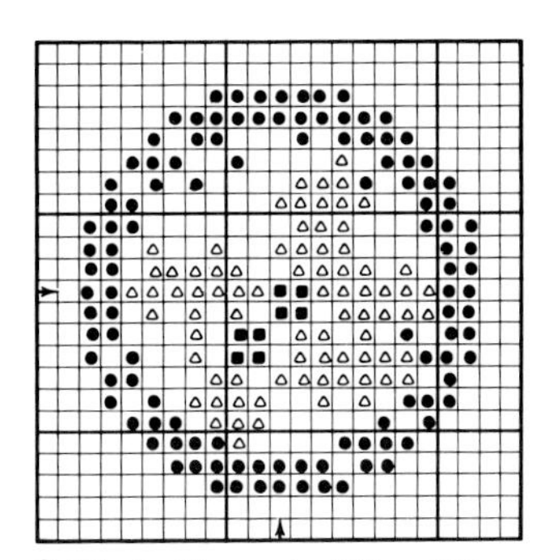

Stitch Count: 19 x 19

Design 5: Stitched on 8 pieces of seacrest Hardanger 22 over two threads, the finished design size is 1¾" x 1¾".

Bates		DMC (used for sample)
	Step 1: Cross-stitch (three strands)	
893	○	224 Shell Pink-lt.
70	■	3685 Mauve-dk.
878	●	501 Blue Green-dk.

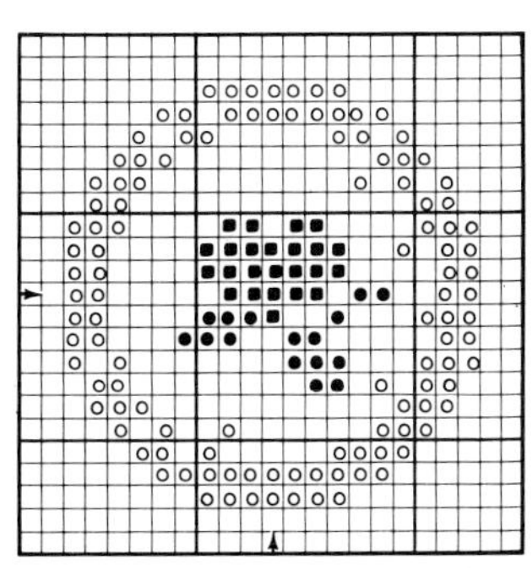

Stitch Count: 19 x 19

Design 6: Stitched on 8 pieces of seacrest Hardanger 22 over two threads, the finished design size is 1⅜" x 1⅝".

Bates		DMC (used for sample)
	Step 1: Cross-stitch (three strands)	
897	▲	221 Shell Pink-dk.
161	∴	826 Blue-med.
859	□	3053 Green Grey
878	●	501 Blue Green-dk.
	Step 2: Backstitch (one strand)	
149	(backstitch)	336 Navy Blue

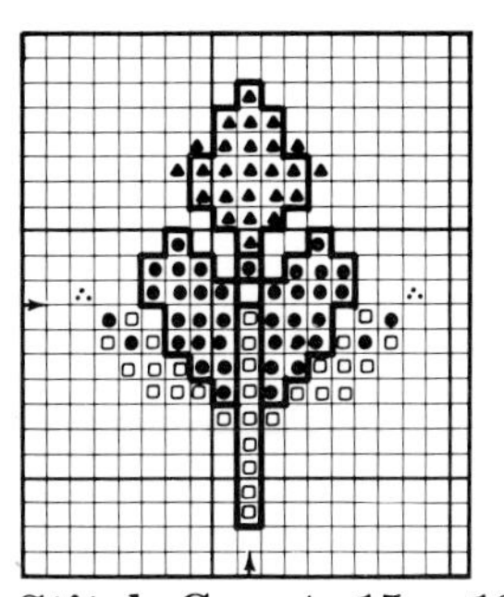

Stitch Count: 15 x 18

MATERIALS

Completed cross-stitch; see sample information for individual designs
1½ yards of 45"-wide burgundy fabric; matching thread
⅝ yard of 45"-wide green print fabric
⅛ yard of 45"-wide dusty rose pin-dot fabric; matching thread
⅛ yard of 45"-wide light green fabric; matching thread
12½" x 12½" piece of burgundy pin-dot fabric
Small amount of pink-and-white fabric; pink thread
Light green embroidery floss (DMC 563)
40" x 40" piece of batting
Pink acrylic paint
Three ½" green buttons
Tracing paper for patterns

continued . . .

. . . Wall Hanging continued

DIRECTIONS
All seam allowances are ¼″.

1. Trace the patterns or make templates for the word *Christmas* and for the year.

2. From the burgundy fabric, cut one 40″ square for the backing. Set aside. Also cut four 12½″ squares.

3. From the green print fabric, cut four 12½″ squares.

4. Cut twelve 2¾″ squares each from the dusty rose pin-dot fabric and from the light green fabric.

5. To construct Block A, cut five pinwheel pieces from evening rose Hardanger and three pieces from the pink-and-white print fabric. With right sides together, sew all eight pieces together (see Diagram). Center the design on one burgundy square. Fold under the seam allowances and slipstitch in place.

6. To construct Block B, cut five 2¾″ squares from the evening rose Hardanger and four squares from the seacrest Hardanger, with designs centered. Sew the pieces right sides together (see Diagram). Center the nine-patch design on the green print square. Fold under the seam allowances and slipstitch. Place a 2¾″ pin-dot square in each corner. Fold under the seam allowance on the inside edges, making sure the inside corner meets the nine-patch design. Slipstitch the squares in place.

7. To construct Block C, cut eight Dresden plate pieces from the pink Hardanger. With right sides together, join the eight pieces. Center the design on one burgundy square. Fold under the seam allowances and slipstitch in place.

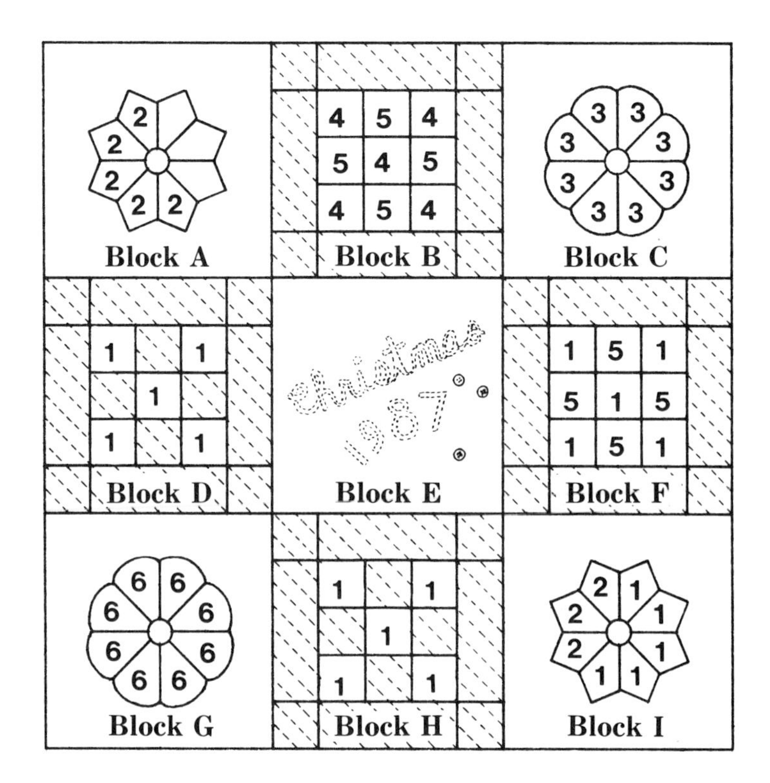

8. To construct Block D, cut five 2¾″ squares from pink Hardanger with the designs centered. With right sides together, join four pin-dot squares to make the nine-patch design (see Diagram). Complete the block according to the directions in Step 6.

9. To construct Block E, transfer the lettering pattern onto one burgundy block. Paint *Christmas* with pink paint.

10. To construct Block F, cut five 2¾″ squares from pink Hardanger and four from seacrest Hardanger, with the designs centered. Complete the block according to the directions in Step 6, using light green pieces for the corners.

11. To construct Block G, cut eight Dresden plate pieces from the seacrest Hardanger. Complete the block according to the directions in Step 7.

12. To construct Block H, cut five 2¾″ squares from pink Hardanger with designs centered. With right sides together, alternately sew a light green square to a pink square to make the nine-patch design (see Diagram). Complete the block according to the directions in Step 6, using light green pieces for the corners.

13. To construct Block I, cut five pinwheel pieces from pink Hardanger and three pieces from evening rose Hardanger. Complete block according to directions in Step 5, centering pinwheel on square of burgundy *pin dot.*

14. Stitch the nine blocks together (see Diagram).

15. Mark the quilting lines on the fabric (see Diagram).

16. Place the wall hanging backing wrong side up on a flat surface. Center the batting and the quilt top right side up on the backing;

baste together. Quilt on every seam between blocks, between pieces, and on the diagonal lines. Use burgundy thread between blocks, around designs on burgundy blocks, and around *Christmas*. Use green thread on green print blocks. Machine-stitch around *1987* with pink thread.

17. Sew three buttons onto the center block with green thread (see Diagram).

18. To finish edges, fold backing fabric and batting double to front edge, making a 1″-wide binding. Slipstitch to quilt top, carefully overlapping corners.

19. Mark ¾″ intervals along the binding on the edge that meets the quilt top. Using two strands of embroidery floss, secure the floss and stitch a spiral, pulling slightly tighter than the binding.

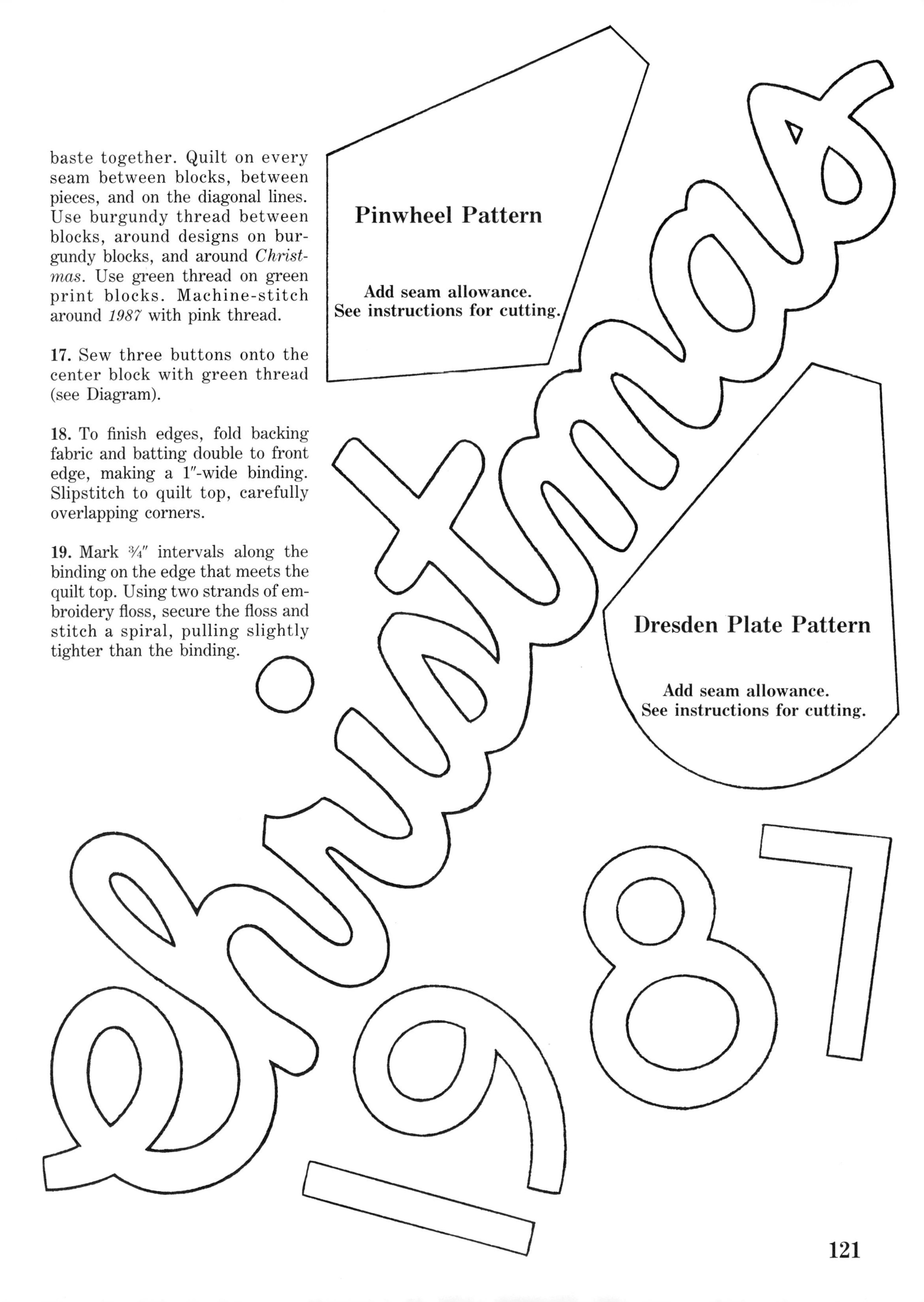

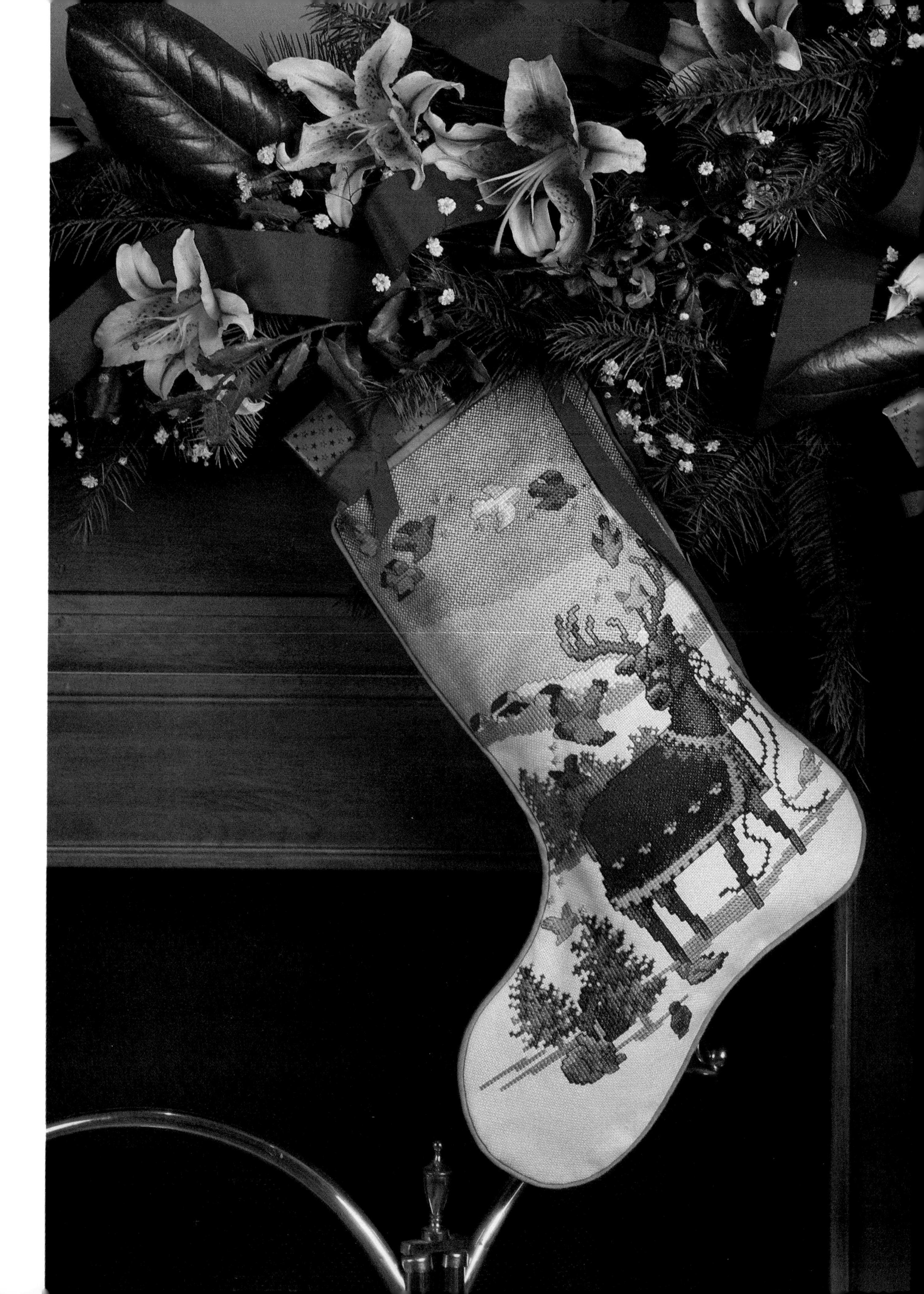

Forest Friends Stocking

SAMPLE

Stitched on white Hardanger 22 over two threads, the finished design size is 11½" x 14½". The fabric was cut 14" x 20". (A fabric with this stitch count must be used so that design will fit stocking.)

continued . . .

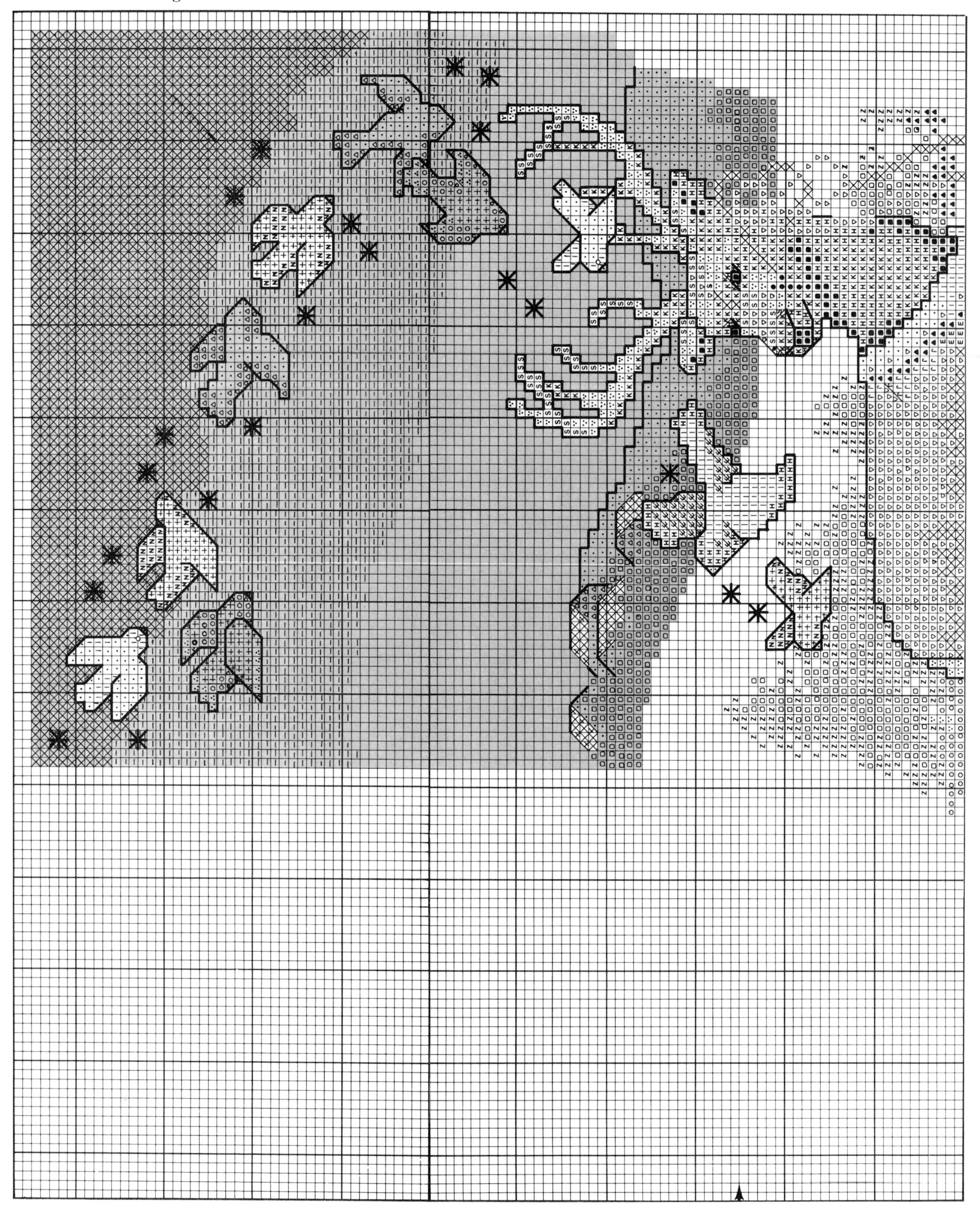

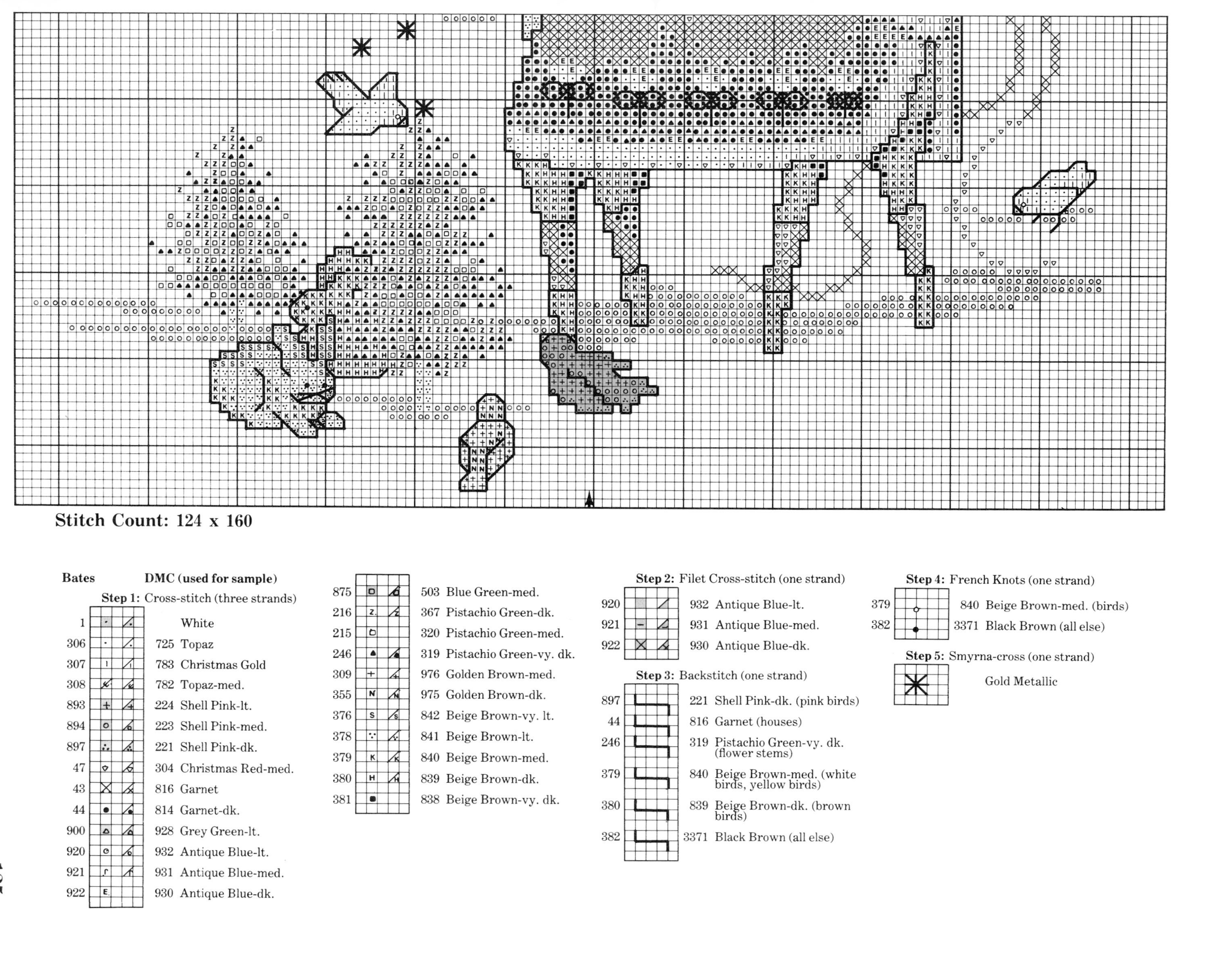

Stitch Count: 124 x 160

Bates	DMC (used for sample)
Step 1: Cross-stitch (three strands)	
1	White
306	725 Topaz
307	783 Christmas Gold
308	782 Topaz-med.
893	224 Shell Pink-lt.
894	223 Shell Pink-med.
897	221 Shell Pink-dk.
47	304 Christmas Red-med.
43	816 Garnet
44	814 Garnet-dk.
900	928 Grey Green-lt.
920	932 Antique Blue-lt.
921	931 Antique Blue-med.
922	930 Antique Blue-dk.
875	503 Blue Green-med.
216	367 Pistachio Green-dk.
215	320 Pistachio Green-med.
246	319 Pistachio Green-vy. dk.
309	976 Golden Brown-med.
355	975 Golden Brown-dk.
376	842 Beige Brown-vy. lt.
378	841 Beige Brown-lt.
379	840 Beige Brown-med.
380	839 Beige Brown-dk.
381	838 Beige Brown-vy. dk.
Step 2: Filet Cross-stitch (one strand)	
920	932 Antique Blue-lt.
921	931 Antique Blue-med.
922	930 Antique Blue-dk.
Step 3: Backstitch (one strand)	
897	221 Shell Pink-dk. (pink birds)
44	816 Garnet (houses)
246	319 Pistachio Green-vy. dk. (flower stems)
379	840 Beige Brown-med. (white birds, yellow birds)
380	839 Beige Brown-dk. (brown birds)
382	3371 Black Brown (all else)
Step 4: French Knots (one strand)	
379	840 Beige Brown-med. (birds)
382	3371 Black Brown (all else)
Step 5: Smyrna-cross (one strand)	
	Gold Metallic

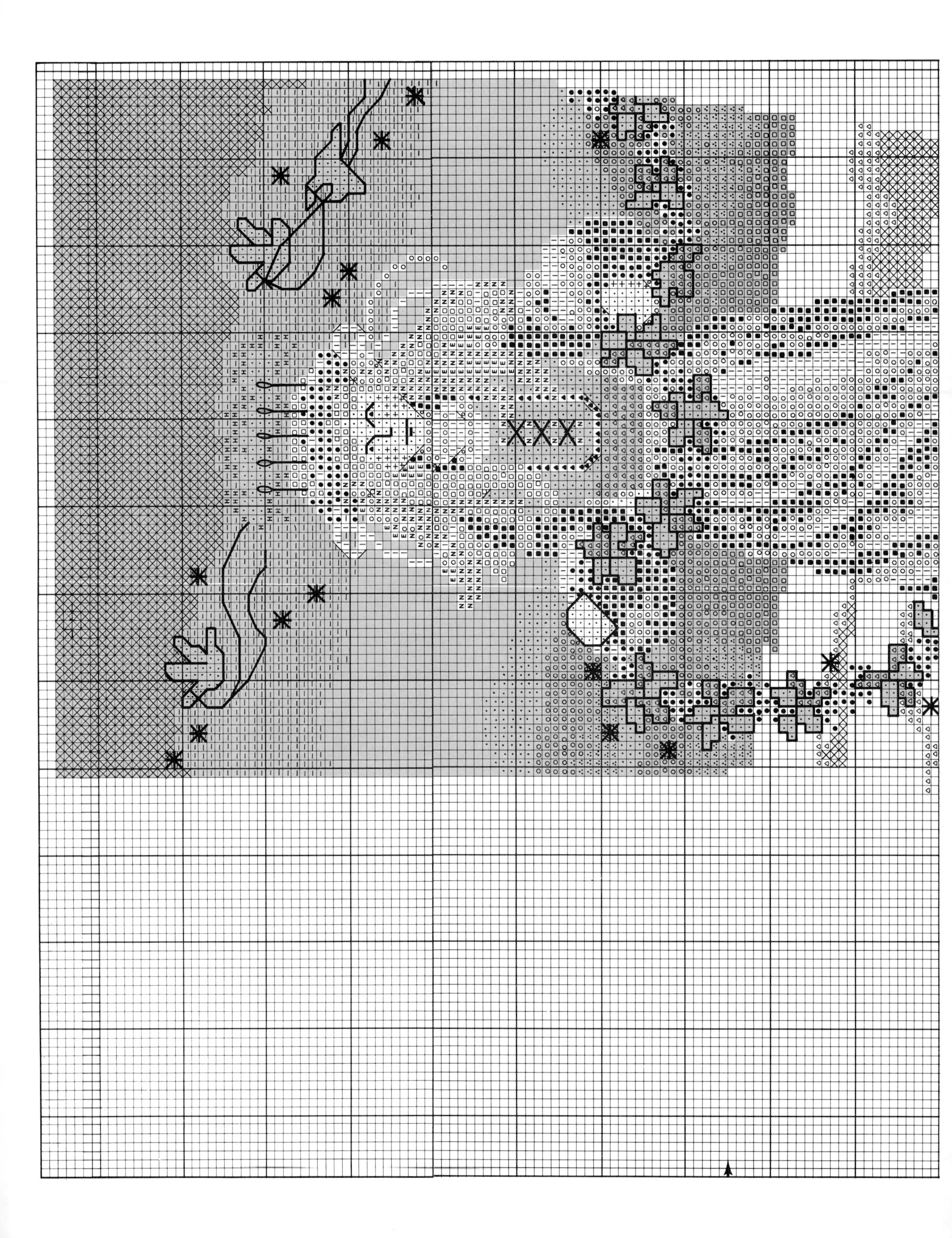

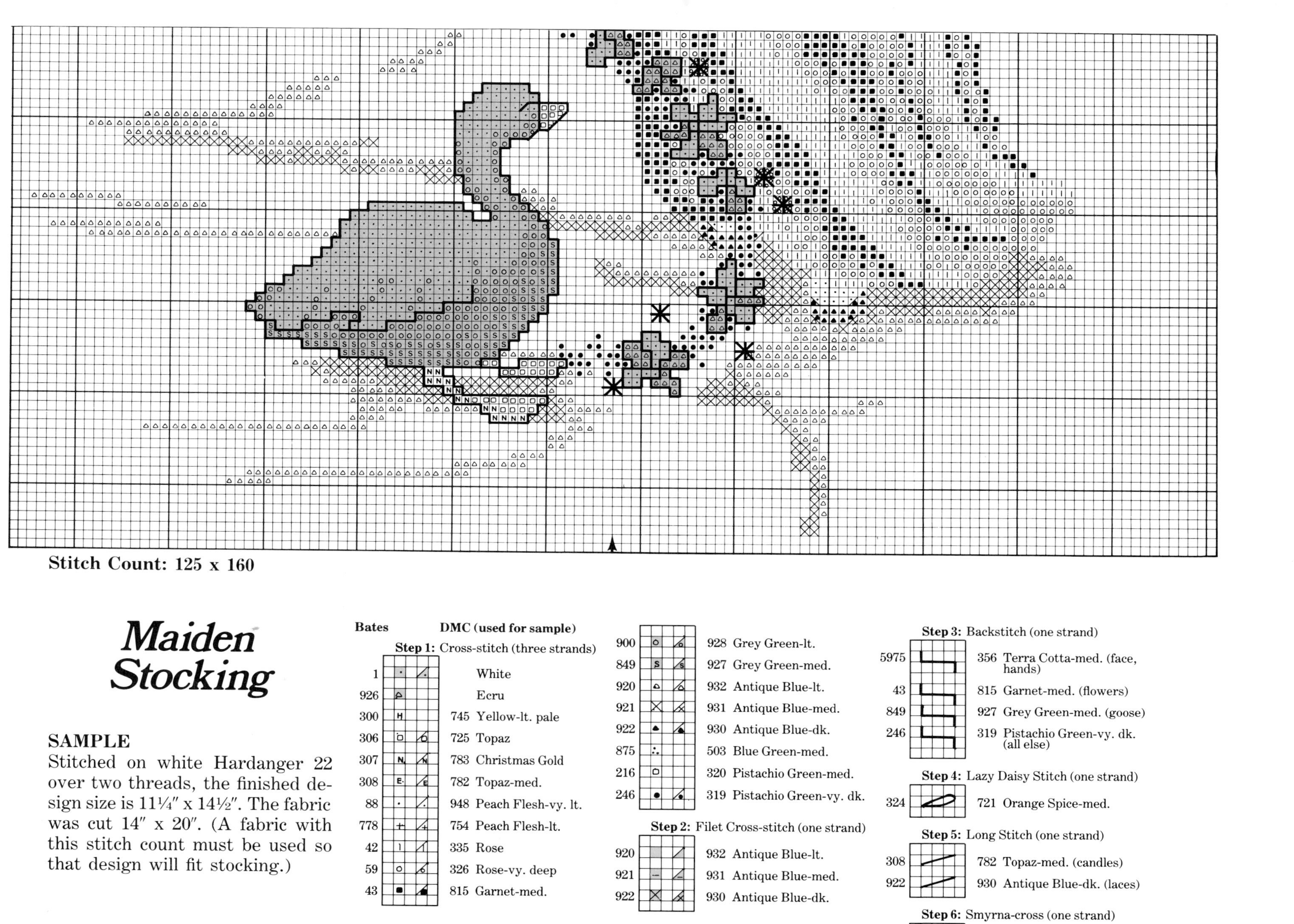

Stitch Count: 125 x 160

Maiden Stocking

SAMPLE

Stitched on white Hardanger 22 over two threads, the finished design size is 11¼" x 14½". The fabric was cut 14" x 20". (A fabric with this stitch count must be used so that design will fit stocking.)

Bates	DMC (used for sample)
Step 1: Cross-stitch (three strands)	
1	White
926	Ecru
300	745 Yellow-lt. pale
306	725 Topaz
307	783 Christmas Gold
308	782 Topaz-med.
88	948 Peach Flesh-vy. lt.
778	754 Peach Flesh-lt.
42	335 Rose
59	326 Rose-vy. deep
43	815 Garnet-med.
900	928 Grey Green-lt.
849	927 Grey Green-med.
920	932 Antique Blue-lt.
921	931 Antique Blue-med.
922	930 Antique Blue-dk.
875	503 Blue Green-med.
216	320 Pistachio Green-med.
246	319 Pistachio Green-vy. dk.
Step 2: Filet Cross-stitch (one strand)	
920	932 Antique Blue-lt.
921	931 Antique Blue-med.
922	930 Antique Blue-dk.
Step 3: Backstitch (one strand)	
5975	356 Terra Cotta-med. (face, hands)
43	815 Garnet-med. (flowers)
849	927 Grey Green-med. (goose)
246	319 Pistachio Green-vy. dk. (all else)
Step 4: Lazy Daisy Stitch (one strand)	
324	721 Orange Spice-med.
Step 5: Long Stitch (one strand)	
308	782 Topaz-med. (candles)
922	930 Antique Blue-dk. (laces)
Step 6: Smyrna-cross (one strand)	
	Gold Metallic

. . . **Stockings continued**

MATERIALS (for one stocking)

Completed cross-stitch on Hardanger 22 over two threads; see sample information
One 13″ x 18″ piece of unstitched white Hardanger
¾ yard of 45″-wide powder blue fabric; matching thread
1½ yards of ⅜″-wide hot pink grosgrain ribbon for Maiden Stocking or 1¼ yards for Forest Friends Stocking; matching thread
¼ yard of ⅜″-wide pink grosgrain ribbon for Maiden Stocking; matching thread
1¼ yards of narrow cording
Tracing paper for pattern

DIRECTIONS

All seam allowances are ¼″.

1. From the stitched Hardanger, cut one stocking for the front. Also cut one stocking from the unstitched Hardanger for the back.

2. From blue fabric, cut two stocking pieces for lining and one 2″ x 4″ piece for loop. Cut 1¼″-wide bias strips, piecing as needed, to equal 45″. Cover cording.

3. For Maiden Stocking only, cut one 8″ length of hot pink ribbon and one 8″ length of pink ribbon. Slipstitch side by side above the top edge of cross-stitch.

4. Stitch cording to right side of stocking front. With right sides of stocking front and back together, stitch on cording stitching line. Trim seams. Turn.

5. Stitch the two lining pieces, right sides together, leaving a 4″ opening in the back seam.

6. Fold loop piece, right sides together, to measure 1″ x 4″. Stitch 4″ side. Trim and turn. Fold loop in half and pin to top edge at back seam, matching raw edges.

7. Slide the lining over the Hardanger stocking, right sides together, seams matching. Stitch the top edge, securing the loop, raw edges matching, in the seam. Turn stocking through opening in lining. Stitch opening closed.

8. Tuck the lining inside the stocking, allowing ¼″ of the lining to show along the top edge (see the photo). Secure the lining to the seam allowance by hand.

9. Cut the remaining hot pink ribbon in half and, handling the two pieces as one, tie a knot. Secure the knot to the stocking (see the photo). Trim ends.

each square = 1 inch

Nine-Square Pillows

SAMPLE
The designs are stitched on Hardanger 22 over two threads. (A fabric with this thread count must be used so that the designs will fit the pillow.)

Heart: Finished design size is 1½″ x 1¼″. The fabric was cut 6″ x 6″.

Goose: Finished design size is 1⅜″ x 1¾″. The fabric was cut 6″ x 6″.

Tree: Finished design size is 1⅞″ x 1⅝″. The fabric was cut 6″ x 6″.

Bates	DMC (used for sample)
	Step 1: Cross-stitch (three strands)
44	816 Garnet
189	991 Aquamarine-dk.
	Step 2: Backstitch (one strand)
401	413 Pewter Grey-dk.
	Step 3: French Knots (one strand)
401	413 Pewter Grey-dk.

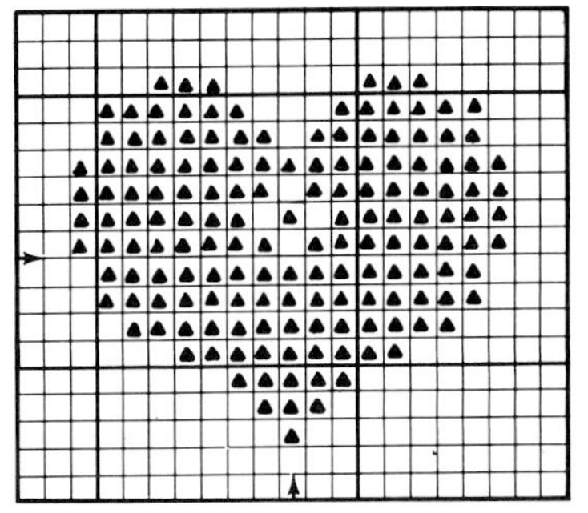

Stitch Count: 17 x 14

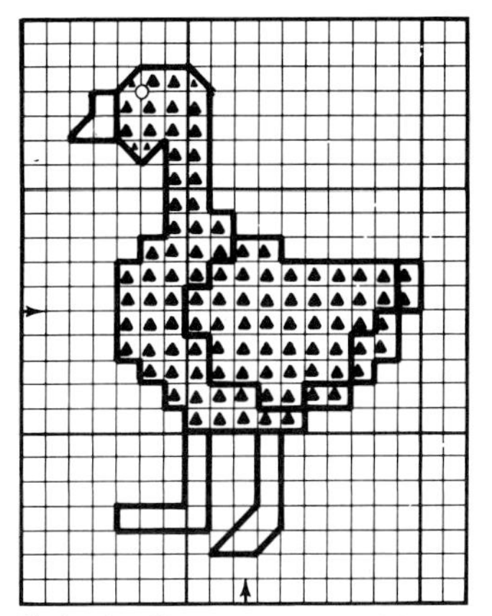

Stitch Count: 15 x 20

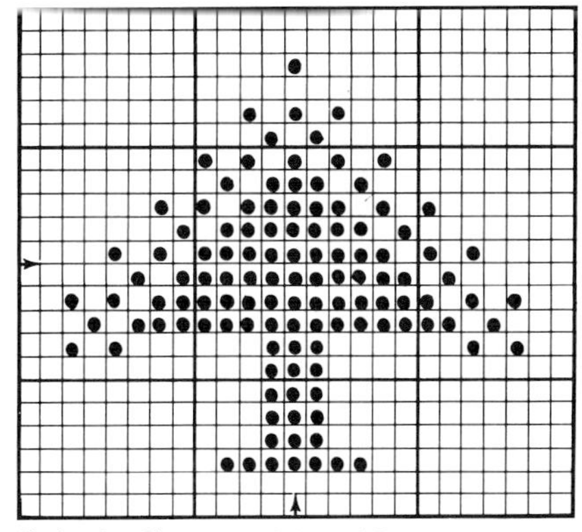

Stitch Count: 21 x 18

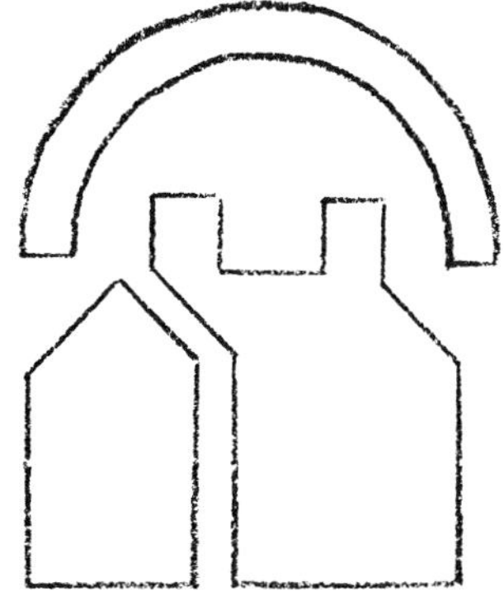

continued . . .

. . . Pillows continued

Materials (for one pillow)

Completed cross-stitch squares on white Hardanger 22 and matching thread; see sample information

Additional small pieces of unstitched white Hardanger 22 for stenciled squares (for pillow with stenciling)

½ yard of 45″-wide print fabric for border and back; matching thread

⅜ yard of 45″-wide contrasting print fabric for sashing and cording; matching thread

Small pieces of fabric for corner squares in sashing; matching thread

14″ x 14″ piece of polyester fleece

½ yard of ⅛″-wide green ribbon; matching thread (for pillow with stenciling)

14″ x 14″ knife-edge pillow form

14″ x 14″ piece of muslin

1⅝ yards of medium cording

Stenciling materials (for one pillow)

Light green thread for quilting

Large-eyed needle

Dressmakers' pen

DIRECTIONS

All seam allowances are ¼″.

1. Make the stencils (see General Instructions).

2. Stencil the house design on the white Hardanger three times or as many times as desired.

3. From the Hardanger, cut nine 3½″ x 3½″ pieces, centering a design in each square.

4. From the border fabric, cut one 14″ x 14″ piece for the back and four 15″ x 1¾″ strips.

5. From the sashing fabric, cut twenty-four 3½″ x 1″ pieces. Also cut a 1¼″-wide bias strip, piecing as needed, to equal 56″. Cover the cording (see General Instructions).

6. Alternating four sashing strips with three design squares, sew a horizontal row for the top of the pillow front (Diagram A). Press the seams away from the designs. Stitch the remaining two rows, combining stenciled designs and stitched designs as desired.

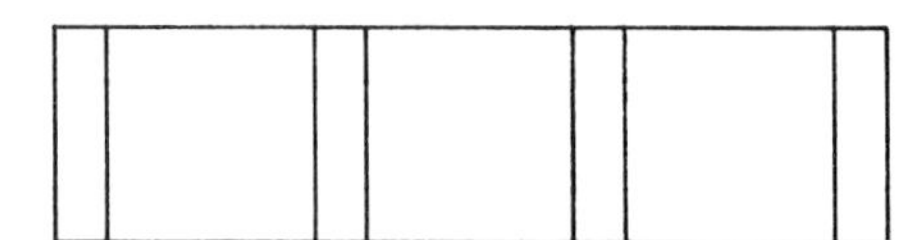

Diagram A

7. Alternating four sashing squares and three sashing strips, sew a horizontal row (Diagram B). Press the seams toward the squares. Sew to the top edge of the top design row. Make three more rows of sashing and sew them to the design rows. Press the seams away from the designs. Note: For a unique effect, sew a few of the corner squares wrong side up.

Diagram B

8. Mark the center on each edge of the nine-square front. Mark the center of one long edge on each border strip. With right sides together and center marks matching, sew a border strip to one edge of the front piece, stitching to within ¼″ of the corner. Press the seam toward the border. Repeat for the remaining border pieces.

9. To miter the corners, fold the right sides of two adjacent border strips together and stitch at a 45-degree angle (Diagram C). Trim the seam. Repeat for the remaining corners.

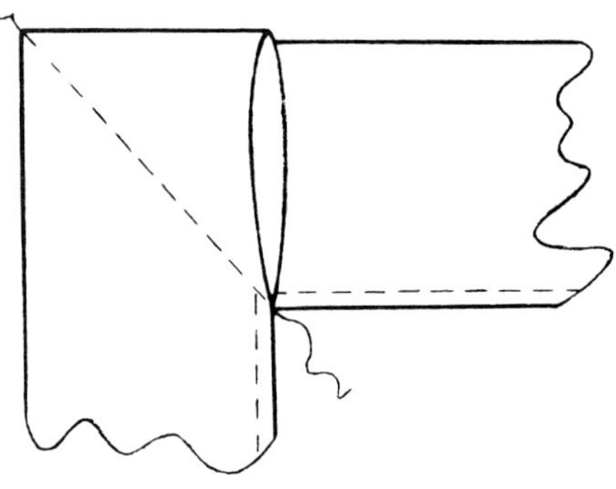

Diagram C

10. Using a dressmakers' pen, mark quilting lines on the pillow front (Diagram D). Layer the pillow front, right side up, over the fleece and muslin; baste together. With green thread, hand-stitch on the quilting lines. Thread the large-eyed needle with the ribbon and run it behind the goose's neck. Tie a knot and hand-tack to keep from slipping (see the photo).

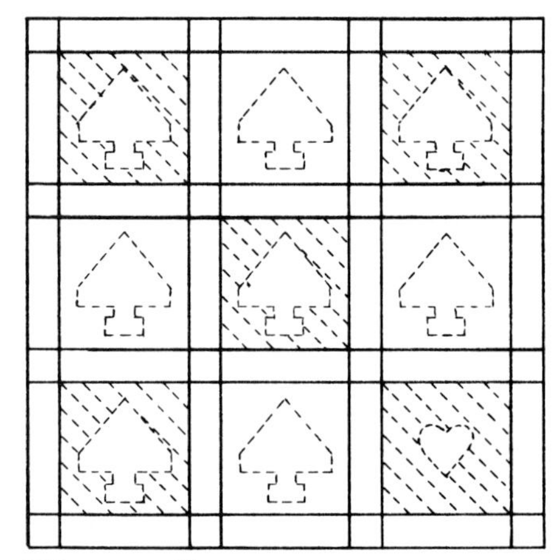

Diagram D

11. With the raw edges matching, pin the cording to the pillow front; stitch.

12. With right sides together, stitch the pillow front to the pillow back, sewing on the stitching line of the cording. Leave a 10″ opening. Turn right side out and insert the pillow form. Stitch the opening closed.

Nutcrackers in a Row

SAMPLE
Stitched on white Aida 14, the finished design size is 12⅞" x 7¾". The fabric was cut 19" x 14".

continued . . .

. . . Nutcrackers continued

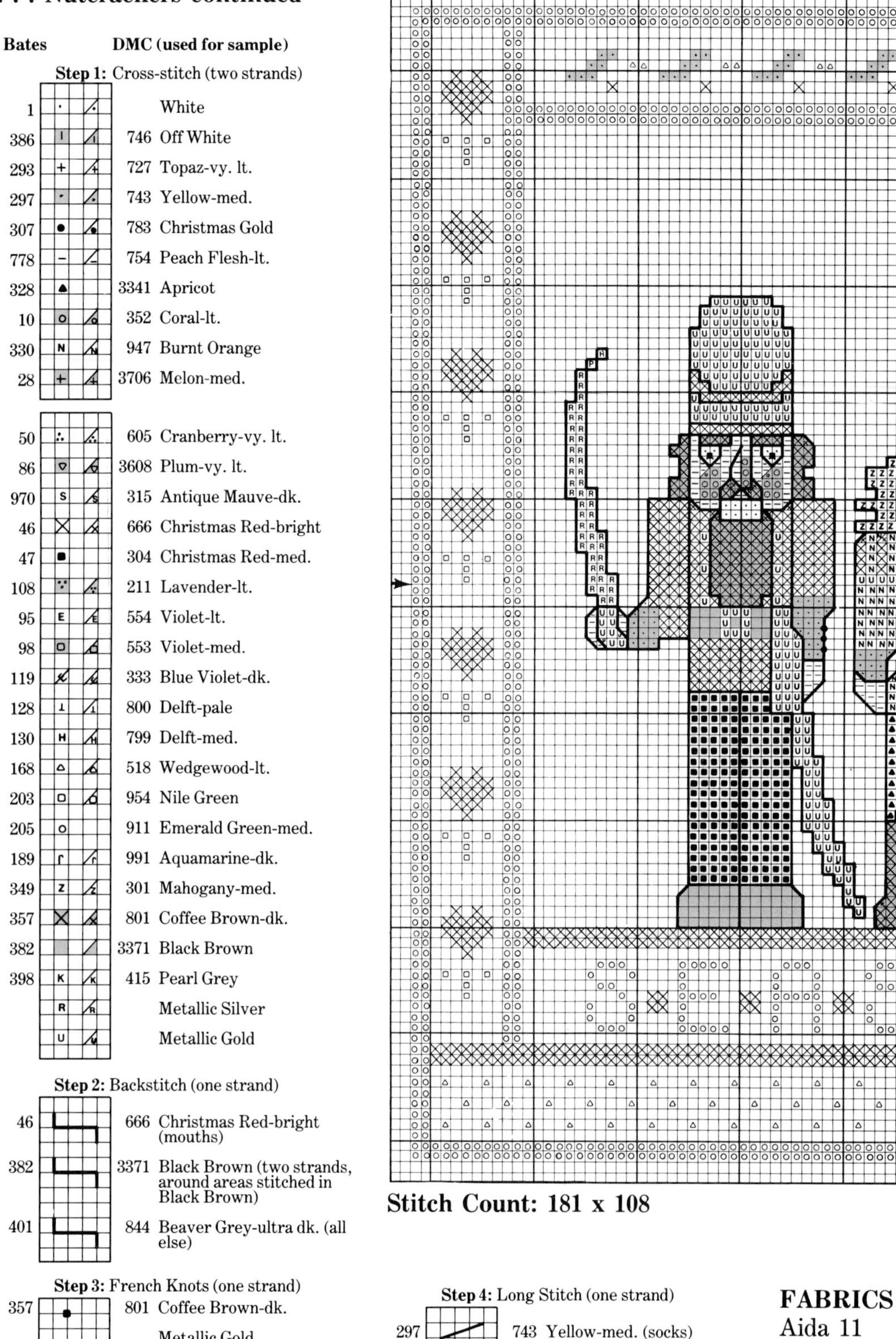

Bates	DMC (used for sample)	
Step 1: Cross-stitch (two strands)		
1		White
386	746	Off White
293	727	Topaz-vy. lt.
297	743	Yellow-med.
307	783	Christmas Gold
778	754	Peach Flesh-lt.
328	3341	Apricot
10	352	Coral-lt.
330	947	Burnt Orange
28	3706	Melon-med.
50	605	Cranberry-vy. lt.
86	3608	Plum-vy. lt.
970	315	Antique Mauve-dk.
46	666	Christmas Red-bright
47	304	Christmas Red-med.
108	211	Lavender-lt.
95	554	Violet-lt.
98	553	Violet-med.
119	333	Blue Violet-dk.
128	800	Delft-pale
130	799	Delft-med.
168	518	Wedgewood-lt.
203	954	Nile Green
205	911	Emerald Green-med.
189	991	Aquamarine-dk.
349	301	Mahogany-med.
357	801	Coffee Brown-dk.
382	3371	Black Brown
398	415	Pearl Grey
		Metallic Silver
		Metallic Gold

Step 2: Backstitch (one strand)

Bates	DMC	
46	666	Christmas Red-bright (mouths)
382	3371	Black Brown (two strands, around areas stitched in Black Brown)
401	844	Beaver Grey-ultra dk. (all else)

Step 3: French Knots (one strand)

Bates	DMC	
357	801	Coffee Brown-dk.
		Metallic Gold

Stitch Count: 181 x 108

Step 4: Long Stitch (one strand)

Bates	DMC	
297	743	Yellow-med. (socks)
46	666	Christmas Red-bright (socks)
		Metallic Gold (blue jacket, lantern)

FABRICS	DESIGN SIZES
Aida 11	16⅜" x 9⅞"
Aida 18	10" x 6"
Hardanger 22	8¼" x 4⅞"

General Instructions

Cross-Stitch

Fabrics: Most fabrics used in this book are even-weave fabrics made especially for cross-stitch and are available in needlework departments or shops. If you cannot find the fabrics in your area, refer to Suppliers. Fabrics used for the models in the photographs are identified in the sample information by color, name, and thread count per inch.

Finished Design Size: To determine the finished size of a design, divide the stitch count by the threads per inch of the fabric. When designs are stitched over two threads, divide the stitch count by half of the threads per inch.

Needles: Use a blunt tapestry needle that slips easily through the holes and does not pierce the fabric. With fabric that has eleven or fewer threads per inch, use needle size 24; with fourteen threads per inch, use needle size 24 or 26; with eighteen threads or more per inch, use needle size 26.

Preparing Fabric: Cut the fabric 3″ larger on all sides than the finished design size, or cut as indicated in sample information. To keep the fabric from fraying, whipstitch or machine-zigzag the raw edges.

Hoop or Frame: Select a hoop or stretcher bars large enough to hold the entire design. Place the screw or the clamp of the hoop in a 10 o'clock position (or 2 o'clock, if you are left-handed) to keep from catching the thread.

Floss: Cut the floss into 18″ lengths. For best coverage, run the floss over a damp sponge and separate all six strands. Put back together the number of strands recommended for use in sample information. If the floss becomes twisted while stitching, drop the needle and allow the floss to unwind. The floss will cover best when lying flat.

Centering Design: Find the center of the fabric by folding it from top to bottom and again from left to right. Place a pin in the point of the fold to mark the center. Locate the center of the graph by following the vertical and horizontal arrows. Begin stitching at the center point of the graph and fabric. Each square on the graph represents one complete cross-stitch. Unless indicated otherwise in the sample information, each stitch is over one unit of thread.

Securing Floss: Never knot floss unless working on clothing. Hold 1″ of thread behind the fabric and secure the thread with the first few stitches. To secure the thread when finishing, run it under four or more stitches on the back of the design.

Backstitching: Complete all cross-stitches before working backstitches or accent stitches. When backstitching, use the number of strands indicated in the code or one strand fewer than was used for cross-stitching.

Stitching Method: For a smooth stitch, use a "push and pull" method. Push the needle straight down and completely through the fabric before pulling it up.

Carrying Floss: Do not carry floss more than ½″ between stitched areas because loose threads, especially dark ones, will show through the fabric. Run the floss under worked stitches on the back when possible.

Cleaning Completed Work: After making sure fabric and floss are colorfast, briefly soak the completed work in cold water. If it is soiled, wash it gently in mild soap. Roll the work in a towel to remove excess water; do not wring. Place the work face down on a dry, lightweight towel and press it with a warm iron until it is dry.

Stitches

Cross-Stitch: Bring the needle and thread up at A, down at B, up at C, and down again at D (Diagram A). For rows, stitch all the way across so that the floss is angled from the lower left to the upper right; then return (Diagram B). *All the stitches should lie in the same direction.*

Diagram A

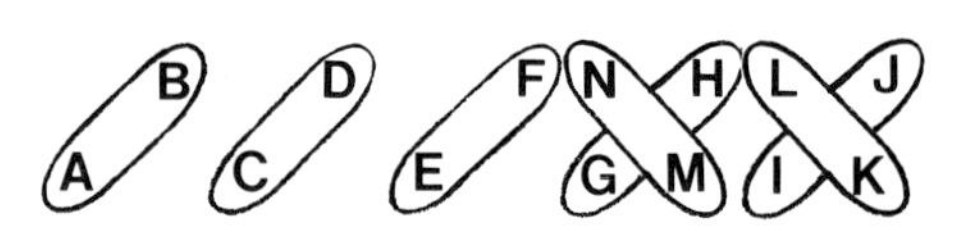

Diagram B

Filet Cross-Stitch: Filet Cross-stitch is a modern interpretation of a lace-making technique called "filet brode." When complete, the background resembles a delicate net. The design is cross-stitched with enough strands of embroidery floss to cover the fabric, while the background is ordinarily cross-stitched with one strand. Designs having a definite positive and negative pattern work best.

Beadwork: With one strand of embroidery floss, attach beads to fabric with a half-cross, lower left to upper right. Secure the beads by returning the thread through the beads, lower right to upper left. Complete an entire row of half-crosses before returning to secure all the beads.

Half-Cross: Indicated on the graph by a slanted line with the color symbol beside it; make the longer stitch in the direction of the slanted line. The stitch actually fits three-fourths of the area (Diagram C). Bring the needle and thread up at A and down at B, up at C and down at D.

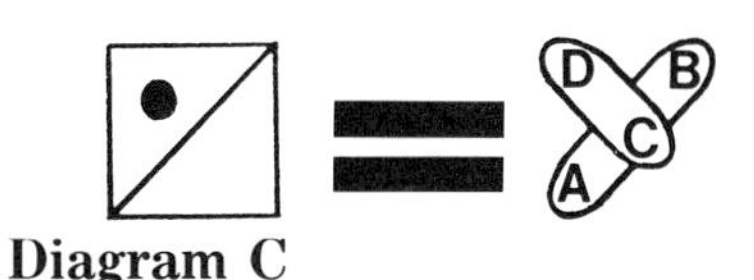

Diagram C

In cases where two colors meet, the graph will indicate how both colors make up the completed stitch (Diagram D).

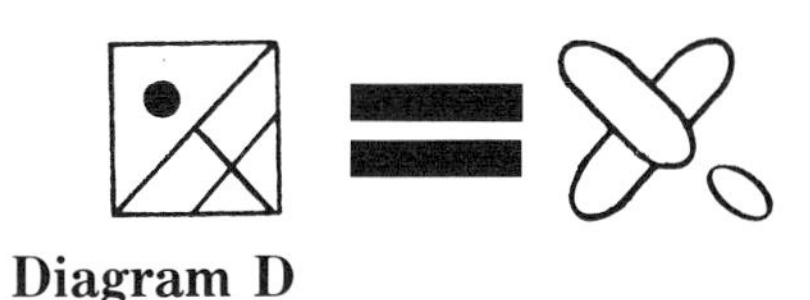

Diagram D

Lazy Daisy Stitch

Couching Stitch

French Knot

Smyrna Cross

Herringbone Stitch

Turkish Tufting Stitch

Satin Stitch

Backstitch: Work from left to right with one strand of floss (unless designated otherwise in the code). Bring needle and thread up at A, down at B, and up again at C. Going back down at A, continue to stitch in this manner (Diagram E).

Slipstitch: Working from right to left, insert needle at A, slide it through the folded edge of the fabric for about ⅛″ to ¼″, and bring it out at B (Diagram F). Directly below B, take a small stitch through the second piece of fabric.

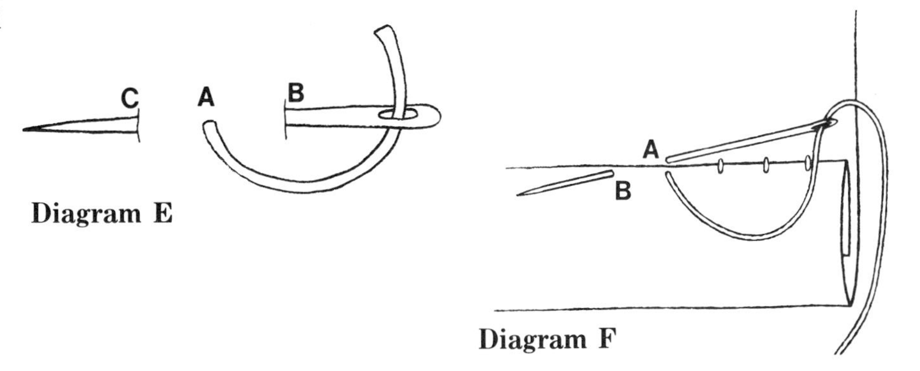

Diagram E

Diagram F

Working with Waste Canvas

Cut the waste canvas 1″ larger on all sides than the finished design size. Baste the waste canvas to the fabric or paper to be stitched. Complete the stitching; each stitch is over one unit (two threads) except on paper gift bags. When stitching is complete, use a spray bottle to dampen the stitched area with cold water. Pull the waste canvas threads out one at a time with tweezers. It is easier to pull all the threads running in one direction first; then pull out the opposite threads. Allow the stitching to dry; then place face down on a towel and iron.

Stenciling

Preparation: Select a moderate-weave or tight-weave natural fabric without a nap. Preshrink all fabrics and press.

Supplies: Acrylic paint; stiff brush with ½″ bristles; stencil board (available at an art supply store); craft knife or single-edged razor blade; small containers for mixing paints; water for cleaning brushes; tracing paper; carbon paper; pencil; dressmakers' pen.

Making Patterns: Cut pieces of stencil board at least 1″ larger on all sides than the finished design size. Copy the entire pattern onto the stencil board one time for each color being used. With a craft knife, cut one template for each color. Cut smaller areas first. Once you start cutting, rotate the stencil board and follow the design clockwise (if right-handed). Do not lift the knife until that line of the design is completed.

Colors: Acrylic paints come in a variety of colors, but may need to be mixed to achieve the desired shade to match the fabrics being used. (Mix enough of a color to complete the project because it is very difficult to match a color later.) Use small containers for mixing colors. Acrylic paint in a tube is a good consistency for fabric stenciling. Add only a few drops of water, if needed.

Applying Paint: Pin, tape, or staple the fabric to a flat surface to keep it taut. Position the stencil and tape in place. Begin working at the top of the design. Use small amounts of paint and a brush that is almost dry. Dab the paint, applying it first to the edges of the design and then the center, covering the entire area evenly. Allow it to dry; then apply the second color using the next template.

Cleaning: Iron the stenciled work from the wrong side. Hand-wash in cold water, but do not wring. Dry flat.

Ribbon Flowers & Leaves

Flowers: For each flower, place a 3″ or 4″ length of ribbon, wrong side up, on a flat surface. Fold both ends at a right angle to the ribbon. Hand-stitch a gathering thread across the bottom edge, leaving the needle threaded (Diagram A). As you slightly gather the ribbon, wrap it to make a flower (Diagram B). Force the needle through the lower edge of the ribbon and secure the thread. Trim any excess ribbon.

Leaves: For each leaf, place a 2″ length of ribbon, wrong side up, on a flat surface. Fold the right and then the left side forward, to form a point at the top (Diagram C). Tightly gather and secure the thread (Diagram D). Trim any excess ribbon.

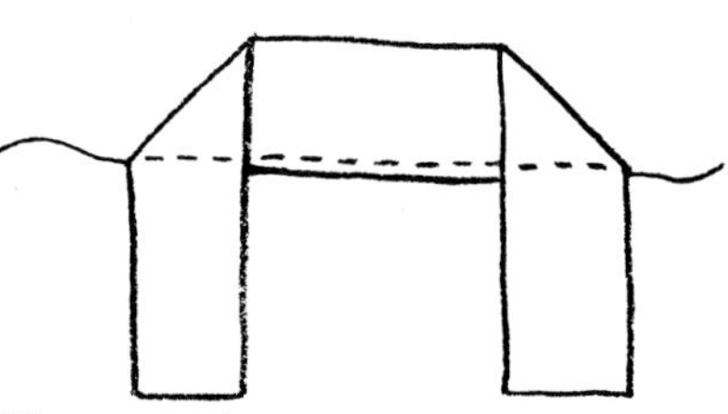

Diagram A

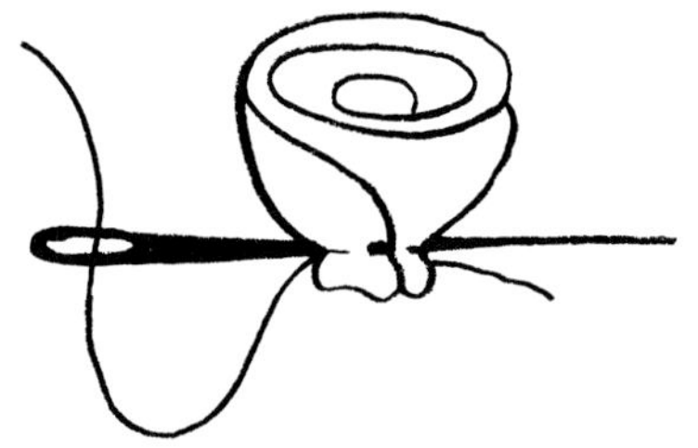

Diagram B

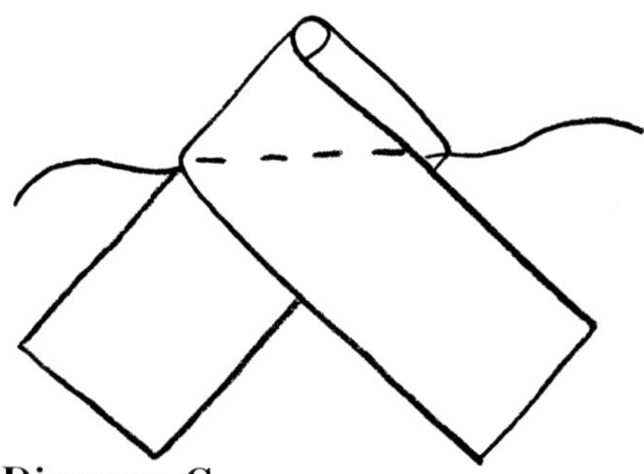

Diagram C

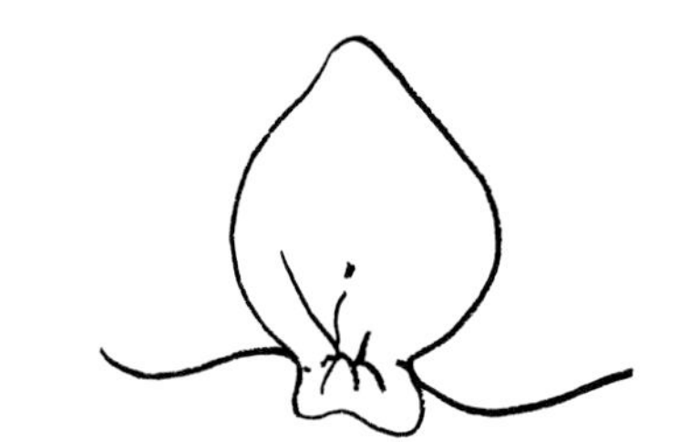

Diagram D

Sewing Hints

Bias Strips: Bias strips are used for ruffles, binding, or cording. To cut bias, fold the fabric at a 45° angle to the grain of the fabric and crease. Cut on the crease. Cut additional strips the width indicated in instructions and parallel to the first cutting line. The ends of the bias strips should be on the grain of fabric. Place the right sides of the ends together and stitch with a ¼″ seam (Diagram A). Continue to piece the strips until they are the length indicated in instructions.

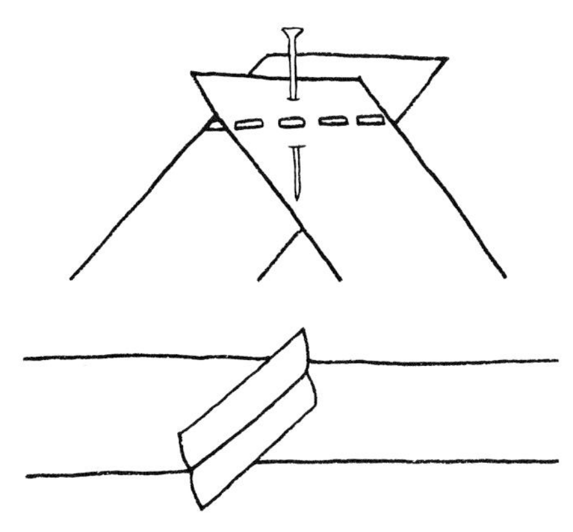

Diagram A

Cording (also called welting or piping): Piece bias strips together to equal the length needed for cording. Place the cord in the center of the wrong side of the strip and fold the fabric over it. Using a zipper foot, stitch close to the cord through both layers of fabric (Diagram B). Trim the seam allowance ¼″ from the stitching line.

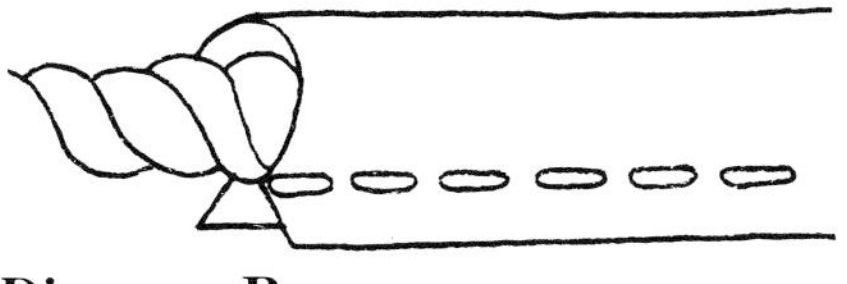

Diagram B

Clipping Seams: Clipping seam allowances is necessary on all curves and points and on most corners, so that the finished seam will lie flat. Clip into the seam allowance at even intervals, ¼″ to ½″ apart, being careful not to cut through the stitching (Diagram C).

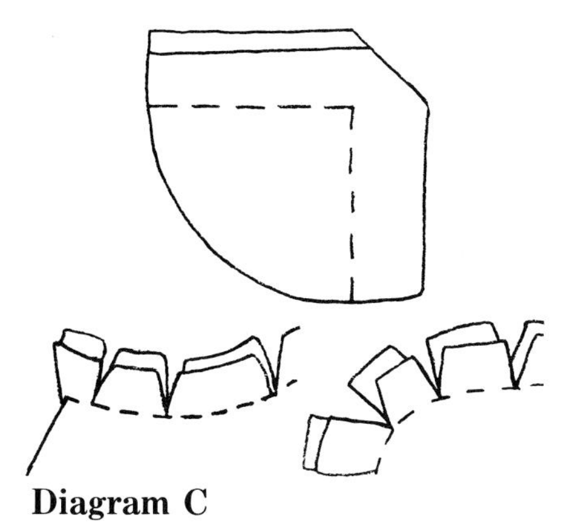

Diagram C

Gathers: Machine-stitch two parallel rows of long stitches ¼″ and ½″ from the edge of fabric (unless instructions say differently). Leave the ends of the thread 2″ or 3″ long. Pull the two bobbin threads and gather to fit the desired length. Long edges may need to be gathered from both ends. Disperse the fullness evenly and secure the threads in the seam by wrapping them around a pin in a figure eight (Diagram D).

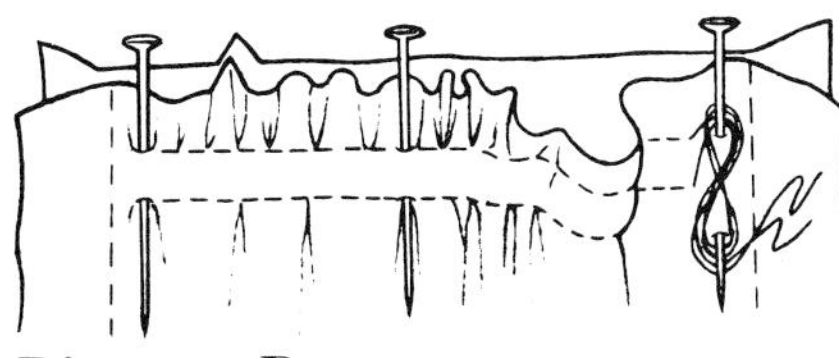

Diagram D

Doll Instructions

Doll Body

MATERIALS

Porcelain doll (see Suppliers)
⅛ yard of white fabric; matching thread
Stuffing
Glue
Dressmakers' pen
Tracing paper for patterns

DIRECTIONS

All seam allowances are ¼″.

1. Trace patterns for the doll body front, back, arms, and legs, transferring all information. From the white fabric, cut out pieces.

2. With right sides together, fold one arm piece and stitch along the outside edge, leaving the bottom edge open. Turn and stuff. At the opening, turn fabric under ¼″. Insert a porcelain arm; glue. Repeat for second arm. Repeat for legs.

3. Sew darts in the body pieces. With right sides together, stitch front and back along the side edges of body piece, leaving 2″ at top and entire bottom unstitched.

4. With the body piece wrong side out, place the legs inside the body so that the raw edges on the legs align with the raw edges on the bottom of the body. Sew across the bottom. Turn body right side out through top opening. Stuff. Slipstitch opening closed.

5. Tack the arms to the body at the shoulders. Glue the head to the top of the body.

continued . . .

. . . Doll Body continued

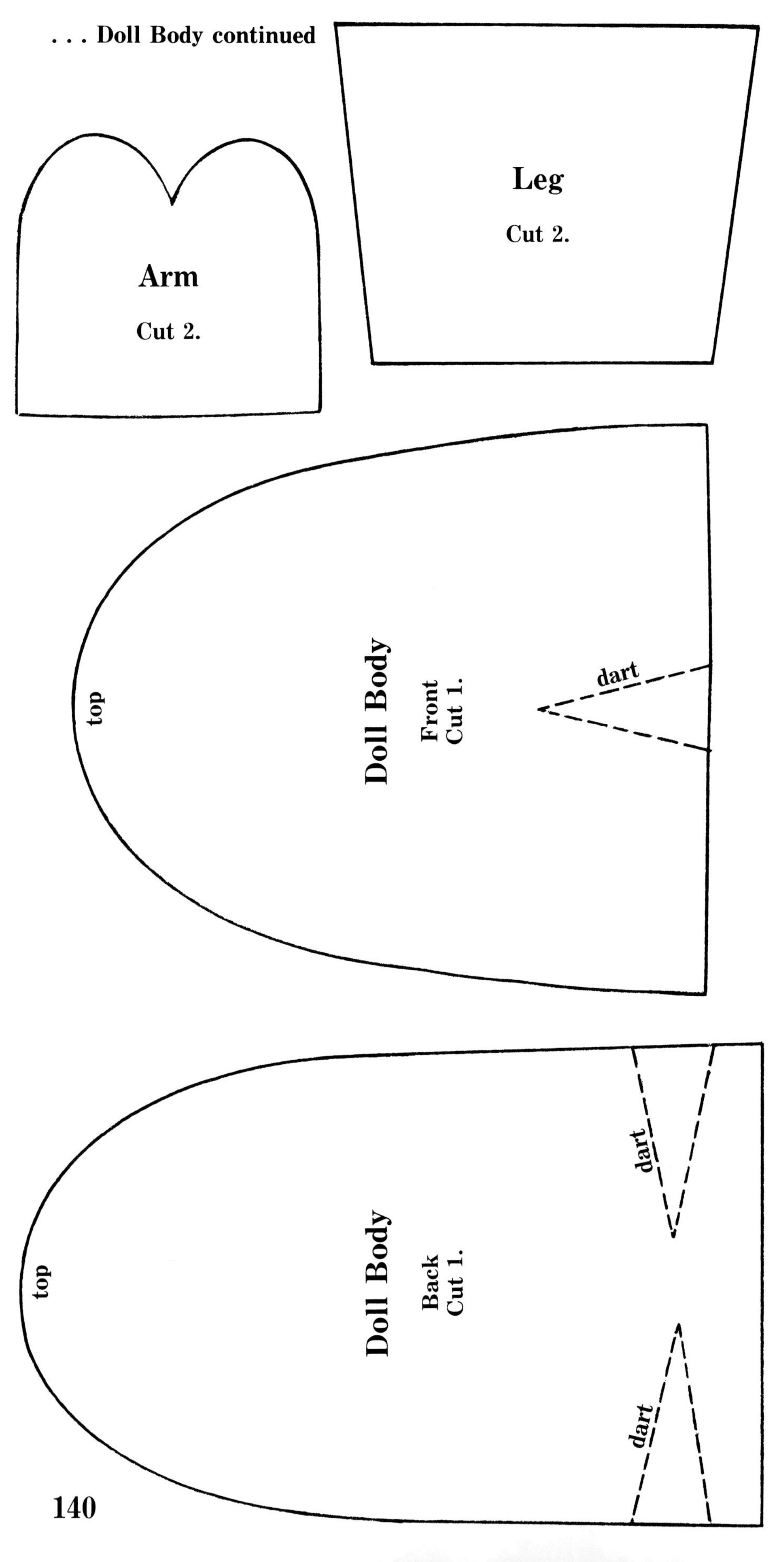

Doll Dress

MATERIALS
¼ yard of 45″-wide fabric; matching thread
Two small snaps (optional)
Elastic thread (optional)
Tracing paper for patterns
Dressmakers' pen

DIRECTIONS
All seam allowances are ⅛″.

1. Trace the dress patterns for the bodice front, bodice back, sleeve, and skirt, transferring all information.

2. From the fabric, cut pieces for the dress, according to the information on the patterns.

3. With right sides of one bodice front and two bodice back pieces together, stitch the shoulders. Repeat for the remaining bodice front and bodice back pieces.

4. With the right sides of the two bodices together and the shoulder seams matching, stitch the center back, around the neck, and the second center back. Clip the curved edges. Turn right side out. Proceed to handle both layers of the bodice as one layer of fabric.

5. Stitch a narrow hem in the wrist edge of each sleeve.

6. Stitch two rows of gathering threads in one sleeve cap. Gather the sleeve to fit the armhole. Stitch the sleeve cap to the bodice. Repeat for the remaining sleeve cap.

7. With right sides together, stitch one side seam and one sleeve. Repeat for the remaining side seam and sleeve. By hand, sew elastic thread ¼″ from the hem at the wrist. Gather to fit the doll and secure.

8. Fold the skirt right sides together, and stitch to within 2″ of the top edge; backstitch. (This seam is the center back; the long edge with the opening will be the waist.) Fold the edges of the opening double to the wrong side and stitch with a narrow hem.

9. Mark the center of the top of the skirt. Stitch gathering threads along the edge. Stitch a ¼″ deep hem in the bottom edge of the skirt.

10. Mark the center front of the bodice at the waist. Gather the skirt to fit the bodice. Match the center of the skirt to the center of the bodice and stitch.

11. Sew snaps on the center back opening at the neck and the waist of the dress.

12. Option: If the doll is to be for display only, the clothes can be attached permanently. Instead of using elastic thread at the wrist, sew gathers with matching thread and secure, making an exact fit. Also, omit the snaps at the back opening and slipstitch the opening closed.

Doll Pinafore

MATERIALS

Completed cross-stitch; see sample information for individual pinafores
Small pieces of additional cross-stitch fabric for pinafore; matching thread
⅛ yard of 45″-wide matching fabric for lining of pinafore
Two small snaps
½ yard of ⅜″-wide blue satin ribbon (for Schoolgirl Doll)
Tracing paper for patterns

DIRECTIONS

All seam allowances are ⅛″.

1. Trace patterns for the pinafore bodice front, bodice back, skirt front, and skirt back, transferring all information.

2. Position the pattern carefully on the cross-stitch fabric, before cutting. Cut out pinafore pieces.

3. From the lining fabric, cut out pinafore pieces.

4. To form the bodice, stitch the bodice front and back pieces, right sides together, at the shoulders and along the sides. Repeat for the lining.

5. With the right sides of the bodice and bodice lining together and the shoulder seams matching, stitch the center back, around the neck, and the second center back. Clip the curved edges. Turn right side out. Proceed to handle both layers of the bodice as one layer of fabric.

6. Turn the edges of the armhole opening of the bodice and the lining to the inside. Stitch by hand. Repeat for the other armhole.

7. With the right sides of the pinafore skirt front and lining front together, stitch the side and bottom edges. Trim the corners. Turn right side out.

8. With the right sides of the pinafore skirt back pieces together, stitch to within 1½″ of the top edge. Repeat for the lining. With right sides of the pinafore back and lining back together, stitch the side and bottom edges. Trim the corners. Turn right side out. Fold the edges of the opening of the pinafore back twice and carefully topstitch through all layers.

9. To join the bodice and pinafore skirt, follow the directions in Step 10 of the Doll Dress.

10. Fold bodice lining over raw edges at the waist and slipstitch.

11. Sew snaps on the center back opening at the neck and the waist of the pinafore.

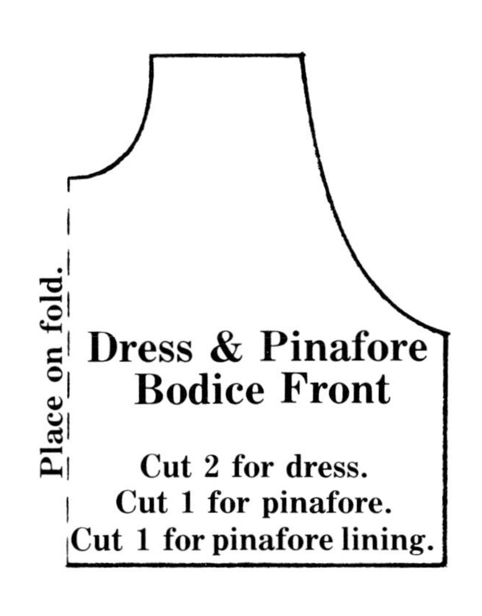

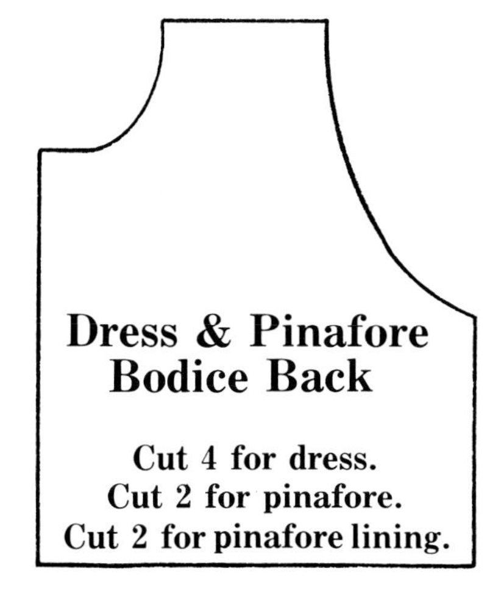

continued . . .

. . . Dress & Pinafore continued

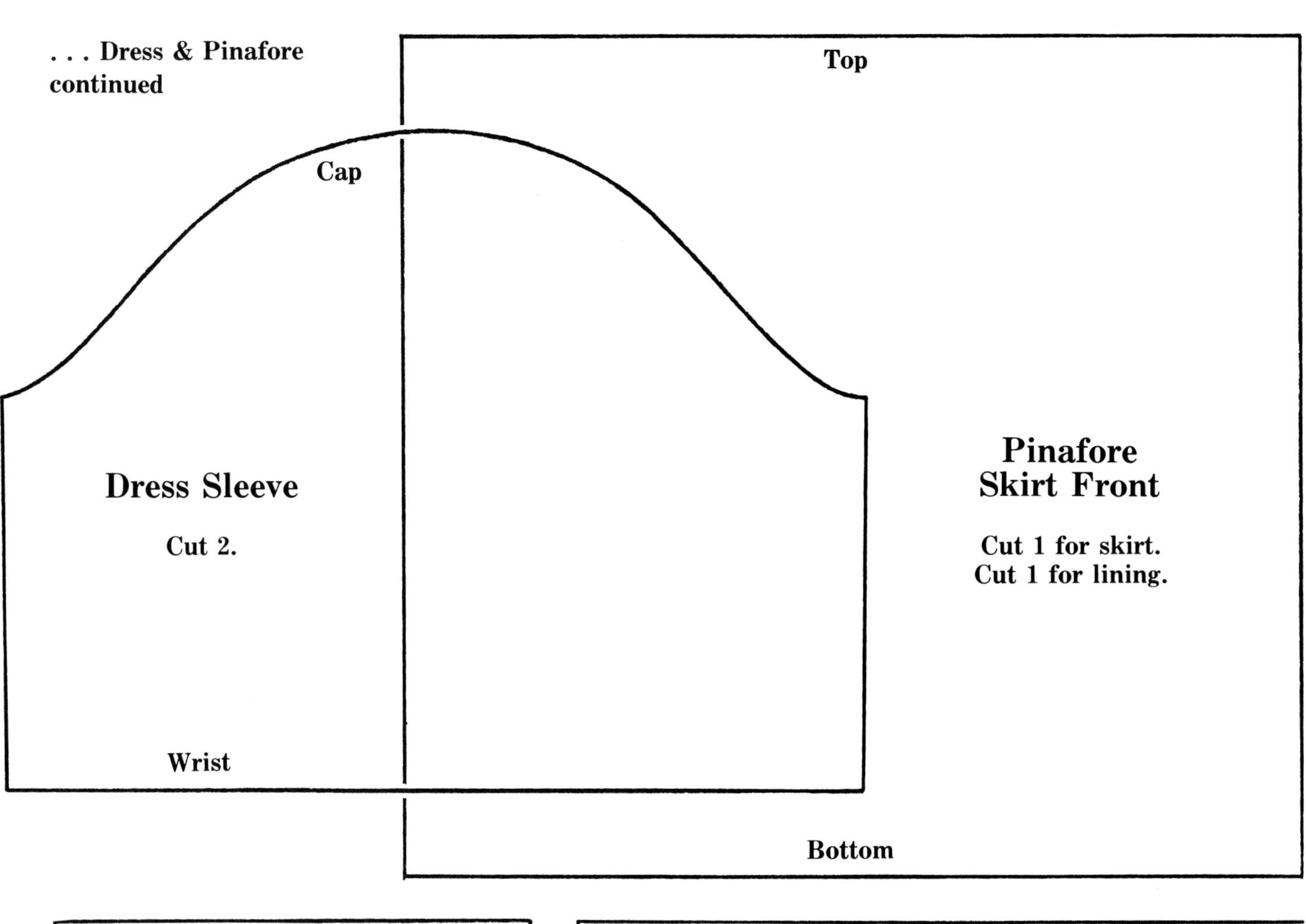

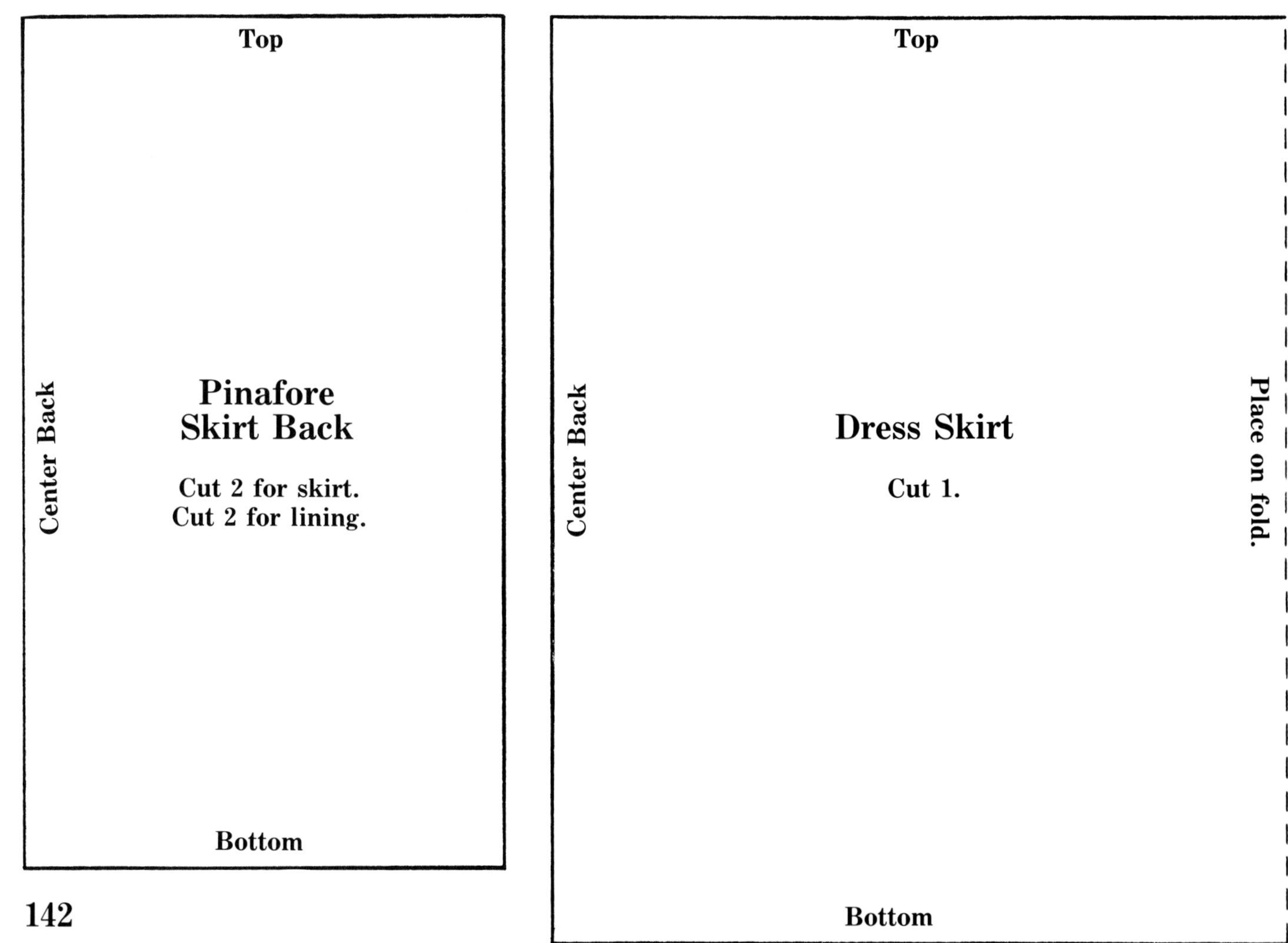

Jacket Motifs

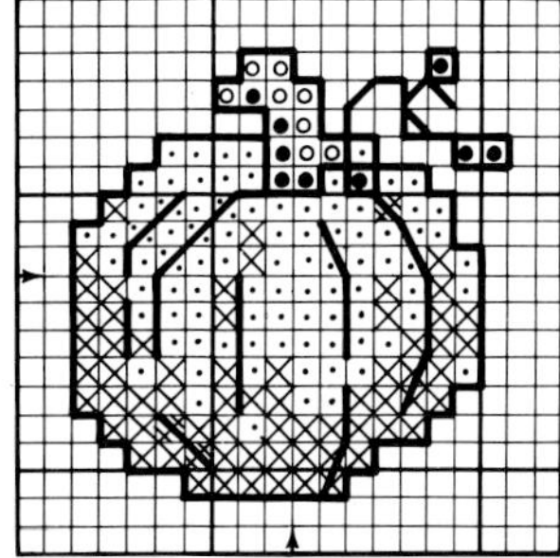

Stitch Count: 16 x 16

Bates	DMC (used for sample)
Step 1: Cross-stitch (two strands)	
303	742 Tangerine-lt.
316	740 Tangerine
209	913 Nile Green-med.
228	910 Emerald Green-dk.
Step 2: Backstitch (one strand)	
228	910 Emerald Green-dk. (stems)
401	844 Beaver Grey-ultra dk. (all else)

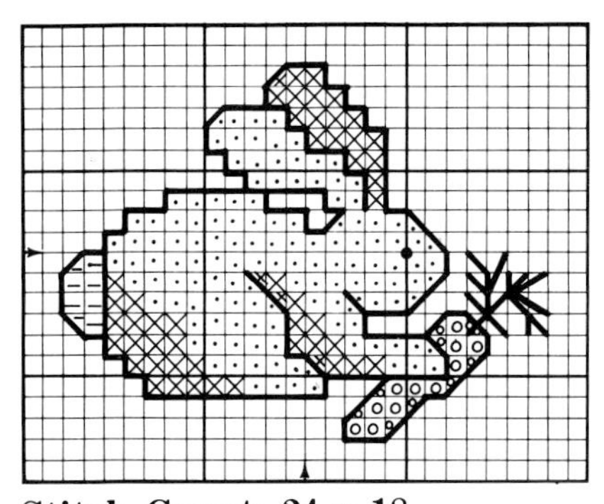

Stitch Count: 24 x 18

Bates	DMC (used for sample)
Step 1: Cross-stitch (two strands)	
1	White
48	818 Baby Pink
24	776 Pink-med.
316	740 Tangerine
Step 2: Backstitch (one strand)	
228	910 Emerald Green-dk. (stems)
401	844 Beaver Grey-ultra dk. (all else)
Step 3: French Knots (one strand)	
401	844 Beaver Grey-ultra dk.

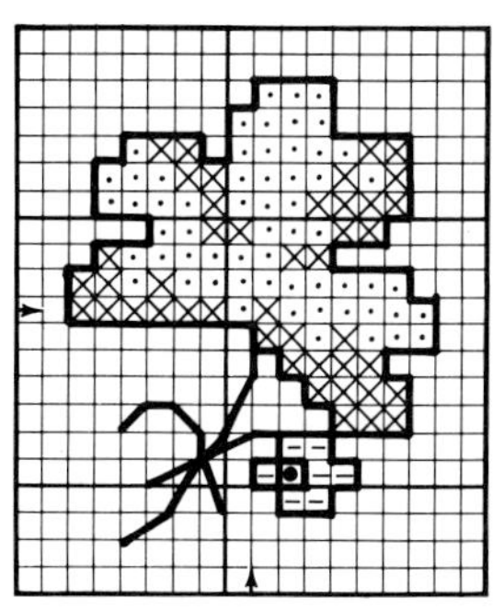

Stitch Count: 14 x 17

Bates	DMC (used for sample)
Step 1: Cross-stitch (two strands)	
1	White
26	894 Carnation-vy. lt.
209	913 Nile Green-med.
228	910 Emerald Green-dk.
Step 2: Backstitch (one strand)	
228	910 Emerald Green-dk. (stems)
401	844 Beaver Grey-ultra dk. (all else)

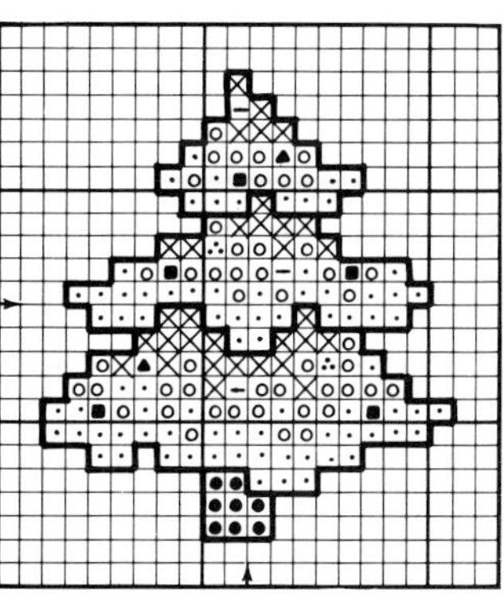

Stitch Count: 18 x 20

Bates	DMC (used for sample)
Step 1: Cross-stitch (two strands)	
1	White
297	743 Yellow-med.
316	740 Tangerine
26	894 Carnation-vy. lt.
47	321 Christmas Red
209	913 Nile Green-med.
228	910 Emerald Green-dk.
380	839 Beige Brown-dk.
Step 2: Backstitch (one strand)	
401	844 Beaver Grey-ultra dk.

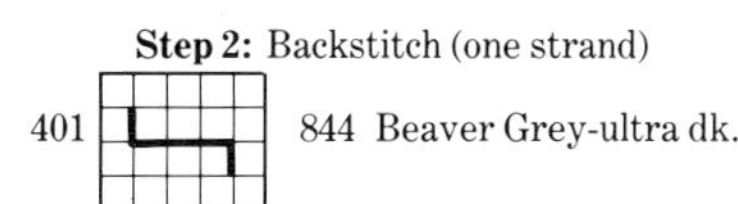

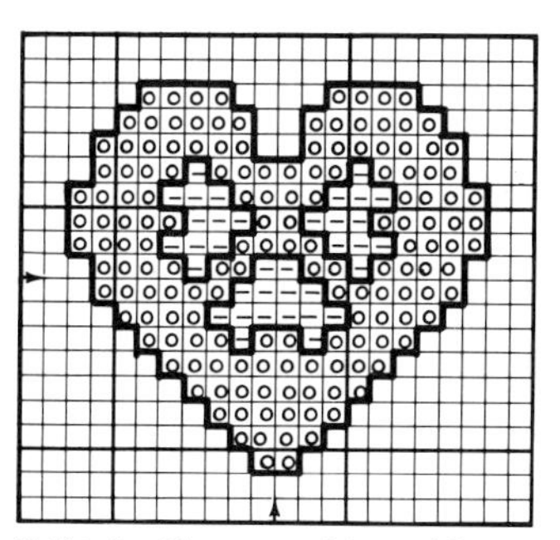

Stitch Count: 18 x 16

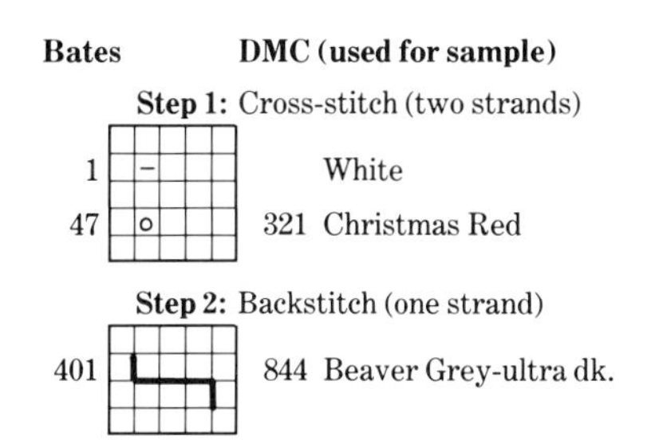

Bates	DMC (used for sample)
Step 1: Cross-stitch (two strands)	
1	White
47	321 Christmas Red
Step 2: Backstitch (one strand)	
401	844 Beaver Grey-ultra dk.

Suppliers

If you are unable to locate a particular material in your local needlework store, you may write to the following manufacturers for a list of distributors in your area.

Glenshee Egyptian Cotton and Linen 29—Anne Powell Heirloom Stitchery, P.O. Box 3060, Stuart, FL 33495.

Dublin 25—Wichelt Imports, Inc., Rural Route 1, Stoddard, WI 54658.

Linaida—Charles Craft, P.O. Box 1049, Laurinburg, NC 28352.

Other fabrics—Joan Toggitt, 35 Fairfield Place, West Caldwell, NJ 07006. (For retail orders, write to Hansie's Haus at the same address.)

Metallic thread—Kreinik Manufacturing, P.O. Box 1966, Parkersburg, WV 26101.

Perforated Paper—Astor Place, 239 Main Avenue, Stirling, NJ 07980.

Beads—MPR Associates, P.O. Box 7343, High Point, NC 27264.

Ribbon—C. M. Offray & Son, Route 24, Box 601, Chester, NJ 07930-0601.

Porcelain, wooden, and music boxes—Anne Brinkley Designs, Inc., 21 Ransom Road, Newton Centre, MA 02159.

Porcelain doll parts and a booklet of patterns for additional doll clothing—Chapelle Designers, P.O. Box 9252, Newgate Station, Ogden, UT 84409.